RESTORATIVE JUSTICE

AF722034

Restorative Justice: Society's Steady March Towards a Civilized Justice Paradigm

by

Ezzat Fattah, PhD, DHC (Liège), FRSC
Professor Emeritus, School of Criminology
Simon Fraser University

ISBN-13: 978-1-9992156-0-6

Copyright ©2019 Ezzat A. Fattah.
All rights reserved, including the right to reproduce this book
or portions thereof in any form.

Design by Robert Grey.

Restorative Justice

Society's Steady March towards a Civilized Justice Paradigm

Ezzat A. Fattah
PhD, DHC (Liège), FRSC

CONTENTS

Part III
The Search for an Alternative Paradigm and a Humane Criminal Policy

Part IV
Is a Non-Punitive Society a Utopian Dream?

Preface

My Conversion *to* Restorative Justice

Admitted to the Faculty of Law at the University of Cairo in 1944, I obtained my LL.L. degree in 1948. The following year I was appointed an assistant prosecutor in the city of Alexandria. The next twelve years brought about several promotions as well as rotations to different Egyptian cities and towns. By the end of the 1950s I was chief prosecutor in Cairo.

Although I practised law as a public prosecutor for twelve years, it did not take me long to realize that the law, particularly in a non-democratic society, can be an instrument of injustice rather than a tool of justice. It became clear to me that criminal law can be and is often used by the powerful to oppress the powerless and to enforce and strengthen the privileges and advantages of the ruling classes. I witnessed first-hand how the law, instead of being used as an engine for reform, was used as a weapon for domination, oppression and suppressing dissent. While a prosecutor in small Egyptian towns I was tormented by the fact that peasants and labourers who could neither read nor write were dragged before the courts and were being punished for violations of laws they did not understand and, if understood, did not agree with. Even when the sentence was a monetary fine, they were unable to pay and were thrown in jail. The administration of justice was a sham.

The disillusionment with the law, the vagaries of an ill-equipped, understaffed justice system were disheartening. And with them came the realization that crime is a social and cultural problem that cannot be solved by passing a law or by dispensing punishment, even the most severe punishment. Vendetta, just as an example, was a widespread custom in Upper Egypt as it was in parts of Southern Europe. I soon realized that no criminal law and no punishment, be it the death penalty or life imprisonment, was going to solve the problem or change the custom. I strongly believed that only a major cultural, attitudinal and evolutionary change could lead to gradually abandon such an entrenched barbaric tradition.

Another eye-opener early in my career as a prosecutor confirmed my conviction that neither the criminal code nor penal sanctions are the solution to deep-rooted social or political problems, be they crime, drugs, violence (and nowadays we can add terrorism). Then there was an experience in the early

1950s that totally changed my views of punishment. The use of hashish and opium (both of them were imported drugs) was endemic, although understandable. Living in squalid conditions with no hope of any kind, the masses tried to escape their miserable lives. As alcohol was prohibited by their religion, they turned to other mood-modifying drugs. As a result, the use of drugs became a widespread and alarming problem. When the military came to power after the overthrow of the monarchy in 1952, the new government decided that something had to be done. The approach, typical of the mentality of army and police officers, was to get tough, in fact extremely tough. The maximum penalty for drug trafficking at the time was three years imprisonment and there was no minimum. The law was changed and overnight a minimum mandatory sentence of life imprisonment with hard labour and no possibility of extenuating circumstances (the new law took away any discretion the judges had) replaced the old penalty. As the prosecutor dealing with drug cases in Alexandria, I was able to observe first-hand the consequences of the new draconian law, and it was exactly the opposite of what the makers of the law thought it would be.

Trafficking in drugs became much worse, and it was not difficult for me to see why. Except when very large quantities of drugs were seized, members of drug squads were very reluctant to formally proceed with the charges. Offenders caught with small amounts (or even medium amounts) were given a couple of slaps on the face, had their drugs informally confiscated and warned not to do it again or else! As the prosecutor, I was incensed that the penalty for drug trafficking was now more serious than the conventional/usual penalty meted out for wilful homicide and tried to find some way of not proceeding with the cases to court. In the few cases where I had little choice but take them to court, the three judges presiding over felony proceedings were extremely reluctant to convict and quite often acquitted the accused, either under pretext that the evidence was insufficient or simply on a technicality. The rules of search and seizure made such acquittals rather simple. As the new drug law made the sanction (for the reasons explained above) much less certain than it used to be when the maximum punishment was three years, any deterrent effect the law may have had was reduced rather than increased!

But with the new, though rather theoretical, risk of life imprisonment the price of drugs on the illicit market skyrocketed and the prospect of larger profits attracted hundreds of new traffickers to the drug scene to take advantage of the lucrative opportunities. A greatly increased risk for border patrols was another side effect of the new mandatory minimum sentence. Drug smugglers (and all drugs were brought into Egypt from abroad, particularly from Lebanon) who faced the prospects of being arrested were now willing to shoot-to-kill those trying to catch them. They had nothing to lose, since the penalty for drug smuggling was now the same as the prescribed punishment for murder! Whatever faith I might have had left in the deterrent effect of punishment, particularly harsh punishment, was not only utterly shattered but totally vanished.

Half a century ago, in the heated struggle to get Canada to abolish capital punishment, I decided to test the popular and widely held, though unproven, belief that the death penalty is a unique deterrent. To do so, I conducted a study of the quantitative and qualitative regional variations in criminal homicide rates across Canada. It would take too long to summarize here the details of the study or its findings. Suffice it to say that the results showed that the faith placed in the deterrent effect of the death penalty lacked any scientific or empirical support. Actually, it suggested strongly that the supposedly unique deterrent effect is not fact but fiction.

One of the lessons the study taught me is that homicide research can in many ways be very enlightening for the discipline of criminology, much more so than other offences against property or against the person. So when shortly afterwards I was visiting the Ivory Coast as a guest professor at the University of Abidjan, I decided to do a study of African homicide to gain a better understanding of the impact culture has on the rates, the nature and the types of criminal homicide. As a former French colony, the Ivory Coast inherited a good system of record-keeping and this, I thought, would both facilitate and enhance the validity and reliability of the study. So with the usual diligence of an enthusiastic researcher, I carefully examined the national police records on criminal homicide during the previous ten years.

Very soon I noticed that there were few, if any, cases recorded in the rural areas and the small villages of the Ivory Coast. Could it be that the rural population in the country was much too peaceful to kill one another? I thought, well, no! There was in fact another explanation. Once I probed further into the possible reasons for such a flagrant discrepancy, it did not take me long to realize that there were two, almost parallel, systems of justice operating in the Ivory Coast. One was the Western punitive system, inspired by the expiatory and retaliatory teachings of the Old and New Testaments, a system that was imposed on the Ivorian population by the colonial power, France. The system used mainly a two-pronged weapon in its response to crime: death and imprisonment. The second was the indigenous, tribal system, or call it patriarchal if you want, which used customary rules and traditions to solve conflicts and to settle disputes of all kinds between the members of the community.

Getting no satisfaction from the Western system of punitive, retributive justice and unable to comprehend why the state should steal the conflicts from their rightful owners (to use Nils Christie's idea) while doing nothing to compensate the victim's family or to achieve reconciliation between the feuding clans, those victimized simply did not report the homicides to the police, preferring instead to have the matter dealt with according to their norms and their customs. The two elements of this indigenous justice were compensation (for the death, injury or harm done) and reconciliation aimed at restoring the peace disrupted by the offence and at ensuring a future of harmonious coexistence.

All this was an eye-opener. It convinced me that punishment is not and can never be the answer. It convinced me that there must be a better solution, a better response to harmful, injurious acts. I was fascinated by the tales of cultural anthropologists who studied what Western scholars denigrate as "primitive societies." Those were societies that have escaped the influence of Judaism, Christianity and Islam, and thus were not inspired or affected by the religious notions of expiation and penitence.

What I found remarkable was the quasi-universality of the historical evolution of social reaction to harmful and injurious acts. The reports of social and cultural anthropologists show that in every society studied there was an evolution from private vengeance to group vengeance to a system of compensation, which is the earliest form of restorative justice. Moving from vengeance to compensation was a normal progression because retaliation proved detrimental to the group.

As Barnes (1972:48) pointed out: "The most serious shortcoming of the system of clan retaliation was that it provided no satisfactory method of bringing a quarrel to an end... Therefore an injury once perpetrated started a perpetual vendetta which was likely to render life extremely precarious to members of both clans."

In view of this, I find it rather amazing that despite enormous social evolution and vast intellectual progress in the last two centuries, our criminal justice system remains frozen in the era of retaliation. It continues to be fixated on the notion of retribution and the need to inflict pain and suffering on the offender by way of making him pay for the injury or harm he has done. It has always baffled me that in this day and age, in the twenty-first century, we continue to accept the punishment response as a given and fail to see its destructive and nefarious consequences, whether the penalty is death or imprisonment.

But my favouring of restorative justice over punishment is not merely a humanitarian stance. It is based on a deep conviction that it is a better, viable, constructive and more effective response to harm than the deliberate infliction of pain and suffering. This is why any attempt to discuss restorative justice or to extol its merits must inevitably address what is fundamentally wrong with society's current response to violent and harmful acts. This is why, instead of praising restorative justice and highlighting its positive aspects, the emphasis in the early chapters of this book will be on the failures, the futility and the detrimental effects of the current approach, namely the use of punishment and penal sanctions as the sole or the dominant response to undesirable and illegal behaviour.

The early practices of mediation, restitution and attempted reconciliation appealed to me because they were inspired by and similar to those found in the societies I was referring to.

Early on in my criminological career my thinking was deeply influenced by the writings of many justice reformers, like Beccaria, Bentham, Romilly, Victor Hugo, Fyodor Dostoyevsky and others. One book that touched me deeply was George Bernard Shaw's *The Crime of Imprisonment*, published in 1946 by Philosophical Library.

Throughout my long career I applauded every attempt, every move, to move away from punishment or to use alternatives to incarceration. I certainly hope that my writings on the issue have had some influence on those reforms.

I am proud that Canada has been in the forefront of pioneer initiatives in restorative justice, and we certainly have to thank indigenous nations for this positive development. As early as 1974, almost half a century ago, the first mediation program was started in Kitchener, Ontario. It is also true that in the following couple of decades things were slow to develop and innovative practices were modest, few and far between. But close to the end of the century the pace picked up considerably.

So in 1995 the Canadian Criminal Code was amended to reflect the importance of restorative justice practices and alternative sanctions to the criminal justice system, adding section 742.1, which allowed judges to impose a conditional sentence that can be served in the community. Two years later the code was amended again, altering section 718.2 which required judges to consider restorative justice options during the sentencing process. The modified section reads "...all available sanctions other than imprisonment that are reasonable in the circumstances should be considered for all offenders..." (Criminal Code, RSC 1985, c C-46, s. 718.2(e).

In 1999 the federal throne speech contained an explicit acknowledgement of the importance of restorative justice in Canadian society.

One of the most important decisions pertaining to restorative justice in Canada was rendered by the Supreme Court in *R v Gladue*. In it the Supreme Court endorsed the notion of restorative justice and a sentencing regime that pays fidelity to healing as a normative value. Responding to the widely held, yet erroneous, belief that restorative justice is lenient and much too soft on offenders, the court also made it clear in the same decision that sentences involving restorative justice were not more lenient than incarceration. In fact the court argued that, when combined with appropriate probationary conditions, restorative justice may "...impose a greater burden on the offender than a custodial sentence," (*R v Gladue* 1999 1 SCR 688 at para. 72).

One important development worth mentioning is the establishment of First Nations Courts or Indigenous Courts. The first was in Toronto in 2001, and here in British Columbia the one in New Westminster has been operating since November 2006.

Things are progressing but they are too little and too slow and surely decades away from my dream of having a fully institutionalized restorative justice system in place of the punitive/retributive system that we have right now.

Last year (2018) there was a senate open caucus forum on restorative justice, but to my knowledge it has not led to concrete results in practice. Be this as it may, according to a recent CBC (Canadian Broadcasting Corporation) broadcast, there are currently 500 different restorative justice programs running in communities across the country, primarily for youth offenders. And in June 2018, Nova Scotia became the first Canadian province to open a superior court on a reserve, a court that will incorporate indigenous restorative justice traditions and customs.

Another recent initiative worth mentioning is the Federal-Provincial-Territorial Meeting of Ministers Responsible For Justice & Public Safety, held in St. John's, Newfoundland, in November (15/16, 2018). The government ministers discussed restorative justice and issued a statement enumerating what they saw as key elements of success and followed that by four concrete recommendations, the first of which is to recognize restorative justice as an investment in an effective and efficient criminal justice system.

References

Barnes, H.E. (1972). *The Story of Punishment: A Record of Man's Inhumanity to Man* (second edition revised). Montclair, NJ: Patterson Smith.

Canada (1995). *Criminal Code.* RSC 1985, c C-46, s. 781.2(e).

Canada, Supreme Court (*R v Gladue* 1999 1 SCR 688 at para 72).

Christie, N. (1977). "Conflicts as Property." *British Journal of Criminology,* I. 17(1):1-19

Fattah, E.A. (2017). "From the Land of the Pharaohs to Lotus Land: The Life and Criminological Achievements of Ezzat A. Fattah." In J. Winterdyk (ed.) *Pioneers in Canadian Criminology,* pp. 44-75. Oakville, ON: Rock's Mills Press.

Acknowledgements

PARTS OF THIS book were previously published as articles in reviews, journals or as book chapters. I wish to acknowledge the cooperation of the publishers and the organizations listed below and to thank them for making it possible to reproduce or reuse in full or in part the material below. Since the previously published material, as well as the new material, deals with the same topics: justice paradigms, justice models, justice philosophy and justice practice, some overlap and redundancies seem inevitable. A special effort was made to reduce these to a minimum. Readers' tolerance and understanding would be appreciated.

I wish to offer my sincere thanks to Robert Grey, who made this book possible through the superb technical assistance he provided.

1982 Ezzat A. Fattah. "Making the Punishment Fit the Crime: The Case of Imprisonment: The Problems Inherent in the Use of Imprisonment as a Retributive Sanction." *Canadian Journal of Criminology*, vol. 24, no. 1, pp. 1-12, January 1982. Ottawa: Canadian Criminal Justice Association.

1993 Ezzat A. Fattah. "Beyond Metaphysics: The Need for a New Paradigm: On Actual and Potential Contributions of Criminology and the Social Sciences to the Reform of the Criminal Law." Originally published in *Criminal Law Theory in Transition/Finnish and Comparative Perspectives*, edited by Raimo Lahti and Kimmo Nuotio, published in 1992 by the Finnish Lawyers Publishing Company. My sincere thanks to Alma Talent, Helsinki, Finland, for the kind permission to reuse this article.

1999 Ezzat A. Fattah. "From a Handful of Dollars to Tea and Sympathy: The Sad History of Victim Assistance." In J.J.M. van Dijk, Ron G.H. van Kaam and Jo-Anne Wemmers (eds.) *Caring for Crime Victims: Selected Proceedings of the 9th International Symposium on Victimology*. Monsey, NY: Criminal Justice Press, pp. 187-206.

1991 Ezzat A. Fattah. "From Crime Policy to Victim Policy: The Need for a Fundamental Policy Change." *Annales Internationales de Criminologie*. Published by the International Society of Criminology (Paris), vol. 29 (nos. 1 & 2), pp. 43-60.

1998 Ezzat A. Fattah. "A Critical Assessment of Two Justice Paradigms: Contrasting the Restorative and Retributive Justice Models." In Fattah, E.A. and Peters, T. (eds.) *Support for Crime Victims in a Comparative Perspective*. Leuven, Belgium: Leuven University Press, pp. 99-110.

2012 Ezzat A. Fattah. "The Dawning of a New Era in Social Reaction to Crime: Promise, Potential and Limitations of Restorative Justice." In *Archiwum Kryminologii*, tom xxxiv, pp. 7-42.

2007 Ezzat A. Fattah. "Is Punishment the Appropriate Response to Gross Human Rights Violations? Is a Non-Punitive Justice System Feasible?" In E. van der Spuy, S. Parmentier, A. Dissel (eds.) *Restorative Justice: Politics, Policies and Prospects*. Cape Town: Juta and Company (PTY) Ltd., pp. 209-227. Originally published in *Acta Juridica*, 2007.

"People commit crimes, not because they are pathological or wicked, but because they are normal."

Hiroshi Tsutomi

Introduction
A Basic, Fundamental Question: What Is Justice?

See my article in *Archiwum Kryminologii*, TOM XXXIV, 2012, pp. 11-20.

"JUSTICE" IS ONE of those terms that is so frequently and so abundantly used that no further attempt is made to define it or to analyze it. This is the reason why the focal interest in this introductory chapter will be on exploring and understanding what justice really is. It seems rather axiomatic that one cannot talk about, discuss or advocate restorative justice or, for that matter, any other justice model or paradigm without first understanding what justice is. The terminology of justice has expanded exponentially in the last three or four decades. One can hardly keep up with the terms used to describe various types of justice. A very quick search yielded at least three dozen justice types: divine justice, heavenly justice, natural justice, social justice, traditional justice, formal justice, ordinary justice, criminal justice, retributive justice, punitive justice, vindictive justice, retaliatory justice, distributive justice, restorative justice, peacemaking justice, transitional justice, transformative justice, informal justice, healing justice, harsh justice, lenient justice, blind justice, satisfactory justice, real justice, relative justice, relational justice, commutative justice, procedural justice, contributive justice, instrumental justice, corrective justice, organizational justice, adversarial justice, procedural justice, legal justice, rough justice, street justice, community justice, vigilante justice, poetic justice, etc., etc. This is by no means an exhaustive list. Much ink is spilled by the authors trying to describe and explain each adjective, but hardly any effort is made to define the noun itself, as if justice can be universally defined or uniformly applied, as if the term "justice" is self-evident or self-explanatory (Fattah, 2002:312). This is surprising because to my knowledge there is no agreed upon or universal definition of justice! Dictionaries' definitions of justice are very disappointing. One such definition says that "justice is the upholding of what is just" or "the quality or fact of being just." So what exactly is just? Similarly, to define injustice as "that which is not just" does not seem to be very enlightening or very explanatory. Those definitions bear a great resemblance to the highly criticized definition of crime, "crime is what the law says it is."

Is there such a thing as natural justice, divine justice? Is justice a biological instinct, is it a psychological imperative? Is the thirst for justice an innate need, an inborn yearning, and if so, how and why is it that so many human beings are not moved by the social and economic injustices that they see all around them all the time? Or is longing for justice an acquired rather than an inbred desire? Is justice a transcendental notion, an immutable concept or is it an evolutionary idea that changes with the times in order to adapt and become congruent with the cultural and moral thinking of the era? If justice is evolutionary, how is it that the notions of retribution, vengeance, retaliation and punishment are as alive today as they were hundreds of years ago?

Yes, what exactly is justice? Is justice a universal concept? Do people in different cultures share a common understanding of what justice is? Are there cultural variations in the perceptions of justice and in defining its requirements? How exactly do people who somehow escaped the influence of Western theological and moralistic teachings understand the term "justice"? Do they have in their native language a word equivalent to the word "justice"? Is justice a theological notion, a philosophical idea or is it simply a legal concept? Is justice an abstract notion like heaven and hell or is it a concrete, tangible and measurable entity? Is justice a philosophical abstraction, a legal fiction or is it a cultural and a sociological construct? Is justice an absolute or a relative concept? Is justice a subjective feeling or an objective reality? Can justice be quantified and mathematically measured? Can justice be theorized? Is a general universal theory of justice possible?

Despite the dearth of sociological, anthropological and cross-cultural studies aimed specifically at discovering the notions, the conceptions and the ideas of justice among various communities, in particular communities that are as close to the state of nature as can be, some authors (for example, Rawls, 1971) have attempted to formulate a Western ethnocentric justice theory. But how successful could such valiant attempts be? A theory is a scholarly construct aimed at explaining a natural, social or behavioural phenomenon. It is a construct that lends itself to empirical testing and validation. According to *Webster's Twentieth Century Dictionary*, a theory is "a formulation of apparent relationships or underlying principles of certain observed phenomena which has been verified to some degree." A theory requires valid proof of its acceptance, and this is what distinguishes theory from a hypothesis or mere speculation. It is possible, therefore, to develop a criminological theory formulated to explain crime or delinquency or a penological theory such as "deterrence theory," which maintains that fear of punishment or the actual experience of punishment does deter people from committing crime.

Justice, however, is neither a phenomenon nor a theory. It is an idea, or better still, an ideal, a desideratum. Justice is a subjective feeling, and this is precisely why a theory of justice seems no more possible or feasible than a theory of love or hate. This is not to say that it is not possible to study, analyze and compare methods of conflict resolution and dispute settlement in different communities. It is not to deny the possibility of discovering what may be described as a philosophy of justice or developing a justice paradigm or a justice model (Fattah, 2002).

But justice is not something tangible or cognizable. Justice is an abstract notion, a vague concept, it is not something you can touch, taste, smell or hear. Abstract concepts are difficult to grasp. They are hard to define or to describe. They do not have objective or universal meaning. They are perceived differently, interpreted subjectively and understood in completely diverse ways.

Like justice, retribution is an abstract notion, not a theory. To equate retribution with justice denotes faulty logic. Retribution is nothing other than a philosophical or theological justification for the deliberate infliction of pain and suffering on a fellow human being. And the justification is not only ethically flawed, it is morally indefensible. Others may agree or disagree, but I personally believe that there is a huge difference between philosophizing and theorizing.

How Abstract Can the Concept of Justice Be?

To illustrate the extent to which justice is an abstract concept, here is a concrete example from Canada. Twenty-five years ago, Canada's federal government decided that the criminal justice system needs a complete overhaul and set up a "sentencing commission" charged with "...the responsibility of examining sentencing in Canada and of making recommendations on how the process should be improved." After conducting a thorough review, the commission concluded "...that there are serious problems with sentencing in Canada and that these problems cannot be eliminated by tinkering with the current system or exhorting decision-makers to improve what they are doing. The system is in need of fundamental changes in its orientation and operation. Unfortunately, these are not novel assessments. The problems have existed for a very long time and in recent years have become the source of extensive discussion and debate. Yet the changes that have occurred have been piecemeal in nature while the overall context in which sentencing takes place has remained virtually unchanged for over a century. Over the course of time, various commentators, federal commissions and committees have identified many of the same problems identified by the Canadian Sentencing Commission. Problems – such as the over-reliance on custodial sanctions and the existence of unwarranted disparity in sentencing – do not require almost two and a half years of inquiry by a nine-member commission to be discovered. Identifying the problems may be relatively easy. Determining the solution is not. The government of Canada established the Canadian Sentencing Commission in recognition that there exist serious problems in the structure of sentencing and that these problems could only be resolved by a comprehensive set of recommendations which reflected the complexities of the criminal justice system as a whole. The members of the commission accepted this assessment and were mindful of what had been said about sentencing over the past century," (p. xxi).

A few million dollars and thousands of printed pages later, the commission reached the "earth-shattering conclusion" stating in no uncertain terms that "The fundamental purpose of sentencing is to preserve the authority of and to promote respect for the law through the imposition of just sanctions... The paramount principle governing the determination of a sentence is that the sentence be proportionate to the gravity of the offence and the degree of responsibility of the offender for the offence."

In other words, the most appropriate philosophy for criminal justice is "just deserts"! Not a mention of victims, their needs and/or their rights, not a word about providing redress to those victimized, nothing! The commission's conclusion was hardly a surprise to me. Having appeared before the House of Commons Standing Committee on Justice and the Solicitor General, in 1988, and been accused by one of its members of wanting to revolutionize the justice system simply because I called for an end to punishment, it would have been too optimistic to expect something truly progressive or other than reactionary from such a backward-looking body. In my comments on the Sentencing Commission report and recommendations contained in a brief submitted to the Standing Committee in March 1988, I wrote:

> "In an era meant to become the golden age of the victim, there seems to be a growing obsession with punishment, euphemistically called "just deserts." Yet having punishment as the central focus of our criminal justice system is neither morally legitimate nor practically effective. It can only act to the detriment of the victim. Dispute settlement, mediation, reconciliation, arbitration and reparation are concepts foreign to a system based on punishment, a system that regards the crime not as a human action but as a legal infraction. The operation of such a system acts to intensify the conflict rather than solving it. And instead of bringing the feuding parties together, it widens the gap that separates them," (Fattah, 1988).

Some years later, Todd Clear (1994) expressed similar views affirming that penal harm does not help the victim and cannot make the victim whole again. Instead, the focus on getting even with the offender could in some ways divert the victim from his/her personal path of recovery. Clear adds:

> "In this way, the emphasis on penal harm may actually be a disservice to the victim, in that it promises that if the state is only able to impose a penalty severe enough, the victim will be able to overcome the crime. The focus is placed on what happens to the law violator, not what happens with the victims. The victim's victory at sentencing is eventually exposed as a pyrrhic conquest, for the problem faced by the victim does not centre on the offender," (1994:173).

Reflections on the Social Reaction to Crime in the Twenty-First Century

As a lawyer and social scientist I have always been fascinated and intrigued by the phenomenon of social reaction to crime: its history, its manifestations and forms, its current state and its possible future. It always perplexed me that despite the ever-growing secularization of society and the quasi-complete separation of church and state, social reaction remains dominated by theological teachings and religious philosophy. Despite its historic failure in preventing crime or reducing offending rates and despite its horrendous human, social and financial costs, punishment continues to thrive and flourish. How could this be explained? How is it possible that in this day and age, in the twenty-first century, an advanced, civilized society such as the United States continues to practise the archaic relic of the death penalty?

Not long ago, one of the Republican candidates aspiring for the nomination to the presidency of the U.S.A., Mr. Rick Perry, could not hide during the nomination debates his pride at having signed more death warrants than any other governor in the history of the state of Texas. Mr. Perry was deeply proud of his record despite the fact that the innocence of some of those for whose execution he was responsible was proven in spite of the overwhelming hurdles needed to overcome and to prove that a judicial error was made.

What If Beccaria Were to Come Back?

If eighteenth-century Italian philosopher and justice reformer Cesare Beccaria were to be resurrected and were God to send him back to earth to check and report on the state of criminal justice in post-industrial twenty-first-century societies, there is little doubt that he would be utterly shocked to find out that criminal justice has changed little, if at all, in the two-and-a-half centuries since his immortal essay *Dei Delitti e Delle Pene* was published in 1764! Surely he would be overwhelmed by the drastic social changes and the technological innovations he would see all around him, but he would also be amazed that penal philosophy has undergone little change and is still dominated by the theological teachings of the Old Testament. He would certainly be at a loss to understand that retribution continues to be the key principle in sentencing and that criminal court judges continue their futile and hopeless struggle to make the punishment fit the crime!

A confirmed abolitionist, Beccaria would undoubtedly be disheartened to learn that the talion law principle of life for life is still being practised in the two most powerful countries on earth, namely the U.S.A. and China, as well as in a host of developing countries, such as Iran and Saudi Arabia.

Beccaria would be dismayed to find out that legal vengeance is the current norm of criminal justice. Probably what would shock Beccaria most would be to discover that the two main punishments meted out by the criminal courts in his time, namely fines and incarceration, remain the main punishing tools in present-day courts of law.

As a libertarian and staunch defender of the rights of the individual, Beccaria would have a hard time comprehending that in supposedly free democratic societies people are being punished and incarcerated for using mind-altering drugs, such as marijuana, cocaine, ecstasy, amphetamines, etc. when the use of other mind-altering and mood-modifying drugs, such as alcohol, tobacco and caffeine, are perfectly legal and rampant.

Having forcefully stressed the need to protect the citizens against the despotism of power, one has to wonder what Beccaria would think when he found out that the richest and most powerful country on earth practises targeted assassinations and extra-judicial killings of suspects who were never charged or faced justice in a court of law.

Beccaria would be devastated when he learns that 2,284,000 Americans are behind bars and that six million others are under correctional supervision. Even more shocking to Beccaria would be the statistics showing that 50,000 Americans are daily in solitary confinement while 70,000 are raped in American prisons every year (see Gopnik, 2012; and Stewart, 2012).

Beccaria, who must have been very familiar with the Roman practice of throwing early Christians to the lions, would undoubtedly be horrified to discover that in this day and age in the Louisiana State Penitentiary, nicknamed Angola, hard-core inmates sentenced not only to life imprisonment but to sentences of 90, 100 or 150 years are being thrown to angry bulls under pretext that it is a rodeo.

Beccaria would seek leading criminologists and Stockholm prizewinners in his attempt to understand and to find some explanation for why, despite social upheavals, despite the technological revolution, the criminal justice system has remained archaic in its philosophy, its outlook and its tools. He would want to know why the criminal justice system has remained insulated from whatever progressive changes and advances that have taken place in society and why the system has resisted every attempt to modernize and change.

Alas! Beccaria would be bound to be terribly disappointed, as very little in-depth research has been done to adequately explain the real reasons for criminal justice misoneism and resistance to change. And he definitely would want to understand why it is that despite the ever-growing secularization of society, criminal justice has been totally unable, even unwilling, to free itself from the shackles of religion, to shed its retributive mantle, to adopt new progressive policies and philosophies and to pursue new avenues and horizons.

Yes, Beccaria would undoubtedly be distressed to discover that whatever changes have taken place in the past two centuries have been few, minor and cosmetic. He would wonder at the absence of bold, progressive, earth-shattering changes aimed at revolutionizing the criminal justice system and bringing it to the standards of the Space Age. He surely would be surprised at the regressive changes that continue to drag the criminal justice system ever closer and closer to state vengeance. Beccaria would be deeply puzzled that a society which made spectacular advances, achievements and unbelievable innovations in every sector and every aspect of human life has been totally lacking in imagination when dealing with offenders and law violators. He would be perplexed that a society that managed to send astronauts into space can find no other solution to crime and conflict but sending offenders to prison.

Beccaria's report to God would surely not be flattering to the human race. He would report that while humans showed enormous ingenuity in inventing and practising methods of torture and modes of punishment they are totally unimaginative when it became necessary to find more humane and less barbaric means of dealing with wrongdoers and law violators.

A Puzzling Question: Is Punishment Synonymous with Justice?

What the Canadian Sentencing Commission's report, mentioned earlier, did was to revive a troubling question that has haunted me throughout my professional life. How could it be that punishment, the deliberate infliction of pain and suffering, the deprivation of liberty or deliberately putting a human being full of life to death be called or perceived as justice? Even more incomprehensible to me is that the death row inmate has to be physically healthy and of sound mind to be executed!!

For over half a century I have been trying desperately to find the answer. Finally I came to the painful conclusion that support for punishment is not a reflection of *the monstrous side of human nature* (which is the title of the new book I am working on) nor to the sadistic impulses of politicians and lawmakers. It is above all an expression of exasperation, helplessness, hopelessness that creates an attitude of total resignation and leads to the mistaken belief that punishment is indispensable and irreplaceable.

Nothing exemplifies more this total resignation and utter lack of imagination than a paper signed jointly by Dan Prefontaine and Yvon Dandurand of the International Centre for Criminal Law Reform and Criminal Justice Policy. The paper entitled *New Directions in Sentencing: Is Punishment Working?* is based on a seminar organized by the National Judicial Institute on Criminal Law, Procedure and Evidence held in Vancouver in March 1996 (13-15). A quotation from the paper will hopefully help to illustrate what I mean. It reads:

> "The organizers of today's seminar are challenging us to reflect on 'whether punishment works.' We would suggest, however, that the obvious answer to that question is, 'It better work,' because we have not yet invented anything that can replace it as a credible response to wrongful and harmful social behaviour. If punishment does not work, then we surely have to abolish our whole criminal justice system because the whole system is predicated on the assumption not only that punishment does work, but also that it is necessary to restore and maintain peace and harmony in the community," (p. 4).

Is it not surprising that a seminar bringing together some of the brightest and learned judges and lawyers in Canada would tell us that punishment better work because nothing has been invented to replace it and since the whole system is built on it, if it is shown that it does not work, the whole system would crumble. Well, with all due respect to the authors and all the fine legal minds who attended the seminar, I would like to strongly affirm without any hesitation that punishment does NOT work and that there are better, more constructive and less devastating methods of restoring and maintaining peace and harmony in the community than punishment.

If the view expressed in the above quotation is that of the learned judges, lawyers, legal scholars and researchers, is it any wonder that no one seems to dare denounce the punishment mania or to challenge the institution of punishment as an archaic, antiquated, anachronistic or as a barbaric and inhumane mode of social reaction to harmful, injurious social acts? Is it any wonder that the criminal law has remained frozen in the era of vengeance and continues to be fixated on punishment and to have it as its cornerstone?

How is it that almost three centuries later the abstract notions of the Enlightenment era that underlie the penal law of Western societies, such as free will, moral guilt, moral responsibility, *mens rea*, malicious intent, malice aforethought, premeditation (not to mention fictitious concepts such as *dolus eventualis*, or so-called indirect intention) remain immune to challenge or even criticism? How is it that no one is bold enough to declare those notions and concepts outdated, unscientific and in flagrant conflict with the findings of the behavioural and social sciences?

How is it that punishment has become synonymous with justice and that justice has become a euphemism for punishment? How is it that justice and punishment have become almost interchangeable terms? How is it that slogans such as "*justice for victims*" are invariably interpreted as demands for more and harsher punishments?

How is it that victims who, as Nils Christie said, are the primary owners of the conflict (Christie, 1977) whose property rights were usurped and whose rightful dues paid to them in the form of "*weregild*," or composition, were expropriated by the state, were led to believe that justice is vengeance and retaliation and that the harsher the punishment the more just is the judgement?

How is it that the theological and abstract notions of retribution, expiation, atonement and penitence became so entrenched in people's minds that no rational thinking, no scientific evidence, no economic crisis, no humanitarian endeavour seems to be capable of shaking such religious beliefs or lessening the incessant demands for punishment?

How is it that punishment has become so universally accepted, extremely popular and so widely practised that people and governments, even in the hardest economic times, are more than willing to waste billions and billions of dollars for no other reason but to inflict pain and suffering on those fellow citizens who have violated man-made laws?

To find the answer to these difficult questions, one needs to look at those rare places on earth where the inhabitants are as close to nature as could be, where overzealous missionaries did not venture and to the very few communities and cultures that somehow escaped or were shielded from the teachings of the Old and New Testaments and the Koran. In those communities, like the Canadian North prior to European settlements, one will discover different practices, different modes of dispute settlement and conflict resolution, peaceful and more harmonious methods of doing "justice." One will find the true origins of the restorative justice paradigm.

References

Beccaria, C. (1764). *Dei Delitti e Delle Pene.* First edition published anonymously!

Christie, N. (1977). "Conflicts as Property." *British Journal of Criminology*, 17(1):1-19.

Canada, Sentencing Commission (1986). *Sentencing Reform: A Canadian Approach* (report). Ottawa: Justice Canada.

Clear, T.R. (1994). *Harm in American Penology: Offenders, Victims and Their Communities.* Albany: State University of New York Press.

Fattah, E. A. (2002). "From Philosophical Abstraction to Restorative Action: From Senseless Retribution to Meaningful Restitution – Just Desert and Restorative Justice Revisited." In H.J. Kerner and E. Weitekamp (eds.) *Restorative Justice, Theoretical Foundations.* Willan Publishing, Culmcott House, Devon, UK, pp. 308-21.

Gopnik, Adam (2012). "The Caging of America: Why Do We Lock Up So Many People?" *The New Yorker Magazine*, January 30.

Prefontaine, D. and Dandurand, Y. (1996). *New Directions in Sentencing: Is Punishment Working?* International Centre for Criminal Law Reform and Criminal Justice Policy.

Rawls, J.A. (1971). *Theory of Justice.* Cambridge, MA: Belknap Press.

Stewart, Brian, Canadian Broadcasting Corporation (2012). "America's 'Prison Nation': Must We Follow Suit?" Broadcast on *CBC News*, February 2, 2012 and updated February 3, 2012.

PART ONE

An Antiquated Justice Paradigm in Urgent Need of Replacement

"The degree of civilization in a society can be judged by entering its prisons. A society should be judged not by how it treats its outstanding citizens but by how it treats its criminals."

Fyodor Dostoyevsky

Chapter I
Making *the* Punishment Fit *the* Crime

The Case of Imprisonment: The Problems Inherent in the Use of Imprisonment as a Retributive Sanction

In *Canadian Journal of Criminology*, 24:1, pp. 1-12.

> "In the age of electronics it will be possible to exercise effective control over criminal offenders outside prisons. Cheaper, simpler and, in the opinion of many, more humane substitutes for prison walls will be provided by radio transmitters fastened to criminal offenders, by radiolocaters, by telephone reports from criminal offenders to a controlling apparatus with facilities for voice analysis, etc., etc. The enforcement of an order to stay within a defined geographical area will be carried out so effectively that a stay in prison can be avoided," Nils Christie (1968).

What Do We have Prisons For?

WHAT DO WE have prisons for? This is a simple, basic question. Yet, despite a prospering prison system, Canadians have never sat down to determine what functions should be assigned to their prisons and what goals they want their penal institutions to serve. They never took the trouble to define what should be the aims and purposes of prisons and what type of offenders they want to see sent to them. In a country which makes excessive use of imprisonment (when compared with other Western nations) and at a time when the costs of incarceration are soaring, this comes as a startling revelation. Prisons continue to exist and thrive despite fundamental changes in penal philosophy, astronomic rise in operating costs, and despite a substantial social evolution and great progress in the social and behavioural sciences. Somehow, prisons seem to transcend any changes in human, social or economic values.

As a result of growing valuation of human life, the death penalty was abolished in many countries and a definite decline in its use and imposition in others occurred. With an increasing valuation of physical integrity and deepening respect for the human body, torture and bodily mutilations disappeared and the use of physical and corporal punishments was considerably reduced. One would have expected that, with increasing valuation of personal freedom, with an existence characterized by greater security against need, by greater comfort, by more leisure and more possibilities for enjoying life, the use of deprivation of liberty as a means of punishment would also decline and eventually disappear. In Canada, where the dollar is regarded as the most valuable commodity, where money is the yardstick against which people's success is measured, one would have expected monetary penalties, such as fines, restitution and compensation to replace imprisonment and to become the exclusive or at least the predominant mode of punishment for both serious and minor offences. Since the trend in penal policy has been to move away from the infliction of physical pain (torture, mutilations, corporal punishments) and emotional suffering (degradation, humiliation), one would have expected society to abandon imprisonment with all the pain, suffering and humiliation it entails to monetary sanctions which simply involve the deprivation of what money can buy. Yet the situation in Canada and the U.S.A. seems to contradict these logical assumptions. Here in Canada there seems to be a steady move towards more and more imprisonment and, at present, offenders are being incarcerated at a higher rate and for longer periods than before. The reasons for the current trend are beyond the scope of this paper and, in any case, they are only open to speculation, since no study has been done of the issue. Rather than discussing the causes for a resurgent popularity of imprisonment, this paper will examine some of the problems inherent in its use as a retributive sanction.

The Retributive Function of Imprisonment

Over the years, prisons were built and used for multiple and varied purposes. They originated as establishments for detention. Later on, they were used as substitutes for mutilations and corporal punishments, as places for religious contemplation and penitence, as institutions for separating and isolating the dangerous and the contaminating, for re-educating and re-socializing the wayward and the deviant, as symbols of fear to deter and intimidate the offender and others who may be tempted to follow his example.

Although at one time rehabilitation was seen as one of prisons' major functions, they never succeeded in achieving this goal. In fact they proved to be schools of crime. Instead of developing a sense of personal worth in the prisoner and instead of teaching the inmate self-reliance and responsibility, prisons bred dependence, hate, anger, frustration and hostility. The Law Reform Commission of Canada is, therefore, correct in stating that "It is difficult to show that prisons rehabilitate offenders or are more effective as a general deterrent than other sanctions."[2 & 9]

The high rate of recidivism speaks eloquently for prisons' failure in the domain of special deterrence. Jaffary (1963)[14] reports that four-fifths of prisoners in Canadian penitentiaries have served at least one prison sentence in a penal institution and many have served repeated terms. The fear of imprisonment is probably greatest among those who have never experienced it, precisely those most unlikely to be sentenced to prison once they commit their first offence. Criminological studies assessing the differential impact of various legal sanctions in preventing recidivism found that, for many offenders, probation is likely to be as effective as an institutional sentence. Some researchers also reported that fines and discharges are more effective than either probation or imprisonment for first offenders and recidivists of all age groups.[13] Furthermore, there are reasons to believe that longer institutional sentences are no more effective in preventing recidivism than shorter ones.[3] This led the Assembly Committee on Criminal Procedure of the California State legislature[8] to conclude that for deterrence and intimidation purposes, imprisonment and in particular lengthy imprisonment, is not only ineffective but is a clear misuse of public funds.

Many people, including many criminologists, see retribution as the primary function of imprisonment. If asked why offenders are sent or should be sent to prison, most people would probably answer that "they ought to be punished for what they have done" or that "they ought to pay their debt to society" or simply "because they deserve it." And in many of the models and principles recently proposed for criminal justice, such as the "justice model," "the principle of commensurate deserts" and "the presumptive sentence," imprisonment figures prominently as the retributive sanction par excellence. No one would argue with the view that sending a man to prison is a punishment. Prisons are ideal places for punishment. Whether they are old dungeons or modern constructions, they admirably serve the purpose of inflicting pain and suffering upon the offender. Paradoxically, the use of imprisonment as a retributive sanction was introduced as a humane measure to replace the then-prevalent physical and corporal punishments. Nils Christie (1968) quotes the Norwegian Act, of October 15, 1815, to illustrate the transition from physical torment to loss of liberty:

> "Where the law now in force punishes a crime with the loss of two fingers, the courts should in the future impose on the guilty person imprisonment for life; and instead of loss of a hand, imprisonment for ten years; and instead of piercing the hand and rending it, imprisonment for two years; and instead of piercing the hand, imprisonment for one year."[4]

The Changing Value of Fines and Imprisonment

The use of fines or imprisonment as means of retribution implies an equation between the wrongfulness of the offence, the loss, harm or injury suffered by the victim and the amount of the fine or the period of imprisonment to which the offender is sentenced. Since the punitive value of fines and imprisonment does not remain constant but considerably changes over the years, it follows that for the purpose of the equation it is necessary to regularly readjust the penalties as prescribed in the law and as meted out by the courts. These re-adjustments are not taking place. The sanctions provided by the Criminal Code have remained virtually unchanged since it was enacted in 1892. There is every reason to believe that judges hardly take into account, when determining their sentences, the changes in the value of penal sanctions. At a time when the emphasis in sentencing was placed on rehabilitation rather than punishment, this might have been forgivable. With the present resurgence of the ideas of the Classical and the Neo-Classical schools, the matter takes a wholly new significance.[5]

Despite the importance of this topic to any theory of punishment or to a retributive model of criminal justice, there has been almost no discussion of it in the criminological literature. In all the literature consulted, no other study was found dealing specifically with the changes in penal values except an article published by Nils Christie in 1968. And it is rather surprising that none of the economists, who in recent years have turned to criminology in increasing numbers, has paid any attention to this topic. In his article, Christie (1968)[11] states the problem as follows:

> "The value of money decreases or increases as a result of inflation or deflation. But the same thing applies to the penal value of different means of punishment. When the value of an existence free from physical pain increases when improved hygiene, medical care and anaesthetics give better assurance of such an existence, we can probably inflict a little less physical pain to compensate for the same crime. When the value of human life increases, we more seldom pay with it for the same type of offence. Or since life and death are dichotomies that fit badly into a graded scale of punishments, the offences that require the death penalty must be correspondingly graver when the value of life increases. When daily existence is characterized by greater security against need, more leisure and fewer limitations on self-development, then a lesser deprivation of these benefits will compensate for the same crime. The penal value of a day in prison has increased. But, on the other hand, when the value of money goes down, one must pay an increased fine to compensate for the same offence."

With a rapidly increasing rate of inflation in recent years, the value of money has been decreasing at an ever-accelerating pace. A thousand- or a hundred-dollar fine does not have today the punitive value the same fine had ten, twenty or fifty years ago. It is fair to say, therefore, that a constant devaluation of monetary penalties is taking place as a result of the continuing erosion in the value of money. It might be argued that, although the statutory fines have not changed, judges have been consciously or unconsciously making the necessary adjustments when determining the amounts of fines within the minimum and the maximum prescribed by the law. It is difficult to test the validity of such hypothesis in the absence of Canadian data. But though rates and figures are not available, there is a general impression that fines handed out by the courts nowadays are not substantially higher than those meted out several years ago.

In Scandinavia, the day-fine system[6] although not meant originally to adjust the amount of fines to actual changes in the value of money but rather to establish a degree of fairness in penalties given to offenders of varying incomes, does in fact, at least to a certain extent, achieve the purpose of adjustment. Unfortunately, Canada has not yet seen fit to adopt an identical or a similar system.

The opposite of what has been taking place with regard to fines has been occurring in relation to imprisonment. Imprisonment, as it is practised today, is not merely a deprivation of liberty. It also entails the deprivation of many pleasurable things that life outside the walls has to offer and which a free person with reasonable income is able to enjoy. Several attempts have been made in recent years to measure the quality of life using a long list of social indicators. Most of these indicators point to an improvement in the quality of life in Western countries, particularly since the end of the Second World War. Since life outside the prisons has changed for the better, the pains of imprisonment have grown and so did the deprivations associated with incarceration. In the absence of necessary legislative adjustments to statutory prison terms and the lack of judicial adjustments to actual prison sentences, imprisonment has become a much more severe penalty than it used to be. At the same time, the relative seriousness of the majority of offences for which imprisonment is being used (that is, property offences without violence) has declined as a result of growing prosperity, inflation and an abundance of material goods.

It might be argued that over the years life in prison has also substantially improved, that the living conditions in penal institutions now are far better than they were in the last century or in the early half of the twentieth century. This is undoubtedly true. It might further be argued that the improvement in life conditions inside the walls has kept pace with the improvement in the quality of life on the outside and that the gap between the two has not widened even it has not necessarily narrowed. This is rather doubtful.

The Practical Implications of the Changing Value of Penal Sanctions

What are the practical implications of the changing value of penal sanctions? There are several. For the sake of brevity, the discussion of these implications is limited to the two foremost functions of penal sanctions, namely deterrence and retribution.

Deterrence

The issue of deterrence is a very controversial one and research on the deterrent effect of criminal sanctions, despite some progress in the last decade, is still in its infancy. More reliable data, sophisticated methodology and complex research design are needed to gain insight into the dynamics of deterrence. But for the purpose of the present discussion it is assumed that punishment, be it imprisonment or fine, is a deterrent and that the severity of punishment is, as many claim it to be, an important variable that is significantly associated with the efficacy of deterrence. If this is the case then it follows that the deterrent value of monetary penalties is declining while the deterrent value of prison sentences is increasing. Consequently, those who expect to be sentenced to a fine if caught and convicted will be less deterred, while those who expect to be sentenced to a prison term will be more deterred. This is, needless to say, an over-simplification because a host of other variables exercise a non-negligible impact on the effectiveness of punishment as a deterrent. It is clear, however, that if the maintenance of dissuasive and intimidating functions of penal sanctions at a constant level is desired then regular adjustments in Statutory and actual penalties have to be made to take into account the ever changing value of these penalties.

Retribution

The implications of the changing value of penal sanctions on retribution are more serious and more far-reaching. Although the legislative task of prescribing a certain penalty for a specific offence, and the judicial task of imposing a penalty within the range provided by the legislator, are necessarily arbitrary exercises, the principle of justice requires a certain measure of uniformity and individualization in the administration of penalties. Disparity of sentences, on the other hand, strikes at the heart of justice itself and constitutes an affront to the principle of equality before the law. It is fairly easy to document the differential treatment the rich and the poor, those from high and those from low social strata, get at the hands of justice. The preference of the criminal courts has always been to sentence high-class criminals and white-collar criminals to fines, while using prison sentences more frequently for the poor and blue-collar offenders. Many arguments are made to justify this apparently inequitable practice. It is argued, for instance, that sentencing the poor, the unemployed and the have-nots to fines is a futile exercise, since they are unable to pay and will thus end up in prison anyway. It is also argued that imprisonment when applied to the wealthy and the upper class constitutes a much harsher punishment than when applied to the poor and the lower-class offenders. It is often said, in cases where a white-collar criminal is sentenced to a fine for an offence for which the poor is usually sent to prison, that he has suffered a lot from loss of reputation, status or standing within the community and that a prison sentence is, therefore, unwarranted. The accuracy and truthfulness of such assertions or rationalizations are irrelevant to the topic under discussion. What is of particular relevance is the fact that however unfair this practice may be, the unfairness is being accentuated and aggravated by the changing value of fines and imprisonment. As a result of the declining value of fines and the growing severity of imprisonment, upper-class and white-collar criminals are getting away with milder and milder penalties (fines), while poor, lower-class offenders are being more severely punished (prison sentences).

The Problems Inherent in Using Imprisonment as a Retributive Sanction

1. Making the Punishment Fit the Crime: The Eternal Problem

Private vengeance in primitive societies is, quite often, unlimited in scope and quite disproportionate to the harm done. The great progress achieved through the law of talion saw the establishment of a balance between the wrong and the punishment, the legitimizing of the sanction only if it is in proportion to the harm done. Imprisonment as a retributive sanction lacks the fairness and proportionality of *lex talionis*. The eternal and insoluble problem facing legislators using imprisonment as a means of retribution is to determine what term of prison should expiate an attack on property or to equate physical and sexual assaults with a number of days, months or years in prison. The arbitrariness of such equation is both evident and inevitable. It is certainly possible to grade various criminal offences according to their objective and/or perceived seriousness. However, to come up with a prison term equivalent to theft or robbery, to assault or rape, is a completely different matter. It is one thing to state and to empirically demonstrate that people regard robbery as more serious than theft or that they view forcible rape as much more serious than indecent exposure, but to stipulate that the punishment for theft or that for rape be so-and-so many years in prison is a totally different matter. Any such stipulation is inevitably arbitrary, capricious and despotic. Since *lex talionis,* no criminal law has ever succeeded in making the punishment fit the crime. Faced with this problem, penal reformers of the eighteenth and nineteenth century, such as Cesare Beccaria, advocated that punishment be made as much in conformity with the nature of crime as possible. For this reason, Beccaria recommended that crimes against the person be punished by corporal punishment and that thefts not involving violence be punished by a fine. Later on, however, most legislators decided to make imprisonment the primary penalty for nearly every crime. Since the dilemma of equating the amount of deprivation of liberty with the degree of moral guilt or with the extent of harm done had never been solved, the determination of the length of imprisonment was left either to the arbitrariness of the legislators or to the discretion of the sentencing judge, with all the disparities and inequities that ensued.

As a vehicle for retribution and as an instrument for expiation, imprisonment poses insurmountable problems of justice, fairness and equity. If, as a nation, Canada decides that punishing criminals is the ultimate goal of the criminal justice system, then, as a civilized, technocratic society, it must be able to find a more humane and less arbitrary way of punishing criminals and of demonstrating society's disapproval and condemnation than imprisonment.

2. Measuring the Pains of Imprisonment for Each Individual Offender

The problem of making imprisonment fit the crime is not the only insurmountable obstacle in the way of the use of imprisonment as a retributive sanction. At the heart of retributive justice are the notions of fairness and equality. But fairness and equality are not achieved if the allocation of punishment is made solely by reference to the nature and the seriousness of the offence of which the offender has been convicted. Fairness and equality do not mean sentencing people guilty of similar crimes to identical or similar terms of imprisonment. Like the philosophers of the Classical School, proponents of principles such as "just deserts," "determinate sentence" and "presumptive sentence" see their proposals as the only way to remedy current sentencing disparities and to restore fairness and equity. In this they seem to be guided by the same naive optimism that led Classical thinkers to believe that only a system of fixed punishments can and will eliminate the injustices and iniquities of the old regime. The revival of the Classical ideas is quite evident in the report of the Committee for the Study of Incarceration in the U.S.A. As many others, the members of the committee could not conceive of individualization without disparity, and therefore retreated from a concept of individualized justice and discretion in sentencing. Rather than suggesting solutions to the problem of sentencing disparity or remedies to cope with it, they chose to abandon individualization and to opt for a greater mechanization of justice. Mechanization may be a workable proposition for distributive justice-dispensing fines, compensation or ordering restitution. It is hardly feasible when the punishment meted out to various offenders is imprisonment.

By proportioning the amount of fine to the defendant's income, the Scandinavian day-fine system comes close to achieving the ideal of fairness. But with imprisonment it is a totally different matter.

Retributive justice requires that offenders convicted of the same offence be subjected to the same amount of pain and suffering, to the same degree of unpleasantness, to identical deprivations, and that they be made to suffer similar consequences. But the pains of imprisonment, so well described by Sykes,[17] are not the same for all those who experience it, even when they are kept in the same or similar institutions for the same length of time. The pain of losing one's liberty varies greatly from one individual to the other. The deprivation of material amenities depends on what amenities are available to the person when he is outside. The rupture of family and friendly ties depends on whether the person has a family and friends or not. The loss of status or reputation is not of the same degree and does not carry the same consequences for persons of different standing and from different social classes. The loss of autonomy and choice depends on how much autonomy and choice the person enjoyed before being put behind bars. The forced abstinence from sexual intimacy with the other sex can be a highly traumatizing experience for a heterosexual individual, while a homosexual may have a greater opportunity for sexual activity in prison than on the outside.

As long as it remains impossible to measure the pains of imprisonment and to weigh the sufferings and deprivations resulting from it for each individual offender, the use of incarceration as a retributive sanction will always be an arbitrary, capricious, unfair and inequitable exercise.

The sentence of life imprisonment, whether subject to review by parole authorities or not, poses yet an additional problem. Like the death penalty, life imprisonment fails to take into account the age and life expectancy of different offenders. It thus constitutes a much harsher penalty when imposed upon younger offenders than when imposed upon older ones.

3. The Functional Incompatibility of Retribution and Rehabilitation

The use of prison as a retributive sanction and its use for the purpose of rehabilitation appear to be two mutually exclusive goals. Retribution and rehabilitation are functionally incompatible. Retribution, by definition, requires that pain be inflicted and that the offender be made to suffer for his crime. It implies the humiliation and the degradation of the wrong-doer. Rehabilitation, on the other hand, requires that the offender be treated humanely with dignity and respect, be shown love, kindness and compassion, not cruelty, contempt and hate.

4. The Functional Incompatibility of Incarceration and Restitution to the Victim

In recent years there has been a growing awareness of the plight of crime victims and of the need to redress the wrong and to repair the harm done to them by the offence. Many believe that if the criminal does have a debt to pay, it is not a debt to society but to the victim(s) of his offence(s). The deserving, worthwhile goals of restitution and compensation are hindered and not facilitated by imprisonment. The incarceration of the offender is, in many ways, incompatible with the notion of restitution or compensation to the victim. At the going inmate wages in penal institutions, even the lucky few who are given the opportunity to work in prison hardly earn enough money to satisfy their daily requirements of cigarettes and sundries. In effect, by incarcerating the wrongdoer, the state is making restitution to the victim a virtual impossibility. One of the major advantages alternatives to incarceration have over imprisonment is that they do not interfere with the offender's continuing employment if he is a wage-earner and that in many cases the offender is required to seek employment and to make restitution to the victim as a condition for the non-custodial disposition.

State victim-compensation programs, despite the fanfare with which they were launched some years ago, offer the victims no more than a symbolic or token compensation. Coverage is restricted to less than ten per cent of all crime victims, and the numerous conditions for eligibility reduce this further to a handful of individuals. The major or perhaps the only problem in the way of wider or universal coverage is one of cost. Prisons absorb such a large portion of criminal justice costs that little is left to subsidize other more positive and less wasteful programs. If what is being spent now on our prisons is funnelled to victim compensation, enough funds will be available to ensure universal or quasi-universal coverage. Here is just one example in support of this claim.

According to Waller and Okihiro (1978),[7] the average value of property stolen in their sample of residential burglaries in Toronto in 1973 was $210. Let us assume that as a result of inflation the average value has almost doubled to $400 in 1981. A conservative estimate of the cost of keeping an inmate in a federal penitentiary for two years puts it at $60,000. In other words, the cost of a two-year prison sentence suffices to compensate one hundred and fifty burglary victims!

Conclusion

At the time it was adopted as a retributive sanction, a little more than a century and a half ago, imprisonment might have been a humanitarian measure compared to the sanctions it had replaced. But times have changed and prisons today are living monuments exemplifying man's inhumanity to man. They are constant reminders of the failure to come up with more humane, less wasteful and less destructive ways of dealing with society's criminals. What seems surprising, as the twentieth century draws to a close, that the propriety and inevitability of incarceration are accepted as a given and that the legitimacy of imprisonment as a punishment is never questioned. Neither reform commissions or commissions of inquiry are asking whether society has the right to ever resort to incarceration as a punishment or whether liberty and freedom have reached a degree of sacredness that deprivation of them can no longer be employed or justified. When this degree was reached by human life in many countries, the death penalty simply ceased to be applied. And when physical integrity reached the same level, corporal punishments were removed from the arsenal of sanctions.

Experience shows that the best and perhaps the only way to avoid or to make less use of imprisonment is to reduce the number of prisons. A moratorium on prison construction in Canada might, therefore, be necessary for changing current legal and police practices and for developing innovative non-institutional measures to deal with the bulk of non-violent and non-dangerous offenders. It might also be helpful in changing the attitudes of the public and in gaining wider public acceptance for non-custodial sentences. This is borne out by the experience of many countries. Christie (1968)[11] points out that the transition from physical torment to loss of liberty in Norway early in the nineteenth century resulted in the penitentiaries and other penal institutions becoming full to bursting point. As a result, a long series of amendments to the criminal law were passed from 1842 to the turn of the century, all of which tended in the direction of shortening the periods of imprisonment or avoiding imprisonment altogether. Here in North America, Nagel (1977)[15] found that American states which built prisons during the past twenty years have more overcrowded institutions now than before, while those states which did not build have less crowded prisons.

With the abolition of the death penalty, with the substantial improvement in the quality of life since the end of the second world war, imprisonment has become the most cruel in the arsenal of punishments. And yet this country has no qualms about applying it widely or about practising it in abundance. This attitude is best explained by George Bernard Shaw (1946)[16] when he claimed that, although imprisonment is the most cruel of all punishments, those who inflict it without having ever experienced it cannot believe it to be cruel.

References

1. Despite this, the Canadian public is still asking for more. In 1966, the Gallup interviewers asked a sample of Canadian adults the following question: "In general, do you think the courts in this area deal too harshly or not harshly enough with criminals?" Forty-three per cent of the respondents felt that the courts in their area were not harsh enough. The percentage of those who perceived the courts as being too lenient continued to rise when the question was asked again in subsequent years. It grew to 58% in 1969, to 66% in 1974, to 73% in 1975 and to 75% in September 1977. Only 4% of all respondents in 1977 were of the view that the courts in their area were too harsh.[10]

2. Despite this, the Law Reform Commission of Canada was not willing to recommend the abolition of imprisonment. Instead, it recommended that it should be an exceptional sanction and should only be used for the following three reasons: (1) to separate from the rest of society for a period of time certain offenders who represent a serious threat to the life or personal security of others and or (2) to denounce the behaviour that is deemed highly reprehensible because of its violation of fundamental values or (3) to sanction offenders who willfully fail in carrying out obligations imposed under other types of sentences.

3. A summary of the studies that arrived at this conclusion can be found in the Law Reform Commission's report *Fear of Punishment*, pp. 95-97.[12]

4. *Parliamentary Proceedings 1815*, Vol. I. Christiana, 1819, p. 218 quoted after Christie (1968). Christie notes that there is a seeming inconsistency in the tariff in that the loss of two fingers was commuted to imprisonment for life, whereas the loss of a whole hand was commuted to imprisonment for ten years. This was due to the fact that the loss of two fingers was the traditional punishment for bearing false witness, and this was, in the opinion of the legislative committee, a graver offence than forgery, which had until then been punishable by loss of a hand.

5. The rejection of rehabilitation and the reaffirmation of the principles of the Classical School is nowhere more explicitly stated than in the report of the Committee for the Study of Incarceration chaired by Charles Goodell. In the preface to its report *Doing Justice: The Choice of Punishments,* the chairman makes the following declaration: "What emerges from our study is a conceptual model that differs considerably from the dominant thinking about punishment during this century. The conventional wisdom has been that the sentence should be fashioned so as to rehabilitate the offender and isolate him from society if he is dangerous. To accomplish that, the sentencer was to be given the widest discretion to suit the disposition to the particular criminal. For reasons which this book explains, we reject these notions as unworkable and unjust. We conclude that the severity of the sentence should depend on the seriousness of the defendant's crime or crimes – on what he did rather than on what the sentencer expects he will do if treated in a certain fashion."

6. For a review of the day-fine system in the Scandinavian countries, see Law Reform Commission of Canada: *Restitution and Compensation-Fines, Working Papers* 5 and 6, Ottawa: Information Canada, October 1974, pp. 43-48. See also Home Office: *Report of the Advisory Council on the Penal System,* "Non-custodial and semi-custodial penalties," 1970, pp. 7, 8, 74-76.

7. The mean value of property stolen from the household sample in 1973 was $345. However, the authors note that much of this was due to one large jeweller dy theft involving items worth $8,000 in their relatively small sample of the 57 burglaries resulting in something stolen. Eliminating this case results in an average value of property stolen of $210.

8. California State Legislature, *Deterrent Effect of Criminal Sanctions: Progress Report of the Assembly Committee on Criminal Procedure,* 1968.

9. Canada: Law Reform Commission, *Ottawa Imprisonment and Release.* Information Canada, 1975.

10. Canadian Institute of Public Opinion: *The Gallup Report* (several years).

11. Christie, N. "Changes in Penal Value," in *Scandinavian Studies in Criminology, Volume 2: Aspects of Social Control in Welfare States,* Nils Christie (ed.). Oslo: Universitets Forlaget, 1968.

12. Fattah, E.A. *Fear of Punishment: Deterrence.* Ottawa: Ministry of Supply and Services, 1976.

13. __Hood, R. and Sparks, R. *Key Issues in Criminology.* London: World University Library, 1970.

14. Jaffary, S., *Sentencing of Adults in Canada.* Toronto: Toronto University Press, 1963.

15. __Nagel, W. "On behalf of a moratorium on prison construction." *Crime and Delinquency,* April, 1977.

16. Shaw, G.B. *The Crime of Imprisonment.* New York: Philosophical Library, 1946.

17. Sykes, G.M. "The Pains of Imprisonment." In L. Radzinowicz and M.E. Wolfgang (eds.) *Crime and Justice, Volume III: The Criminal in Confinement.* New York: Basic Books, 1971.

18. von Hirsch, A. *Doing Justice: The Choice of Punishments.* Report of the Committee for the Study of Incarceration. New York: Hill and Wang, 1976.

19. Waller, I. and Okihiro, N. *Burglary: The Victim and the Public.* Toronto: University of Toronto Press, 1978.

Chapter II

Beyond Metaphysics: *The* Need *for a* New Paradigm

On Actual and Potential Contributions of Criminology and the Social Sciences to the Reform of the Criminal Law

Originally published in *Criminal Law Theory in Transition: Finnish and Comparative Perspectives*, edited by Raimo Lahti and Kimmo Nuotio, published in 1992 by the Finnish Lawyers Publishing Company.

My sincere thanks to Alma Talent, Helsinki, Finland, for the kind permission to republish this article.

> "In the criminal justice system we are witnessing the death throes of an old and cumbersome paradigm, one that has dominated Western thought for more than 900 years… Only if we are willing to look at our old problems in a new light do we stand a chance of solving them. This is our only hope and our greatest challenge."
>
> Randy E. Barnett, "Restitution: A New Paradigm of Criminal Justice," in Galaway and Hudson, *Perspectives on Crime Victims* (1981:245)
>
> "Revolutionary though the prospect of abandoning the concept of responsibility may be, it is clear that we are travelling steadily towards it."
>
> Barbara Wootton, *Social Science and Social Pathology* (1959:251)
>
> "Much in the intellectual current of our time has been thought to challenge the validity of the basic postulate of the criminal law: the concept of criminal responsibility."
>
> Francis A. Allen, *The Borderline of Criminal Justice* (1964:126)

Introduction

Few would disagree with the statement that the criminal law is in a state of crisis, that it is lagging behind the times. The malaise is felt by scholars and practitioners alike. The commissions of reform established in many countries on a temporary or permanent basis are the proof that something must be done. The needed reform has to be sweeping and radical. The stage seems to be set for a scientific revolution or a paradigm shift in the sense proposed by Thomas Kuhn (1970). This is because most of the current problems can be traced directly to the old paradigm. As Barnett (1977) points out, many if not most of the ills of the present system stem from errors in the underlying paradigm. Thus any attempt to correct these symptomatic debilities without examination of the theoretical underpinnings is doomed to frustration and failure (p. 245).

Kuhn (1970) defines scientific revolutions as "those non-cumulative developmental episodes in which an older paradigm is replaced in whole or in part by an incompatible new one." A paradigm, he explains, is an achievement in a particular discipline which defines the legitimated problems and methods of research within that discipline. This achievement is sufficiently unprecedented to attract new adherents within that discipline. This achievement is sufficiently unprecedented to attract new adherents away from rival approaches while providing many unsolved questions for these new practitioners to solve (Barnett, 1977, 1981). Another definition of "paradigm" is given in Ritzer (1975), who writes:

> "A paradigm is a fundamental image of the subject matter within a science. It serves to define what should be studied, what questions should be asked, how they should be asked and what rules should be followed in interpreting the answers obtained. The paradigm is the broadest unit of consensus within a science and serves to differentiate one scientific community (or subcommunity) from another. It subsumes, defines and interrelates the exemplars, theories and methods and instruments that exist within it," (1975:7,189).

The present paper will examine the crisis in the criminal law and will offer some views on the principal reasons for the crisis. The various conditions identified by Kuhn (1970) and Young (1988) as necessary for a paradigm shift will be analyzed and this will be followed by an outline of a new paradigm proposed to replace the old one.

Part One: The Crisis

1. The Anachronism of the Criminal Code in Western Societies

Like the Canadian criminal code (enacted in 1892) and many others, the Penal Code of Finland dates back to the nineteenth century, having been passed on December 19, 1889. The kindest thing that could be said about all these penal codes is that they are historical documents that mirror the mentality of the era in which they were enacted. The piecemeal changes they have undergone since they were passed reflect various social and political circumstances occurring over a century. The fact that these codes have neither been overhauled nor replaced by new modern ones speaks eloquently to the criminal law's unmitigated resistance to change. Of all branches of law, the criminal law undoubtedly is the one that demonstrates best society's procrastination and misoneism.

No century has witnessed more scientific and technological advances, more political changes or more social upheavals than the twentieth century. Unfortunately, the criminal code has not kept pace with social and scientific evolution and remains in most countries a relic of the past, as a vestige of a bygone era. It certainly boggles the mind that in the age of science and technology in which we live we continue to have and to accept a criminal law inspired by and based upon concepts, principles, premises and paradigms dating from the Age of Reason, or the Age of Enlightenment. It is simply unbelievable that when we are less than a decade away from the twenty-first century that we seem to see nothing wrong in having an archaic and antiquated criminal justice system, a system trying to dispense justice, not according to earthly criteria, but according to divine criteria. That all the fundamental principles, all the basic notions of the criminal law today have been borrowed from the philosophy and theology of the eighteenth and nineteenth centuries is hard to understand. Such are the notions of evil, wickedness, malice, guilt, culpability, retribution, expiation, atonement, to name but a few. The time has come to ask whether notions such as "free will," "moral responsibility," "criminal intent," "*mens rea,*" "premeditation," "malice aforethought," as well as many others, do have a place in a modern, secular, socially-oriented criminal law like the one needed in the twenty-first century. The fundamental question is whether legal concepts such as "insanity," "diminished responsibility," etc. could withstand the test of science or whether notions such as retribution, punishment, just deserts and so forth have a place in a modern scientific and secular criminal policy.

The obsolescence of the criminal law and the criminal code is decried by scholars and practitioners alike, by criminologists as well as jurists. In a speech delivered to the Canadian Congress of Criminology in 1977, Honourable Justice Antonio Lamer, who was at the time the chairman of the Law Reform Commission of Canada, and who has been recently appointed chief justice of Canada's highest court, stated that:

> "In Canada we still tend to behave as if the ringing declarations of the Age of Reason were the last word in criminal justice and any admission that we have departed from them will be fatal to our system," (1978:128).

To illustrate the state of anachronism of the criminal law, Justice Lamer went on to declare:

> "Among all the areas of public concern for which governments establish departments and ministries, law is unique in one very significant way: legitimacy is measured by how closely what we do today corresponds to what we did in the past. If such thinking dominated other areas of public policy, we would still be training our soldiers to dig trenches, we would still be debating whether smallpox vaccinations are an appropriate public health measure and the tractor would be viewed as a novel and probably dangerous innovation. Modern behavioural science, to say nothing of the eighty per cent recidivism rate in our penitentiaries, has made it absolutely clear that the broad consensus and naive optimism of the nineteenth century has been a disastrous foundation of our approach to the problems of criminality today," (1978:129).

All this points to the urgent need for the Western nations to rethink, reassess and modernize the archaic and antiquated criminal codes of the nineteenth century to bring them to the standards and requirements of the Space Age and to prepare them for the challenges of the twenty-first century.

2. The Persistence of Theological and Metaphysical Notions

A secular society requires and deserves a secular criminal law. Secularization does not simply mean replacing canon law by a man-made criminal code or having a criminal justice system administered, not by the clergy, but by laypersons. Secularization is not achieved just by decriminalizing a few sins or removing irreligious acts, such as heresy or blasphemy, from the list of punishable behaviours. It can only be attained by purifying the criminal law of the theological notions that have dominated it for several centuries. According to *Webster's New Twentieth Century Dictionary* (second unabridged edition), to secularize is "to make worldly or unspiritual; to deprive of any religious character, influence or significance." The same dictionary explains that "secular" means "dissociated from religious teachings or principles." Assessed according to these definitions, Western criminal codes are far from being secular codes. What is surprising is that even the most ardent proponents of a separation of religion and morals from the criminal law seem to see nothing wrong with the persistence of theological notions in that law. It is ironical that the strongest advocates of "punishment" are precisely those who firmly believe that those who do wrong will be subjected in the afterlife to eternal hell. The fact that punishing these "sinners" on earth constitutes double jeopardy is either missed or ignored.

Although most Western societies have managed to effect a complete separation of the state from the church and are no longer dominated by religion, the criminal law remains as one of the few surviving bastions of theocracy. One of the manifestations of this is the way crime is still being regarded. Crime which in a secular society is considered a harmful, injurious behaviour that needs to be redressed in the present and prevented in the future continues to be viewed as wrongful, sinful, immoral behaviour that must be punished. In many quarters it is believed to be the doing of the Devil. Aside from a few insignificant attempts in the last decade, there has been no real effort to replace the theological notions of "moral guilt" and "deserved punishment" by secular ones, such as harm, reparation, restitution and compensation. Despite scientific progress and unprecedented social evolution, social reaction to crime remains largely unchanged. The pagan and theocratic practices of sacrifice (from *sacer*, sacred, and *facere*, to make) and of scapegoating still persist in many codes, including those of the most technologically advanced countries in the world (U.S.A., Russia and Japan) in the form of capital punishment. The religious crusades of the past have now been replaced by moral crusades. The calls "hang them, hang them" and "castrate them, castrate them" are simply the modern versions of the old cry "crucifixion, crucifixion" which was common during Roman times. Excommunication from the church is replaced by expulsion from society. The punishment and stigmatization of deviants and outcasts are not very different from the branding with a hot iron or the burning of witches or heretics. There is hardly any difference between the punishment of epileptics in medieval times and the persecution of drug addicts in modern times. And in psychiatric jargon the preposterous disease of "moral insanity," invented in the nineteenth century, has simply been replaced by the loose diagnostic label of "psychopath."

The resistance to secularization has also had dire practical consequences. The continuing tendency to view crime as moral aberration and as the emanation of a free will has led to naive optimism about the effectiveness of punishment as a deterrent and to exaggerated confidence in the ability of the criminal code to solve social problems and to cure society's headaches. This in turn has resulted in an inflationary criminal law policy, to a crisis of over-criminalization and to an overextended, overburdened and overworked criminal justice system.

Contrary to other branches of law, the reform of the criminal code seems to take one step forward and two steps backwards. Thus the progressive moves aimed at secularizing and modernizing the criminal code in the aftermath of the Second World War have suffered serious setbacks. For example, the positive trend towards secularization, which was quite strong in the 1950s and the 1960s, seems to have been reversed in recent years. It was this trend that led a state committee in Sweden to recommend in 1956 that the word "punishment" be dropped entirely and be replaced by the word "sanction." The suggested reform was one which had already been adopted by the Greenland criminal code of 1954 (Anttila, 1986). Along the same line, one would have expected the theological/philosophical notion of "moral guilt" to be replaced by secular ones, such as "harm," "loss" or "injury." The opposite, however, seems to be the case. Professor Anttila (1986) observed that the shift over the past two decades in Finland has been from a *consequence* orientation to a *guilt* orientation. This trend is particularly evident in the changes made in the provisions on homicide and assault. She points out that the main emphasis is now placed on the guilt manifested by the offender at the time of the act, with the most severe punishment being directed at those who had planned their offence in advance or at least committed the offence deliberately with knowledge of the possible consequences. This guilt-oriented approach led in some cases to the criminalization of mere endangerment, even if no actual harm resulted. It has also resulted in the diminishment of the relative significance of negligent offences where the extent and seriousness of offences often depend on chance factors (Anttila, 1986). Wickedness, it seems, continues to be the prime criterion for punishment.

Another good example of persisting theological practices in the criminal law and criminal justice is the requirement that evidence and testimony be given under oath to be acceptable in court.

The Inadequacy of Metaphysical Notions for the Complex Social Realities of Post-Industrial Societies

The ever-growing complexity of society brought about by the industrial and technological revolutions and the accompanying urbanization led to a gradual, though partial, realization that the metaphysical concepts which dominated European criminal codes in the post-French-Revolution eras are exceedingly inadequate to address and to deal with the rapidly changing social realities. It became abundantly clear that strict adherence to philosophical and abstract notions such as "criminal intent," "*mens rea,*" "free will" and "moral responsibility" makes it impossible to effectively control, sanction and curb a wide variety of socially harmful and dangerous behaviours. These include criminality of negligence, the vast majority of traffic offences, white-collar crime, corporate deviance, crimes against the environment, status offences, offences committed under the influence of alcohol or drugs, and so forth. Instead of overhauling the criminal codes that were enacted in the nineteenth century to adapt them to the realities of post-industrial societies, legal scholars were forced to do some mental acrobatics in order to come up with acceptable deviations, exceptions and exemptions from the metaphysical yet fundamental principles of "*mens rea*" and "free will." As it was necessary in the nineteenth century to invent concepts, legal presumptions and subterfuges that are outright contradictory to the Classical notions of criminal intent and moral responsibility (such as *dolus eventualis*, irresistible impulse, ignorance of the law is no excuse, etc.), contemporary legal scholars had to invent concepts such as technical guilt, objective responsibility, strict liability, absolute liability, vicarious liability and corporate liability, to name but a few.

The inadequacy of the old concepts has been such that a huge number of offences are governed by the newly invented ones. Baroness Wootton (1963) states that the majority of cases dealt with by the criminal courts in England are cases of strict liability in which proof of a guilty mind is not necessary for conviction. More than fifteen years ago, the Law Reform Commission of Canada (1974) reported that Canadian federal laws contain about 20,000 regulatory offences and the laws of the average province about another 20,000, and of the combined total ninety per cent (90%) are offences of strict liability. The commission reported further that each year there are roughly 1,400,000 convictions for strict liability offences and roughly 850,000 persons are convicted of them, that is, a conviction a year for one in twenty-five of the Canadian population. The problem, stated the commission, is enormous, quantitatively speaking. In fact nearly eighty per cent (80%) of all summary convictions are for traffic offences, and in this area of law the proportion of strict liability offences is about ninety-eight per cent (98%). This leads the commission to believe that its estimate of 1,400,000 convictions for strict liability offences is, if anything, conservative.

Greve (1992) reports that a large number of breaches in Denmark are punishable even in the absence of intent on the part of the offender. He places the number of legislative acts in which strict liability for corporations exists at approximately two hundred. In another twenty-five acts, strict liability exists for natural persons. He concludes that whether one looks at the legislation or at the lawbreakers one finds that negligence of one kind or another is what sets the limits for liability to punishment.

These facts and figures clearly demonstrate that in the majority of cases criminal liability is imposed independently of any moral fault. It also means that, while the abstract concept of moral guilt does still have many proponents in the legal community, it has lost any practical significance and could be easily abandoned without dire consequences.

3. The Pursuit of Unattainable Goals

The goals of current criminal codes were set at a time when social sciences, including sociology, psychology and criminology, were woefully underdeveloped. Despite the enormous progress and great strides these disciplines have achieved in the second half of the twentieth century, the goals have neither been reassessed nor redefined. As a result, the criminal code and its executive arm, the criminal justice system, are hopelessly struggling to achieve two impossible goals: justice through retribution and prevention through deterrence. The first, retribution, is ridiculously outdated and morally bankrupt. The second, deterrence, is a common-sense notion that has yet to receive empirical validation. In Finland, for example, retribution remains the guiding principle in sentencing. Commenting on Section 6:1 of the Finnish penal code, Lappi-Seppälä (1992) affirms that:

> "Although the aim is general prevention, the leading principle and criteria in sentencing refer – not to preventive theories – but to ideas that are often linked together with the retributive theories of punishment."

The humanitarian trend which aimed at replacing the philosophical and abstract goal of retribution by the more utilitarian goal of rehabilitation was dealt a heavy blow by the now fashionable doctrine of "nothing works." And as empirical research continues to cast doubt on the effectiveness of traditional criminal sanctions as a deterrent, there is a growing tendency to revert to the old notions of punishment, revenge and retaliation while trying to couch them in more civilized terms, such as "just deserts" and "incapacitation."

The resurgence of religious fundamentalism and under the influence of conservative and right-wing politics that dominated most Western countries in the late 1970s and particularly in the 1980s, the theological view of crime as sin and the normative view that sees criminal behaviour as evil and wicked behaviour are regaining acceptance and are delaying the transition to a modern secular criminal code. One would have expected the switch from the term "penal code" (from Latin *poenalis*, from *poena*, pain, punishment) to the term "criminal code" to be accompanied by a substantial change to the nature of social reaction to crime and the type of criminal sanctions. Such a positive step, however, did not materialize. And while Finland in July 1974 went ahead and abolished imprisonment in the penitentiary, replacing it in all cases with "simple" imprisonment, in Canada we still call our federal prisons "penitentiaries" to emphasize that they are still supposed to be places of penitence and penance.

4. The Faulty Assumption that Crime Is Unique

A. Is Crime Unique?

Critical criminology has questioned the *raison d'être* of the criminal code. The existence of a criminal code separate from the civil one and using sanctions of a different nature, such as imprisonment (and in some countries the death penalty), is predicated upon a doubtful premise. The premise is that crime is a unique or exceptional category of behaviour and that criminal behaviour is more serious or more harmful than other behaviour. The relativity of crime in time and space and the fact that for every behaviour defined as criminal and made punishable by the criminal code there are similar or even identical behaviours that are not clearly indicates that crime is neither unique nor qualitatively different from other categories of behaviour. One can give countless examples to illustrate the claim that criminality is neither an intrinsic quality of the behaviour so defined nor an innate character of that behaviour. Actually, the same material act can be criminal in certain situations but not in others. Killing is allowed in some circumstances (war, self-defence, the death penalty, euthanasia) but strongly prohibited in others. Rape is a serious crime that is severely punished, and yet in many jurisdictions, including Finland, raping one's wife is not a crime. Many acts of violence are criminal while others are condoned or tolerated to the extent that they are culturally legitimate and legally permissible. In many countries the use of the strap in school, of violence to control the behaviour of incarcerated offenders, of corporal punishment by parents against children, are not criminal. Until recently many forms of domestic violence were not subject to any penalty whatsoever. It was not long ago that the California penal code contained a section on wife-beating that only prohibited an assault if it resulted in a "traumatic condition" in the medical sense, i.e. severe physical injury produced by violence (Straus, 1976). The absence of a qualitative difference between behaviour defined as criminal and behaviour that is not may also be observed in the area of property and regulatory offences where the line between legal and illegal, between what is punishable and what is not is, more often than not, quite arbitrarily drawn. This is the case with traffic speed limits, blood alcohol levels, age limits (as the age of consent to sexual intercourse), interest rate levels (determining what is usury, or loan-sharking) and so on. The line separating the criminal offences of theft and fraud from what is normally referred to as "sharp business practices" is particularly thin. For example, many would argue that profiteering, or the realization of excessive gains by companies and businesses, is not qualitatively different from consumers' attempts to exaggerate their losses when claiming from insurance companies. Yet the former is regarded as good business while the latter is defined as fraud! Possession, use and/or sale of certain mood-modifying or pleasure-inducing drugs (such as heroin and cocaine) is criminal and punishable in some countries by death. But the sale and use of other drugs (alcohol, tobacco, etc.) is not criminal. All these examples amply demonstrate that crime is not a unique or exceptional category of behaviour. They show how correct Howard Becker (1963) is when he claims that,

> "Deviance is *not* a quality of an act the person commits, but rather a consequence of the application by others of rules and sanctions to an offender. The deviant is one to whom the label has successfully been applied; deviant behaviour is behaviour that people so label."

The fact is, any historical or comparative analysis of the acts defined as crimes belies the existence of "natural crimes" or acts that could be considered "*mala in se.*" Lady Wootton (1963) addressed this issue in her Hamlyn lectures and declared that it is hard to think of any examples of actions which could, in a strictly physical sense, be said to be bad in themselves. Actions classified as *mala in se*, she suggests, are really only *mala anitiqua* actions, that is to say which have been recognized as criminal for a very long time. Lady Wootton adds:

> "For the origins of the supposed dichotomy between real crimes and quasi-crimes we must undoubtedly look to theology... In the secular climate of the present age, however, the appeal to religious doctrine is unconvincing and unlikely to be generally acceptable," (1963:44-45)

B. Is Crime Qualitatively Different from Tort?

If crime is not a unique or exceptional category of behaviour, if it is not qualitatively different from other behaviours not so defined, then why the insistence on treating it differently and on reacting to it in a substantially different way from the reaction to other harmful, injurious or dangerous behaviours? It is not forgotten that at one time all harmful, injurious behaviours were civil torts treated in more or less the same manner. The emergence of criminal law saw the creation of a new category of behaviour believed to be deserving of punishment. The selection of behaviours to be brought under the realm of the criminal law was guided by political, historical and religious considerations and not by the unique qualities of the behaviours that came to be defined as crimes. As a result, the distinction between crime and tort, between the criminal and the civil code, is both artificial and arbitrary and the demarcation line separating the two is blurred. Very frequently the same act is both crime and tort. And yet, as Morris and Hawkins (1969) point out, no research projects have been conducted to search for the primary cause of tort in our society, and no one has suggested that those who commit torts are biologically inferior to their fellows. They add that a large part of criminal behaviour is perfectly "normal" behaviour, both in the statistical sense and in the sense that it occurs naturally. They write:

> "...the truth is that almost all adults have at some time in their lives committed criminal acts, and it is those who have not who are abnormal. Almost all acts which are defined as criminal in our society have at some time in some society been tolerated and even socially approved. The line between legitimate and illegitimate means of acquiring property is both arbitrary and difficult to define precisely. There are wide differences between states in regard to what sexual behaviour is criminal, and considerable variation in the same state at different historical periods. There is no evidence that the bulk of criminal behaviour is the result of some pathological mental or somatic condition which distinguishes criminals in general from non-criminals," (1969:48)

Parker's (1977) account of the historical development that led to the emergence of the criminal law is identical to what we have traced above. He writes:

> "At this stage of legal development, there was no differentiation between what we know as crime or criminal law and tort or civil liability for damage inflicted. All injuries to persons or property were considered 'wrongs.' The seriousness of the wrong depended upon the disruption caused to the community or the actual or perceived affront to the injured parties. Slowly a distinction emerged between wrongs which were private disputes and required payment to the injured party or his kin, and wrongs which had a public quality and required compensation to the whole group," (1977:28)

C. Is Criminal Victimization More Harmful, More Injurious, More Serious and More Dangerous than Other Victimizations?

The answer to this question is NO. There is no doubt that deaths, injuries and losses from victimization by crime are relatively minor when compared to those caused by other forms of victimization. Unfortunately, there are no accurate statistics for several victimization types. Lady Wootton (1963) insists that the category of strict liability offences illustrates too vividly the fact that in the modern world, in one way or another, as much damage is done by negligence or by indifference to the welfare or safety of others as by deliberate wickedness.

According to Elias (1986), there were 20,000 homicides in the U.S. in 1974 contrasted with 14,200 deaths from workplace accidents, 100,000 deaths from workplace diseases, 219,000 to 328,500 pollution deaths, 16,000 deaths from unnecessary surgery, over 20,000 deaths from improper emergency care, 200 to 10,000 deaths from unnecessary prescriptions, and untold tens of thousands of deaths from symptoms of poverty, such as malnutrition and poor healthcare.

A major study of medical malpractice in the U.S. released in 1990 (*The Vancouver Sun*, March 1, 1990) and reported by Reuter provides some startling figures on one minor type of victimization, namely victimization resulting from medical malpractice. The study, conducted by researchers at Harvard Medical School, reports that in 1984 there were about 7,000 hospital deaths and 27,000 injuries due to negligence of doctors or hospital staff at fifty-one hospitals in the state of New York alone. The study further found that 99,000 patients out of 2.7 million in New York hospitals in 1984 suffered injuries during their hospital stay, and twenty-eight per cent (28%) of those suffered injuries caused by negligence. The study shows that only two per cent (2%) of the patients who suffered malpractice injuries that year sued a doctor or hospital.

Sparks (1981b) observed that, as a cause of injury, crimes of violence in the United States are much less important than motor vehicle accidents, industrial injuries, falls in the home and other natural shocks that flesh is heir to in Western industrial societies.

With the exception of very few and rare types (such as murder, rape or serious injury), most victimizations, even the ones usually termed serious, are actually trivial in nature as well as consequence. That is why they are easily forgotten. One of the major problems of victimization surveys, which by their very nature rely on the memory of the respondents, is the problem of forgetting. Even when the recall period is shortened to six months, the interviewers have to work hard to get the respondents to remember what criminal victimization they have suffered. It is also the trivial nature of most criminal victimization that accounts for the extremely low reporting rates characteristic of most offences. Even fairly serious personal crimes – such as household burglary and personal robbery – are said in most surveys to be reported to the police less than one time in two (Sparks, 1981). The most common reason given in most surveys for not notifying the police is that the victimization was too trivial.

As Hulsman (1986) points out,

> "If we compare criminal events with other events, there is – on the level of those directly involved – nothing intrinsic which distinguished those 'criminal events' from other difficult or unpleasant situations. Nor, as a rule, are they singled out by those directly involved to be dealt with in any way which differs radically from the way other events are dealt with. It is therefore not surprising that considerable proportion of the events which would be defined as 'serious crime' within the context of the criminal justice system remain completely outside the system. They are settled within the social context in which they take place (the family, the trade union, the associations, the neighbourhood) in a similar way as other 'non-criminal' conflicts. All this means that there is no *ontological reality* of crime," (1986:28).

While noting the impact of crime may be less palatable than the impact of other types of victimization, Hough and Mayhew (1983) affirm that, in quantitative terms at least, becoming a victim of robbery, wounding, car theft or burglary is less likely to upset the course of people's lives than the other misfortunes they endure compared with criminal victimization.

Ron Clarke (1981) reports that the average burglary in Britain is committed by a youth under the age of seventeen years who takes less than fifty pounds-worth of property while the occupants are away from the house. The great majority of stolen cars are recovered within a short time of being taken. About half the murders cleared up are committed, not between strangers, but between immediate family members or other close associates, and similarly most assaults take place between people who know each other and who have been drinking (Clarke, 1981).

5. Some Alternative Views on Crime Offered by Criminology and Victimology

A. Crime as a Human Conflict

Victims' current plight stems from the fact that crime is no longer viewed as a conflict or a dispute between two individuals, two human beings, but as a conflict between the offender and society. Viewed as such, crime generates not an obligation to the victim but a debt to society, and once the criminal is punished, the debt presumably is paid. In this scenario there is no place for the victim, no part for him/her to play.

The recent report of the Canadian Sentencing Commission (1988) leads to the painful realization that despite all the current talk about victims this basic outlook has not changed. Instead of stating that the primary goal of sentencing is to repair the harm done to the victim by the offender and to prevent future harm, the commission regrettably declared that:

> "...the fundamental purpose of sentencing is to preserve the authority of, and promote respect for, the law through the imposition of just sanctions," (1988:151).

Such abstract goals are responsible for the depersonalization and dehumanization of the justice system. In an era meant to become the golden age of the victim there is a growing emphasis on the need for punishment, euphemistically called "just deserts." Yet having punishment as the central focus of our criminal justice system is neither morally legitimate nor practically effective. It can only act to the detriment of the victim. Dispute settlement, mediation, reconciliation, arbitration, reparation, are concepts foreign to a system centred on punishment, a system which regards crime not as a human action but as an infraction. Such a system acts to intensify the conflict rather than solving it. And instead of bringing the feuding parties together it widens the gap that separates them. What is needed is a criminal law and a criminal justice system whose primary purpose is to heal the injury, repair the harm, compensate the loss and prevent future victimization. This naturally requires, among other things, a rethinking and a re-examination of the artificial boundaries which have been created over the years between civil and criminal law, between criminal and civil courts as well as the artificial distinctions between crime and tort.

B. Crime as a Social Risk

Modern life is hazardous. The risk a of criminal victimization is but one of the many risks to which people are daily and constantly exposed. Yet while many of the other social risks are covered in the welfare state by some form of insurance, public or private, the risk of becoming a victim of crime is not adequately covered. There is a manifest unwillingness on the part of politicians to even entertain the idea of a social insurance scheme for crime victims similar to health insurance, unemployment insurance, car or labour-accident insurance and so forth. Because of stringent conditions of eligibility, lack of funds or both, less than one per cent of crime victims receive compensation from state-funded programs, and for the few who do get it, it is always too little and too late (see Fattah, 1988). It is not surprising, therefore, that victim compensation programs have been called, and rightly so, political placebos (Chappell, 1973). The awards given to those victimized by crime are ridiculously low when compared with the generous awards that those victimized by civil torts receive. It is a strange anomaly in the present system that if one suffers a serious permanent disability as a result of an intentional crime, be it assault or attempted murder, the person would be lucky to get $3,000 from the provincial compensation program. If the same disability resulted from some form of negligence, medical malpractice or a traffic accident, he/she could get $3,000,000!

The fact that crime is not a unique category of behaviour, that it is not more harmful, more injurious or more dangerous than a multitude of other behaviours shows that there is no valid reason why harm and injury resulting from acts arbitrarily defined as crime should be treated as a distinct category and dealt with differently from other types of victimization. Criminal victimization needs to be viewed as one of the many hazards of modern social life and be dealt with in a way not too different from the way we deal with other risks and hazards to which we are all exposed. Treating it differently results in grave injustices to the ones who victimize and those who are victimized.

How Does the Risk of Crime Compare with Other Risks?

In an attempt to place criminal victimization risks in a proper perspective, researchers in England and the U.S.A. have devised some interesting ways of calculating and presenting those risks. The picture that emerges from these objective risk estimates is drastically different from the alarming one generally transmitted by the mass media or by law enforcement authorities in their relentless pursuit of higher budgets and more manpower.

Clarke (1981) quotes calculations in Britain indicating that at present levels of risk the average householder can expect to be burgled once every thirty years (much longer than the average tenancy) and that the average car owner will have his car taken only once every fifty years (longer than he is likely to be motoring). The risk of a person falling victim to homicide in any year (one in 100,000) was found to be a small fraction of the risks of being killed on the road or dying of cancer. Only one in 175,000 passenger journeys on the London Underground resulted in theft, while one in 8.4 million resulted in robbery.

In another study, Hough and Mayhew (1983) used the findings of the 1981 British Crime Survey (BCS) to estimate the various risks of victimization for an average British citizen. They report that, assuming the rates at 1981 levels, a "statistically average" person aged sixteen or over can expect:

- a robbery once every five centuries (not attempts);
- an assault resulting in injury (even if slight) once every century;
- the family car to be stolen by joyriders once very sixty years;
- a burglary in the home once every forty years.

The same authors compared some risks of victimization to the likelihood of encountering other sorts of mishaps. The chances of burglary were found to be slightly less than the chances (as estimated by questions from the BCS respondents) of a fire in the home. The chances a household runs of car theft turned out to be smaller than the chances it runs of having one of its members injured in a traffic accident. The chances of robbery were smaller than those of being admitted to hospital as a psychiatric patient.

C. Is the Criminal Law's View of Crime Compatible with Science?

There are three leading conceptions of crime; to each corresponds a different criminal policy and a different sentencing philosophy:

1. Viewing crime as the emanation of free will, as the product of a guilty mind and an evil personality. This Classical view which continues to dominate the criminal code of most Western nations leads to a criminal policy centred upon punishment, deterrence and retribution.

2. Viewing crime as a disease, as the product of a sick mind, a diseased psyche or an abnormal personality. This psychiatric/psychological view leads to a criminal justice policy centred upon treatment and rehabilitation and, to a lesser extent, on incapacitation.

3. Viewing crime as a human conflict, as a harmful and injurious behaviour. This sociological view leads to a criminal policy centred upon dispute settlement, conflict resolution, reconciliation, reparation, restitution, compensation and prevention.

The contemplated reform of the criminal law and criminal policy requires a critical assessment of these three conceptions to see how compatible or incompatible each of them is with the findings of modern social and behavioural science. The first view is that of the Classical and Neo-Classical Schools. It is the one that continues to dominate criminal law and has enjoyed a resurgence of popularity in the last decade, even in Scandinavian countries, which have always been in the forefront of penal reform. This philosophical view is, however, incompatible with social and behavioural science.

To accept the metaphysical notion of free will and its philosophical corollary, moral guilt, is to reject the principle of causality, to deny that human actions have natural causes. To admit free will is to ignore the enormous variations in the strength of motives for criminal behaviour, the extreme variations between human beings in their ability to resist temptations, to control their behaviour, to suppress their instincts, urges, drives and impulses, as well as the large differences in people's capacity to hold their emotions in check and not to yield to human passions, desires and fantasies. It ignores the strength of habit, the force of compulsion.

Behavioural sciences teach us that criminal behaviour, like other human behaviours, has causes. Whether the causes are biological or psychological, thus needing treatment and rehabilitation, or whether they are social causes needing social reforms, to base our criminal policy and our sentencing philosophy on abstract notions such as retribution or just deserts is not only an affront to science, it is a wrong response to a complex problem. Whether the criminal is the product of a bad seed or a bad environment, whether crime is the product of nature or nurture, whether its roots can be traced to bad upbringing, abnormal personality, social inequities, inequalities in wealth and power, adopting retribution and punishment as the central focus of the criminal law and the sentencing philosophy, regardless of the euphemisms used, amounts to punishing the victim.

6. Is Retributive Justice Possible and Feasible?

In a retributive system of criminal justice the determination of punishment is supposed to be done according to one or both of the following criteria:

1. The punishment should be proportionate to the gravity of the offence (making the punishment fit the crime).
2. The punishment should be proportionate to the degree of responsibility of the offender for the offence.

As I have pointed out elsewhere (Fattah, 1982; see Chapter I), imprisonment as a retributive sanction can neither be fair nor proportional. It is impossible to fairly determine what prison term is a just desert for an attack on property nor for a physical or sexual assault. It is certainly possible to grade various criminal offences according to their objective and/or perceived seriousness. However, to come up with a prison term equivalent to theft or robbery, to assault or rape is a completely different matter. It is one thing to state and to empirically demonstrate that people regard robbery as more serious than theft or that they view forcible rape as much more serious than indecent exposure, but it is a totally different thing to stipulate that the punishment for theft or that of rape be so or so many years in prison. Any such stipulation is inevitably arbitrary, capricious and despotic. This determination is left either to the arbitrariness of the legislator (fixed, determined, mandatory sentences) or to the discretion of the sentencing judge (choice between a minimum and a maximum) with all the inequities and disparities this entails. The problem is further compounded by the fact that the pains of imprisonment vary enormously from individual to individual. Retributive justice requires that offenders convicted of the same offence be subjected to the same amount of pain and suffering, to the same degree of unpleasantness, to identical deprivations and that they made to suffer similar consequences. But the pains of imprisonment, so well described by Sykes (1971), are not the same for all those who experience imprisonment, even when they are held in the same or in similar institutions for the same length of time. As long as it is impossible to measure the pains of imprisonment and to weigh the suffering and deprivations resulting from imprisonment for each individual offender, it will never be possible to use incarceration in a fair, just and equitable manner.

Trying to apportion the punishment to the degree of responsibility of the offender is not only more problematic, it is an impossible exercise. How can the degree of responsibility of the offender, which is unique for every accused, be quantified or measured? It is a serious scientific error to advocate a sentencing system which supposedly will dispense varying dosages of punishment on the basis of an abstract notion that is neither susceptible to quantification nor measurement. It is even more unscientific to leave such a hopelessly impossible task to the discretion of each judge and to expect that there will be uniformity in the ways they measure the unmeasurable.

The doctrine of free will which is at the heart of our punitive reaction to crime presupposes, as Saleilles (1929) points out, that in the face of an identical act, be it theft, murder or anything else, all those who have committed such an act were equally free and consequently equally responsible. Such a doctrine is contradictory to a theory of causation which recognizes that criminal behaviour is subject to the influence of many endogenic and exogenic factors that result in different degrees of motivation, in varying levels of resistance to temptation and so forth. To admit causation is to deny that those who commit identical or similar acts are equally responsible. And if they are not equally responsible, and if moral responsibility is an abstract notion, how could it be possible to measure it and to quantify it? Attempts to deal with this fundamental problem inherent in the doctrine of free will by introducing notions such as "diminished responsibility" have created more practical difficulties than the dichotomous distinction between those who are responsible and those who are insane.

7. Recapitulation

All the scientific and practical problems outlined above could be traced to the persistence of theological and metaphysical notions in the criminal law and to the justice system's attempt to administer justice, not according to earthly criteria, but according to the "divine" criteria of guilt and punishment.

What is needed is a new system of justice based not on abstract and metaphysical notions of "free will," "moral guilt" and "moral responsibility" but on the secular notion of "harm." What is needed is to replace the notion of retributive justice by the notion of distributive justice. *This should be the new paradigm for the criminal law in the twenty-first century.*

Part Two: Has the Time Come for a Paradigm Shift in Criminal Law?

In his book *The Structure of Scientific Revolutions*, Thomas Kuhn (1970) talks about "paradigm shifts." These, he explains, are "earth-shattering changes in the way we view the world, generated by new discoveries." At the turn of the twenty-first century we are witnessing several sweeping changes that fit Kuhn's definition. One example is the old paradigm of the Industrial Revolution: production, which is in the process of being replaced by a new one: saving the planet, protecting the environment. Paradigm shifts are neither exclusive to the political sphere nor to the natural sciences; they do occur in the social sciences as well. Young (1988) asserts that a successful paradigm shift in the social sciences occurs when:

1. There is a clear empirical problem or anomaly in the dominant paradigm.
2. There is material support for the adherents of the new paradigm to enter the field.
3. There is a material problem for those in power, i.e. a major problem of policy to which the new paradigm offers a solution.
4. There is a politically and culturally conducive context for the emergence of the new paradigm (p. 166).

Hopefully, the above analysis and critique of the present state of criminal law (a law which has changed little since the French Revolution and is still largely based on the philosophy of the Classical and Neo-Classical Schools) has amply demonstrated that the criminal law is in a state of deep crisis and is therefore ripe for a paradigm shift. For obvious reasons, the impetus for this paradigm shift will have to come from that social science most closely linked to the criminal law, namely criminology. To judge whether the time has come for this paradigm shift, let us now examine the four conditions identified by Jock Young as necessary for this to successfully occur.

A. Empirical Problem

As explained above, the criminal law of today is antiquated, archaic and anachronistic, has not kept pace with social and scientific evolution and is therefore lagging behind and is incapable of meeting the challenge of post-industrial society. The empirical problem generated by the obsolete notions of *mens rea*, moral guilt and moral responsibility dictated that they be abandoned in a large number of cases in favour of other ones, such as strict liability or objective responsibility. Another empirical problem is the manifest failure of the criminal law to effectively curb crime or to deal with the plight of crime victims. This is because current criminal law is geared to punishment, not prevention, and reflects a naive and exaggerated optimism in the law's ability to influence people's behaviour through fear and threats. There is also an exaggerated faith in the common-sense assumption that punishment deters. Moreover, the repressive, punitive and retributive nature of the present criminal law means that the victims of crime are left without redress, without adequate financial remedy to the harm, loss or injury they have suffered. This is because the state has usurped the legitimate rights of victims and converted the compensation that traditionally had been paid to them into fines that go to the public treasury. All this created not one but many empirical problems that can only be solved through a paradigm shift.

B. Material Support

Is there sufficient material support for the adherents of the new paradigm to enter the field?

Support for the new paradigm comes from several quarters and from adherents of different (even opposed) political philosophies and ideologies. These range from leftists who are committed to the abolition of punishment to right-wingers who want to see the rights of victims restored and their plight addressed. Several factors have contributed to the growing support for the new paradigm:

1. Ever-growing scepticism about the deterrent effect of punishment and the wisdom of relying on the threat of punishment as the sole (or principal) means of crime prevention.

2. Mounting evidence of the negative and destructive effects of incarceration. In Finland, Bill 66/1988 (quoted by Lahti, 1990b) admits that:

> "...almost always, sentences of imprisonment hamper the possibilities of the future conformity. In addition, the enforcement of sentences of imprisonment is expensive for society."

3. Disillusionment with the medical model and growing scepticism about the efficacy of treatment and rehabilitation programs;

4. Enhanced awareness of the pressing need to secularize and sociologize the criminal law and to bring it up to the scientific standards of the Space Age.

5. Growing concern about a wide variety of extremely harmful actions that cannot be dealt with effectively through adherence to the philosophical notions of criminal intent, moral guilt and moral responsibility.

6. Realization that certain behaviours associated with modern technology can cause such extensive and irreparable harm and damage (nuclear disasters, oil spills, to name but two) that no penalty, not even the death penalty, can be made to fit the crime. Meting out the same punishment to someone who is responsible for the death of one individual and another one who is responsible for the death of half a million shakes the foundations of retributive justice and highlights once again the absolute impossibility of making the punishment fit the crime.

7. Growing concern about the plight of victims and the historical injustice that was done to them when they were unfairly deprived of the compensation that was their due.

C. Major Problem of Policy

The present criminal policy, based as it is on punishment as a means of retribution and an instrument of deterrence, has been pushed to its absolute limit. In the 1980s both traditionally repressive countries, such as England and the U.S., as well as traditionally progressive countries, such as Holland, have seen their prison populations increase, sometimes to new records. And yet none of the salutary effects promised by right-wing politicians materialized. The bankruptcy of these punitive and highly expensive policies can no longer be denied and has been at tremendous social, human and financial costs. Political slogans such as the "war on crime" proved to be hollow, and modest initiatives to help victims such as state compensation or victim-impact statements proved to be nothing more than political palliatives. Clearly there is a major problem of policy on the hands of those in power, a problem to which the new paradigm offers a solution.

In addition to the manifest failure of present policies to curb crime or to reduce crime rates, there are several other realities that illustrate the inconsistencies and deficiencies of the present system:

1. As a result of gross under-reporting, most of the cases that the system is supposed to deal with are handled outside the system!

2. As a result of ridiculously low clearance rates and the attrition in the criminal justice process, only a tiny minority of all those who commit criminal

offences face charges before the courts and an even smaller one is punished. Estimates range between five and ten per cent!

3. As a result of the widespread practice of plea bargaining (common in Anglo-Saxon countries), most of those who are punished are punished for offences other than the ones they have committed or are offered a lenient sentence in exchange for a guilty plea. Ranish and Shicor's (1985) estimate that ninety per cent (90%) of criminal cases in the U.S. are disposed of through plea bargaining gives some idea of the magnitude of the problem!

4. A criminal law system that uses "the ability to distinguish right from wrong" as the prerequisite for criminal responsibility must rely on psychiatric evidence and calls upon the forensic psychiatrist to play an important role in the judicial process. It is the psychiatrist who supposedly enlightens the court on issues such as insanity, partial or diminished responsibility, mental disorder, psychiatric disability, dangerousness and so forth. Psychiatry, however, is not an exact science and is in fact one of the least developed branches of medicine. This explains, at least partially, the frequency of conflicting psychiatric testimonies. A distinguished Australian forensic psychiatrist, Dr. Bartholomew (1986), summarized well the limitations of psychiatric evidence. He wrote:

> "Psychiatrists are unreliable in diagnosis, uncertain as to how to treat those conditions diagnosed and often unable to measure any change that the treatment prescribed may have produced. Finally, they more often than not are unable to make worthwhile predictions," (1986:209).

5. Having noted that present sentencing process is inspired by the example of wise King Solomon, Orloski (1977) writes:

> "...only most judges are not Solomons. On the contrary, judges tend to be provincial, prejudiced, partisan men who evaluate life from their own backgrounds and perspectives and flavour the sentencing of defendants who appear before them with their own social, ethnic and educational biases. Because of this reality, the entire sentencing procedure must be revamped," (1977:104-105).

What Orloski does not realize is that the fundamental problem is not as much a problem of sentencing procedure as it is a problem of sentencing criteria and the type of "divine" and abstract justice that we ask judges to dispense. Is it not preposterous in this day and age to expect judges to have the wisdom of King Solomon and to be able to adapt the punishment (imprisonment; fine) to the crime and to make it commensurate with the degree of responsibility of the offender?

D. Politically and Culturally Conducive Context

With the twenty-first century fast approaching, many countries are in the process of changing and modernizing their criminal law. While none of the new codes has abandoned the old paradigm (moral guilt, moral responsibility, punishment, retribution) in favour of the new one (harm, social responsibility, restitution, compensation), they are deviating more and more from the old paradigm and introducing more and more elements of the new one. This is particularly evident in the way strict liability is replacing moral responsibility. It is also visible in some areas where it was imperative to move from a guilt orientation to a consequence orientation, such as areas of negligence and endangerment. Not only is the time ripe for a paradigm shift in the criminal law, but there are also specific political and social developments that are creating a context conducive to a successful shift. Three developments in particular are worth noting:

1. The Escalating Costs and Diminishing Effectiveness of the System of Punishment

Popular politics of fiscal responsibility, financial restraint and deficit reduction have led to the general acceptance of the economic concept of "cost-benefits" and to its widespread use as a means of evaluating social systems and social programs. Although the criminal justice system has somehow escaped such an assessment, it is quite obvious that its performance is overwhelmingly negative. In an article bearing the provocative title *Dismantling the System,* Jobson (1977) informs us that in some Canadian provinces expenditures within the crime industry (the police sector, the courts sector and the corrections-prison-parole sector) exceed or equal the combined government outlays for environment, natural resources, recreation and culture, and housing. His call for dismantling the system is based on the system's inability to meet most of its avowed goals. He writes:

> "The crime industry, that is, the formal part of the industry set up to deal with crime, is a big industry and an expensive industry. In large part it is an industry teetering on the edge of bankruptcy: its liabilities are many, its assets are few. Most importantly... the industry has not and cannot meet most of its avowed production goals. In part this is due to the fact that production goals are conflicting and antiquated; in addition, neglect of careful accounting procedures and modern management techniques have disguised the extent of the shortfall in reaching production goals and their full cost to the industry," (1977:255).

Jobson adds that the present justice system does not have the technological capacity to deliver on its promises, namely to reform criminals, to deter persons from crime and to prevent crime. He blames the current state of affairs on a set of problems. The first is that the industry is grossly overextended, and the second is that it is overexpanded.

2. *Overwhelming Recourse to Insurance as a Means of Risk Coverage*

One dominant feature of life in a modern, industrial, technological, highly mechanized society and of the social policy of the welfare state is the overwhelming recourse to insurance (public and private) as a means of risk reduction and risk coverage. Recent criminalization literature increasingly stresses the fact that the risk of criminal victimization is a "natural" hazard of modern life, of social relations and social interactions. There is also a growing awareness of a strange anomaly that currently exists: whereas most other risks are covered by some insurance (public or private), the risk of criminalization is not. Actually, one of the ironies of the present system is that those who face the greatest risks of criminal victimization are the ones who can least afford the insurance and the ones most frequently denied coverage by private insurance companies. Joutsen (1987) deplores the fact that state insurance schemes are rarely designed to cover crime risks. Instead they generally cover losses or injuries incurred in certain risky fields of activity, regardless of the cause of this loss or injury, the most notable example being mandatory traffic insurance schemes. The insurance covers risks caused not only by traffic offences per se but also by any traffic accident. Joutsen adds that there is usually a national fund covering parties to a traffic accident who are not covered by insurance.

Slowly but surely we are coming to realize that the distinctions that are made between victimization by crime and other victimizations, between the risk of crime and other social risks, are not only meaningless but also unfair to those who are victimized by actions that happen to be included in the criminal code. This paves the way for a new paradigm whose primary focus is restitution and compensation to the victim.

3. *The Victim Movement*

First espoused by the women's movement and then by the politicians of the new right, the cause of victims of crime has led to the emergence of a powerful pressure group, the victim lobby. Active in many countries, including the U.S. and Canada, the victim movement has focused attention on the plight of crime victims and demanded the re-examination of criminal and penal policies to render them more responsive to the needs of victims. Persistent efforts at the national and international levels culminated in the *United Nations Declaration on the Basic Principles of Justice for Victims of Crime and the Abuse of Power,* which was adopted by the General Assembly on December 11, 1985. The declaration contains twenty-one paragraphs, at least three of which (8, 9, 10) are devoted to restitution. The three paragraphs exemplify the growing acceptance of at least two basic elements of the new paradigm: harm and restitution. Paragraph 8 addresses restitution from the offender or responsible third parties. It declares that:

> "Offenders or third parties responsible for their behaviour should, where appropriate, make fair restitution to their victims, their families or dependents. Such restitution should include the return of property or payment for the harm or loss suffered, reimbursement of expenses incurred as a result of victimization, the provision of services and the restoration of rights."

Commenting on this paragraph, Joutsen (1987) points out that the responsibility of the perpetrator for "making good" is part of the legal tradition of all societies and should be one of the basic elements of any attempt to aid the victim in his recovery.

Paragraph 9 of the declaration recommends the use of restitution as a sanction in its own right. It proposes that:

> "Governments should review their practices, regulations and laws to consider restitution as an available sentencing option in criminal cases, in addition to other criminal sanctions."

Joutsen (1987) draws attention to the confusing wording of this paragraph in that it first calls for restitution as an option and then states that this option should be "in addition to other criminal sanctions." He also points out that, at present, few European countries provide the possibility of restitution as the only sanction in criminal cases, whereas most allow the courts to order the offender to pay restitution in addition to the main criminal sanction. Paragraph 10 of the declaration recognizes the substantial harm that may be caused by environmental offences and the primacy of restitution in cases of this type. It stipulates that:

> "In cases of substantial harm to the environment, restitution, if ordered, should include as far as possible restoration to the environment, reconstruction of the infrastructure, replacement

of community facilities and reimbursement of the expenses of relocation, whenever such harm results in the dislocation of a community."

Joutsen (1987) explains that an environmental offence may be so serious that the community cannot continue to exist in the same place. The air or water may be so polluted as to cause a danger to health or may seriously hamper the livelihood of the whole community. We might add that it is precisely these extremely harmful, injurious actions (Bhopal, Chernobyl, Exxon Valdez, etc.) which very well illustrate the obsolescence of the old paradigm of the criminal law and the total inadequacy of conventional punishments (whether imprisonment or death) as a social reaction or a criminal sanction to these behaviours.

A General Outline of Some Basic Elements of the New Paradigm

A. From a Guilt Orientation to a Consequence Orientation

As will be seen shortly from the following outline, the proposed new criminal law paradigm is not really new at all. It is not a novel invention nor a radical, revolutionary innovation. The proposed model is not one without historical precedent, but one that is historically and sociologically inspired. It derives its fundamental principles and rationale from past and present practices. As mention above, the vast majority of cases dealt with by the criminal courts are offences of strict liability, of negligence, of omission and the like. We need only to ask how this came about and why it was necessary to abandon, on such a large scale, the traditional and deeply anchored notions of criminal intent, moral guilt and moral responsibility. The answer to these questions is not difficult to find. It is evident that the social consequences of these behaviours were held to be more important than the moral considerations which required that wickedness, malice, evil intent be a prerequisite for criminal punishment. The need to regulate these behaviours, because of their actual or potential social harm, overrode the requirement of moral guilt. The growing complexity of society inevitably led to a declining emphasis on criminal intent and to a growing emphasis being placed on the consequences of the act. Naturally this tendency was more pronounced in certain sectors than others.

That harm is slowly becoming the primary criterion for criminalization may be seen in the report of the Finnish Criminal Law Committee, quoted by Professor Lahti (1999a). The first task the committee performed was to try to locate those forms of behaviour that appear to be most harmful when judged in the light of specific goals of each sphere of life. To do so, the committee used a test question: Does a certain behaviour harm or endanger the interests of an individual or of society, and if so, to what extent? In other words, the notion of harm is the yardstick the committee used in order to judge whether a given behaviour should or should not be criminalized. Using this criterion, the committee considered economic crimes to be harmful, as they jeopardized the economy and, in more general terms, the economic viability of society.

A good example of current practice where consequence takes precedence over guilt in determining punishment is that of attempted crime. Current criminal codes punish attempted crime less severely than completed crime. This is in spite of the fact that the same criminal intent is present whether the crime is completed or remained at the stage of attempt because of factors external to the offender's will. The lesser punishment is therefore motivated, not by a lesser guilt, but by a lesser seriousness of consequences.

As the criterion for criminalization, the notion of harm is in perfect harmony with the generally accepted goals of modern criminal law. If we accept that the primary goal of the criminal law in modern Western societies is to prevent the occurrence of socially harmful, socially damaging and socially injurious actions, then it is only logical that the eligibility of any given behaviour for inclusion in the criminal code (and for measuring the seriousness of various actions) be judged according to their actual and potential harm, and not according to the wickedness or the degree of malice of the perpetrator. This, however, is not the way present criminal codes deal with the various categories of criminalized behaviours. Homicide is a good case in point because it illustrates well the difference between a guilt orientation and a consequence orientation. In Canada, in the U.S. and in many other countries, ten times as many lives are lost to negligent manslaughter as to wilful homicide. To treat two categories of harmful behaviour very differently with the less harmful but wicked receiving much harsher punishment than the more harmful but not wicked one does not make much sense in a system of law that claims its primary purpose to be prevention and protection.

As may be seen from this example, and we can give many others, the seriousness of various acts, the need to regulate them and the severity of social reaction to them can be very different when judged according to these two distinct criteria: consequences versus guilt, harm versus intent. The grave problems inherent in or associated with the current guilt orientation of the criminal law have already been explained in some detail. Attention was drawn in particular to the fundamental empirical error of this orientation, namely the futile attempt to quantify the unquantifiable (degrees of moral responsibility) and to measure the unmeasurable (the degree of the freedom of the will, the degree of moral guilt, etc.). This is not to say that the criteria proposed for the new paradigm, namely consequence, harm, injury, are problem-free. However, to measure the harm caused by acts defined as crimes is surely less problematic than trying to measure degrees of moral guilt and moral responsibility. There have been various attempts to empirically measure such harm. In 1975, Patrik Törnudd suggested that crime statistics be changed and that the new ones be based on damages. He quotes Gunnar Fredriksson as saying:

> "Because acts are made punishable because of their harmful consequences, the amount of criminality equals the amount of harmful consequences. The measurement of damages and their variations becomes a primary task for the criminal statistics."

Fredriksson then went on to analyze in detail some problems related to the measurement of direct and indirect damages caused by crime. Another advantage of the notion of harm over the notion of intent, of the consequence orientation to the guilt orientation, is that it allows the regulation of acts of endangerment. There are countless acts in industrial, technological societies that require regulation for the simple reason that they have the potential to cause harm, sometimes quite serious harm. The irony of the present system, based as it is on wickedness and deliberate intent, can lead to preposterous outcomes. Thus grave negligence causing a serious nuclear disaster and claiming thousands of lives or irreparable harm to the environment leads to a much more lenient response than the wilful killing of a single individual, because in the first instance there was no deliberate intent to cause harm.

B. From Moral Responsibility to Social Responsibility

Contemporary criminal law is based on a concept of blameworthiness, which has its foundation in the Judeo-Christian ethic and the notion of free will (Parker, 1977). And although malicious intent applies only at present to a small minority of the workload of the criminal courts, there has been no serious attempt in recent years to discard it and to replace it with a new concept that is compatible with science and more in tune with the times. And yet as far back as the last century, the Italian Positivist School made strong pleas for replacing the abstract notions of moral guilt and moral responsibility by the sociological notions of social responsibility and social accountability. Ferri (1917) argued that moral culpability must be discarded as a prerequisite in crime and suggested that since man's actions may be imputed to him, hence he is responsible for them because he lives in society. To call for replacing moral responsibility by social responsibility is not an attempt to resurrect the ideas of the Italian Positivist School, based as they were on absolute determinism. There are, however, two compelling reasons for abandoning moral responsibility as the fundamental concept of the criminal law: one is scientific, the other is practical.

1. Moral responsibility is based on the notion of free will, which is incompatible with science, as it is the negation of causality (see above).

2. Moral responsibility has always been a major hurdle in the way of dealing effectively with a large number of socially harmful and injurious behaviours, which ultimately led to its rejection in various sectors of criminality, where it has been replaced by other types of liability.

Traffic rules and traffic offences offer a prime example of the anachronism of the notion of moral responsibility. As mentioned earlier, the quasi-totality of these offences are strict liability ones not requiring *mens rea*. The need to require drivers to obey traffic rules, to take certain precautions, to avoid negligence, carelessness or recklessness is based, not on a moral obligation, but on a *social* obligation stemming from the fact that they share the roads with other motorists. It is not a moral duty to respect the rules, it is a *social* responsibility.

The fact that we live in society, that we share the physical environment with others, places several restrictions on our freedom to act and dictates that we respect and obey certain rules of conduct and standards of behaviour. It is our *social* responsibility to refrain from causing harm or injury to others (or to society at large) wilfully or by negligence, by commission or by omission. It is our *social* responsibility not to infringe upon the rights of other members of society.

C. From Legal Fiction to Social Reality

The metaphysical and philosophical notions underlying the criminal law of today are far removed from social reality. And many, including the fundamental notion of free well, are philosophical abstractions that are not susceptible to any scientific or empirical validation. The fact that most of the criminal codes of today were enacted in the nineteenth century means that they were neither inspired nor influenced by social and behavioural science. The result is a hiatus between the criminal law and the disciplines of psychology, sociology, criminology and victimology. The anachronisms of the principles, concepts and notions according to which the criminal law operates necessitated the invention of many legal assumptions and presumptions. Scholars had to perform legal gymnastics in order to adapt an archaic criminal law to the social realities and the exigencies of the twentieth century. As a result, the criminal law today is governed by what may described as "legal fiction." Most of this legal fiction is dictated by the need to find some acceptable justification for the infliction of or exemption from punishment.

Many of the theoretical distinctions are indicative of the quagmire of present criminal law. And yet in many cases the destiny of the accused depends solely on these hair-splitting decisions because the distinction often means the difference between conviction and acquittal, and in some cases between life and death. In her admirable critique of criminal law, Baroness Wootton has demonstrated time and time again how elusive indeed are the criteria by which the "responsibly bad" are to be distinguished from the merely irresponsible (see, for example, Wootton, 1960). But there are many other distinctions, such as those between excuses and justifications; general intent and specific intent; constructive intention and real intention; voluntary acts, involuntary acts and not voluntary acts; purpose, intent and desired result; loss of control, automatism; insane automatism and non-insane automatism; psychiatric disability and diminished responsibility; mental disorder and psychopathic (character) disorder; guilty and sane, guilty but insane and not guilty by reason of insanity; fully responsible, partially responsible, not at all responsible.

These legal distinctions, as well as the distinction between deliberate and negligent actions, are totally meaningless to the person who is killed, injured or harmed by the behaviour. As Lady Wootton (1963) points out, the material consequences of an action and the reasons for prohibiting it are the same whether it is the result of sinister, malicious plotting, of negligence or of sheer accident. A man is equally dead and his relatives equally bereaved whether he was stabbed or run over by a drunken motorist or by an incompetent one.

The new paradigm puts an end to all the practical (and theoretical) problems created by arbitrary, artificial and rather meaningless legal distinctions. Replacing the notion of guilt by the notion of harm, replacing moral responsibility by social responsibility, will remove any need for legal fiction. Yet calls to modernize and sociologize the criminal law by doing away with these outdated legal abstractions, such as free will, moral guilt and moral responsibility, are invariably encountered with the claim that these notions are as vital to the existence of the criminal law as punishment is to the survival of society. An aura is thus created around these principles, giving the false impression that they are somehow transcendental or immutable. What is often forgotten is that these so-called fundamental, basic principles have been sacrificed over and over again for nothing other than purely pragmatic reasons. The invention of a whole series of liability types not requiring criminal intent, moral fault or a proof of wickedness is just one example of both our readiness to circumvent these principles whenever necessary and the implicit recognition that they are outdated, wanting and obsolete. The legal presumption that "no one is deemed ignorant of the law" or that "ignorance of the law is no excuse" exemplifies the willingness to sacrifice even the most fundamental of principles on the altar of pragmatism.

D. From Repression to Regulation

The criminal law has traditionally served a repressive function. In addition to its use as an instrument of power, the theological and philosophical origins of the criminal code led to its use as a means of enforcing religious command and moral standards. As Norval Morris (1973) points out, by tradition America (and the same is true of most other Western nations) has relied on the criminal law, not only to protect persons and property, but also to lead men away from vice and sin, including those vices and sins that injure the sinner. He reports that half of all arrests in the U.S. are for crimes without direct motives, crimes which bring no complainant to the station house, no call to the police switchboard. The fact that everything deviant has been criminalized is equally deplored by Anttila (1984). This, she suggests, is both unpleasant for the average citizen and ineffective from the point of view of the overall interest of society. And it is done in full knowledge that prohibition of deviance prevents creative and innovative behaviour. She adds:

> "Unless we are trying for an Orwellian world where vast resources are expended to control even the most minute actions of individuals, we must choose which forms of behaviour should become the focus of the resources that society is prepared to use for control: Which forms of behaviour deserve so much attention that the cumbersome machinery of the criminal justice system should be taken into play?" (1984:3).

The lucid arguments made by Jerome Hall (1982) for excluding negligence from penal liability and for narrowing punishable guilt to voluntary harm-doing are equally valid for excluding acts that are considered "strict liability offences." And if morality offences, negligent offences and strict liability offences are excluded, what then remains of the criminal law as we know it today?

During the 1960s and the 1970s there was a strong positive trend towards legalization, decriminalization and depenalization. There was a general sentiment that the criminal code had overreached its boundaries and had to undergo a substantial retrenchment. The use of imprisonment as a penal sanction was coming under increasing criticism, and short-term imprisonment was generally considered to be an inappropriate sanction from the social, ethical and economic point of view (Aspelin, 1975; Fattah, 1982). The Scandinavian countries were in the forefront of this wave of reform. It should be noted that the trend towards decriminalization and depenalization was by no means limited to victimless crimes or morality offences. Debates on the depenalization of property offences was in full swing. In Sweden, for example, it was suggested that minor property offences (for example, petty thefts through shoplifting in self-service stores) should lie outside the criminal law and be dealt with by measures other than ordinary punishment. It was held to be unreasonable that society should use its already hard-pressed criminal justice resources to hunt down shoplifters when the firms in question deliberately make crime easy and draw human beings into a "criminal risk zone" (Aspelin, 1975). In Sweden, a government commission which dealt with petty property offences discussed a form of penalization. Aspelin (1975) further reports that in both Denmark and Norway the offence of shoplifting is considered as one punishable by fines. These can be imposed by a senior police officer. In Finland, shoplifting was clearly redefined as an offence punishable only by fines.

In Canada, Jobson (1977) is extremely critical of the criminal justice system's involvement in minor property offences. He notes that the chief victims of petty thefts are corporate persons. These persons include self-service stores of different types, who by the neglect of their wares are in part responsible for their own foreseeable losses. He insists that in the interests of economy and integrity of purpose a retrenchment in this area of criminal justice is needed and alternative servicing of this type of loss is required.

Although the trend towards legalization, decriminalization and depenalization has slowed down in the 1980s and has even been reversed in some instances, there is no doubt that it will be the dominant feature of future criminal codes. Once the paradigm shift has taken place, criminal codes will move from repression to regulation. Already in 1973 Professor Norval Morris proposed that we substitute for our present prohibitions diverse strategies of prohibition, regulation and legalization. He predicted that the criminal law of the future will be predominately an administrative law, reserving punishment only for a persistent flouting of regulatory controls.

E. From Deterrence to Social Prevention

As mentioned earlier, present criminal legislation is based on a common-sense assumption that punishment deters and on an exaggerated faith in the criminal law's ability to influence people's behaviour. This uncritical over-reliance on punishment as a powerful deterrent remains the cornerstone of our crime policy, although it lacks empirical support. As a result, our approach to crime prevention is a totally passive one, as if the mere existence of penalties is sufficient by itself to steer people away from committing crime. The irony of this stand *vis-à-vis* crime is highlighted by Orloski (1977), who writes:

> "Criminal statutes prohibit *nothing*. Instead, the statutes are drafted to punish past behaviour and are applied in factual situations that are *fait accompli*. In short, criminal law punishes the murderer after the victim is dead. It does not prohibit the murder of the victim. It cannot stop the homicide. It merely punishes the perpetrator of the death after it is successfully accomplished. The deterrent effect, if any, comes from the knowledge on the part of the perpetrator of the death that he is liable to be punished if he is discovered, captured and convicted," (1977:43).

Contrary to popular belief, punishment and prevention do not go hand in hand but are two alternative strategies. Placing the emphasis on punishment detracts from the need for active social prevention. And because too much money is being spent on punishment, there is very little, if any, available for prevention. But since it is much easier to punish than to prevent, politicians and the general public have always opted for the former, not the latter. For politicians, punishment is an easy alibi because it gives the impression that something is being done about acts that are a source of fear and anxiety for the public.

Politicians' and the public's overconfidence in the intimidating effect of punishment is both misguided and misplaced. It is misguided because there is ample empirical evidence attesting to the severe limitations of a deterrence policy. It is misplaced because it puts the stick ahead of and above the carrot. Anttila (1984) is critical of the crime control philosophy in Western societies, control which is based one-sidedly on the use of negative sanctions, punishment. This negative means of control, she argues, is preferred despite the fact that recent psychological research has shown that, like with animals, it is easier to have people act in accordance with certain norms by rewarding them for proper behaviour than by punishing them for bad behaviour. She deplores the fact that present criminal codes and current criminal policy scarcely, if ever, use any rewards.

Criminological research has shown that crime rates are closely linked to the available opportunities but are not in the least influenced by variations or fluctuations in punishment. This is not a new revelation. Almost a century ago, Ferri's law of criminal saturation led him to conclude that crimes increase through a sum of causes that are very different from the penalties so easily promulgated by legislators and applied by judges and jailors.

All this suggests that abandoning punishment would likely lead to greater emphasis on social prevention. We should also note that the efficacy of punishment as a deterrent for negligent, careless or inadvertent actions has been the object of great scepticism. One of the sceptics, Professor Glanville Williams, asks: Even if a person admits that he occasionally makes a negligent mistake, how, in the nature of things, can punishment for inadvertence serve to deter?

F. From Intimidation to Mediation; from Segregation to Reconciliation

Christie (1977) has observed that the key element in a criminal proceeding is that the proceeding is converted from something between the concrete parties into a conflict between one of the parties and the state. He points out that in a modern trial two important things have happened. Firstly, the parties are being represented. Secondly, the one party that is represented by the state, namely the victim, is so thoroughly represented that she or he for most of the proceedings is pushed completely out of the arena, reduced to the trigger of the whole thing. The victim, Christie argues, is a double loser: firstly, *vis-à-vis* the offender, but secondly, and often in a more crippling manner, by being denied rights to full participation in what might have been one of the more important ritual encounters in life. The victim has lost the case to the state.

The criminal law which does not cease to broaden its mandate and extend its boundaries has declared a monopoly on every conflict or dispute falling under its jurisdiction. Some codes (Joutsen, 1987, cites the penal code of Cyprus as an example, and we can cite the Canadian criminal code as another) have gone as far as criminalizing the avoidance of criminal procedure by settling a criminal offence privately. And yet private dispute settlement and conflict resolution through mediators and third parties have several advantages over criminal court proceedings which simply end in the punishment of the offender.

Joutsen (1987) cites many factors which speak in favour of informal, private settlements. These generally provide a quick decision at low cost. The individual features of the conflict can be studied to an extent not possible for the authorities of the criminal justice system and there is considerably more discretion in deciding on the proper solution. Instead of the all-or-nothing decision that is often the only option for the criminal justice system (and in which one party is usually held to be the guilty offender, the other the innocent victim), informal settlement can seek a compromise decision that fits the unique features of the case at hand and the parties to the conflict. Joutsen notes further that the parties can be directly involved in the search for the proper outcome to an extent that is not possible in formal criminal proceedings. Finally, he points out that private settlements avoid the legal formalism that typifies criminal procedure. Rather than the black-and-white approach, which characterizes the rules of the criminal procedure, the mediation approach allows a more far-ranging view of the broad circumstances underlying the alleged offence, on the side of both the victim and the offender. Joutsen concludes that the trend towards private settlements will in many cases provide an alternative form of conflict resolution that can be of more assistance to the victim than can the criminal justice system.

Since the current criminal law is centred upon punishment and retribution, and because of its avidity to extract revenue from the wrongdoers (in the form of fines), it naturally shuns any initiative for dispute settlement or conflict resolution, especially when it is done outside the system. As a result, the criminal justice system has missed a golden opportunity to reduce its caseload and to stop the repetition of certain offences through the reconciliation of the feuding parties.

Jobson (1977) asserts that the criminal justice system has overextended itself into conflict situations that are not adequately solved by existing processes. He estimates that almost fifty per cent of crimes are characterized by an ongoing relationship between the offender and the victim. These crimes, argues Jobson, are not committed by strangers but by family members, neighbours, tenants and landlords or within a customer-seller relationship.

> "Yet the adversarial nature of the trial process must treat them as strangers in a duel to the finish. A more satisfactory forum for settling disputes characterized by an ongoing relationship is mediation. Yet the crime industry has not yet generally realized the importance of this alternative dispute-settling service... A general review and expansion of mediation services in the industry would seem to be appropriate at this time," (1977:260).

G. From Retribution to Restitution

Barnett (1977, 1981) insists that the paradigm of punishment is in a "crisis period." This, he believes, is as much because of its practical drawbacks as the uncertainty of its moral status. He further suggests that the alleged absolute justice of repaying evil with evil is really an empty sophism since Christian moralists have always preached that an evil is to be put right only by doing good. Barnett concludes by admitting his inability to find any theory which justifies the deliberate, forceful imposition of punishment within or without a system of criminal justice. To replace the punishment paradigm, Barnett offers the restitution paradigm. This new paradigm views crime as an offence by one individual against the rights of another. The victim has suffered and justice consists of the culpable offender making good the loss he has caused. This new paradigm, argues Barnett, calls for a complete refocusing of our image of crime along the lines of what Thomas Kuhn calls a "shift of world view."

> "Where we once saw an offence against society, we now see an offence against an individual victim. In a way, it is a common-sense view of crime. The armed robber did not rob society: he robbed the victim. His debt, therefore, is not to society; it is to the victim," (1981:251).

Barnett proposes two types of restitution: punitive restitution and pure restitution. He also outlines six advantages that a restitution system has over a system of punishment. These are:

1. The first and most obvious advantage is the assistance provided to victims of crime.
2. The possibility of receiving compensation would encourage victims to report crimes and to appear at trial.
3. Restitution would aid in the rehabilitation of criminals because it is something the offender does, not something done for or to him.
4. Restitution is a self-determinative sentence.
5. Savings to the taxpayers would be enormous.
6. Crime would no longer pay.

One big advantage of a system centred upon restitution is that it would enjoy the unqualified support of most victims. There is in fact overwhelming empirical evidence indicating that victims prefer reparative sanctions (such as restitution) to punitive sanctions, such as imprisonment or fines.

Conclusion

Kuhn (1970) insists that professionalism leads to an immense restriction of the scientist's vision and to a considerable resistance to paradigm change (p. 64). It is not surprising, therefore, that new paradigms encounter a great deal of resistance and that reaction to them can range from outright dismissal to downright hostility. I experienced both these typical reactions when I appeared before the Canadian House of Commons Standing Committee on

Justice and the Solicitor General at its public hearings in Vancouver (March 1988) trying to explain that the criminal law we have at present is totally inadequate for the twenty-first century and is badly in need of a new paradigm. Misoneism is but one explanation for the resistance and hostility. In an attempt to explain the hostile attitude that greets new paradigms, Kuhn (1970) and Barnett (1977, 1981) point out that all the great authorities and teachers were raised with the current paradigm and see the world through it. All the texts and institutions are committed to it. Radical alternatives hold promise but are so untested as to make wary all but the bold. The establishment is loath to abandon its broad and intricate theory in favour of a new and largely unknown hypothesis. They go on to explain how the new paradigm ends up by imposing itself:

> "Gradually, however, as the authorities die off and the problems with the old paradigm increase, the 'Young Turks' get a better hearing in both the journals and in the classroom. In a remarkably rapid fashion, the old paradigm is discarded for the new. Anyone who still clings to it is now considered to be antiquated or eccentric and is simply read out of the profession. All research centres on the application of the new paradigm," (quoted after Barnett, 1981, p. 245).

We get too used to and become too familiar with the system and institutions operating in society to be able to conceive of how society could survive were they to disappear. Few people, for example, can imagine a "society without prisons," and when I chose this as the title for a lecture I gave in the city of Vancouver in 1983, the general reaction was not one of scepticism but of disbelief. It did not help much that I went to great length to explain that no punishment is permanent, transcendental or immutable, and that prisons, as places for punishment, are a relatively recent invention.

We get so used to the systems that we hardly ever look back at their historical origins and historical development. And yet such a retrospective look and analysis can be very beneficial to understanding the present system, why it is the way it is and how it could be reformed. It can also be an enlightening exercise that sheds light on the system's problems, deficiencies and shortcomings. The criminal law is a good case in point. Even a cursory glance at the way it evolved historically suffices to show that it was the product of negative rather than positive historical forces. One need not be a radical, nor a critical criminologist to realize that from the very beginning the criminal law was meant to be an instrument of power and oppression, and not something designed to help or protect the victims. The origins of our present criminal law could be easily traced to the attempts by the kings and feudal lords to consolidate their authority, to enhance their powers and to generate revenue for themselves and their estates by imposing fines and by declaring forfeit the lands and property of convicted persons. The process is related by the Law Reform Commission of Canada (1974) in its *Working Papers* 5 and 6 (pp. 8-9):

> "In Anglo-Saxon England there was no criminal law as we know it. Disputes were dealt with by a process greatly resembling our civil law. When an individual felt that he had suffered damage because of another's wrongful conduct he was permitted either to settle the matter by agreement or to proceed before a tribunal. Restitution was the order of the day and other sanctions, including imprisonment, were rarely used.
>
> "As the common law developed, criminal law became a distinct branch of law. Numerous antisocial acts were seen to be 'offences against the state' or 'crimes' rather than personal wrongs, or torts. This tendency to characterize some wrongs as 'crimes' was encouraged by the practice under which the lands and property of convicted persons was forfeited to the king or feudal lords; fines, as well, became payable to feudal lords and not the victim. The natural practice of compensating the victim or his relatives was discouraged by making it an offence to conceal the commission of a felony or convert the crime into a source of profit. In time, fines and property that would have gone in satisfaction of the victim's claims were diverted to the state. Compounding an offence (that is, accepting an economic benefit in satisfaction of the wrong done without the consent of the court or in a manner that is contrary to the public interest) still remains a crime under the Canadian Criminal Code and discourages private settlement or restitution.
>
> "It would now seem that historical developments, however well intentioned, effectively removed the victim from sentencing policy and obscured the view that crime was social conflict."

This historical development leaves no doubt that it was political ruse by which the legitimate rights of the victims were usurped by the rulers to the latter's benefit. It is this usurpation that Christie (1977) refers to when he states that conflicts have been stolen from the parties directly involved and thereby have either disappeared or become other people's property. It is also a historical fact that with the passage of time the criminal law became a powerful tool of subjugation used by governments and by rulers to consolidate their grip over the population, and it is not a coincidence that many criminal codes begin with the section dealing with offences against the state.

In a paper on the future of criminology (Fattah, 1986), I ventured to make some predictions about the criminal law of the future. I suggested that in an extremely affluent society the right of individual property is bound to lose the central importance it now enjoys. Property offences, which constitute about seventy per cent (70%) of all criminal code offences, will undoubtedly decline. Other things which we now take for granted, privacy and freedom, for example, will become more fragile and hence much more precious commodities than material goods, which will be extremely abundant. One of the primary functions of the criminal law will be to protect these valuable and vulnerable commodities, all the more so because the same technological advances which will make it easy to protect whatever mobile and immobile possessions one has will pose greater and greater threats to human rights and freedoms. In a society obsessed with a never-ending pursuit of wealth and material goods, protection of property becomes one of the primary functions of the criminal code. The major threat to the society of the future will not be, as it is now, the violation of property rights. This threat will pale in comparison to the threats posed by nuclear and other technologies. People's fears in the future will not be to have their property stolen or their houses broken into. Elaborate security systems and comprehensive insurance schemes will take care of that. Their major fear will be that of nuclear or environmental holocaust. Even the fear of losing one's life will not be as great as that created by the prospect of all mankind wiped off the face of the earth. There will be other, though lesser, fears created by the advances in gene technology, genetic engineering and the manipulation of the human embryo. A major part of the criminal codes of the future will be devoted to the regulation of previously unregulated areas, such as organ transplants, artificial insemination, test-tube fertilization, sperm banks, uterus rental and many other issues related to the technical manipulation of human reproduction.

It is almost certain that many of the current forms of property offences will be depenalized; others might even be decriminalized. Many will be transferred from the domain of criminal law to that of civil and administrative laws. The future is likely to see a tremendous expansion of the latter laws at the expense of the criminal law, which will be used less and less as a means of conflict resolution. Future changes in the modes of social control, the abolition of imprisonment as we know it today, the introduction of new measures based on the notions of compensation and restitution, will render the division between the law of crime and the law of torts much less important than it is right now. The boundaries between the criminal law and civil law will be even more blurred in the future than they are today. We should not forget that the vast majority of criminal offences brought to trial end in a sentence to a fine.

A Comparison of the Old and the New Paradigms

Old Paradigm	New Paradigm
Crime is viewed as:	
• a wrongful, sinful, immoral, wicked behaviour that must be punished	• a harmful, injurious behaviour that needs to be redressed in the present and prevented in the future
• a manifestation of the wickedness of the criminal	• a social risk, one of the many hazards of life in a modern, industrial, technological society
• an offence against the Crown, the state, the society	• a human conflict, a dispute between two parties
• a unique, exceptional category of behaviour qualitatively different from civil torts and other uncriminalized behaviours	• neither exceptional nor unique; as not qualitatively different from tort; as less injurious, less serious and less dangerous than many other behaviours that are not brought within the jurisdiction of the criminal law
• there is an ontological reality of crime	• there is no ontological reality of crime
Fundamental concepts and principles:	
• theological, metaphysical, philosophical, abstract concepts	• sociological, positivist, secular
• guilt-oriented	• consequence-oriented
• moral guilt, *mens rea*, malice, wickedness	• harm, injury, loss, endangerment
• free will	• strict liability
• moral responsibility	• social responsibility
Characteristics and goals of criminal law:	
• moralistic, stigmatizing	• neutral, objective
• idealist	• realist
• repressive	• regulatory
• retributive	• distributive, utilitarian
• punitive	• restitutive, preventive
• depersonalized, authoritarian, adversarial	• personalized, conciliatory

Civil cases end in the payment of damages. Thus the only actual difference in outcome between a civil case and a criminal case is that in the latter the damages are paid to the person who suffered the loss, whereas in the former it is the state that benefits at the expense of the victim. And this is what has to change.

Epilogue

In one of his recent papers, Professor Lahti (1990b) asks: "Why does the recodification of the criminal law take too long?" I believe it is because those in charge are desperately trying to integrate conflicting philosophies and to reconcile contradictory, even incompatible goals. Such is the incompatibility between the notions of harm and moral blameworthiness, between a guilt orientation and a consequence orientation. The attempt to reconcile these two very different orientations is quite evident in the works of the Finnish Criminal Law Committee and is exemplified in section 6:1 of the Finnish Penal code, which stipulates that:

> "The punishment shall be measured so that it is in just proportion to the harm and risk involved in the offence and the culpability of the offender manifest in the offence."

The order in which the two criteria are listed might give the impression that harm takes precedence over culpability. However, all other provisions suggest that the opposite is true, since for all purposes *intent* remains the cornerstone of criminalization. Professor Lahti (1990b) reports that a decision was taken at the beginning of the preparation of the criminal law that an act would be punishable under the new criminal law only if committed with intent unless it was clearly stipulated that the offence shall be punishable (also) if committed through negligence. This persisting emphasis on intent overlooks the fact that in modern industrial, technological societies the most harmful actions are not acts of volition (wilful homicide, assault, larceny, etc.) but acts of negligence (Chernobyl, Bhopal, Exxon Valdez, etc.). It seems

Characteristics and goals of criminal law, continued:

• oriented to the past, looks backwards	• oriented to the present and the future, looks forward
• places the discretion in the hands of third parties	• leaves the discretion in the hands of the parties involved
• distances the feuding parties, widens the gap that separates them	• brings the feuding parties together to effect reconciliation

paradoxical to declare that the major aim of the criminal code is to prevent socially harmful behaviour and then continue to use intent, *mens rea* and moral blameworthiness as the primary criteria for criminalization and for fixing the punishment. A similar contradiction exists with regard to sentencing. Thus punishment is judged acceptable, desirable and an effective means of moral education in the case of adults whose behaviour patterns are well established when it is being condemned as a doubtful means of socialization in the case of children and juveniles.

The notions of "guilt" and "punishment" are so firmly entrenched and so deeply anchored in the human mind that they will not disappear overnight. This explains why current criminal code reform attempts in Finland, Canada and most other countries are characterized by a manifest unwillingness to break away from the past, to start from scratch, to admit once and for all that these theological notions have no place in a secular, scientific world, and that philosophical concepts such as free will and moral culpability are totally inadequate for dealing with the complex social realities of the post-industrial society. The unwillingness to abandon the old model of a punitive, repressive penal code, a code that does nothing but dispense punishment, is surprising, particularly when observed in the secular, progressive Scandinavian countries. This is because the notion of criminal law distributing evil in the form of threat and execution of punishment, as Sevón (1990) correctly points out, is antithetical to the concept of the welfare state, a state that distributes goods and material benefits. It is also surprising because other branches of law, such as the civil law and administrative law, are able to deal effectively with many harmful, injurious actions without resorting to the concepts of guilt, moral fault or moral blameworthiness.

References

Allen, F.A. (1964). *The Borderland of Criminal Justice: Essays in Law and Criminology*. Chicago: University of Chicago Press.

Anttila, I. (1984). *Crime Control and Freedom*. Paper presented to the George Orwell Year International Colloquium (Strasbourg, April 2-4, 1984).

Anttila, I. (1986). "Trends in Criminal Law." In J. van Dijk et al. (eds.) *Criminal Law in Action: An Overview of Current Issues in Western Societies*. Arnhem: Gouda Quint BV.

Anttila, I. and Törnudd, P. (1992). "The Dynamics of the Finnish Criminal Code Reform." In this volume.

Aspelin, E. (1975). "Some Developments in Swedish Criminal Policy." In E. Aspelin et al. (eds.) *Some Developments in Nordic Criminal Policy and Criminology*. Scandinavian Research Council for Criminology.

Aultman, M.G. and Wright, K.N. (1982)."The Fairness Paradigm: An Evaluation of Change in Juvenile Justice." *Canadian Journal of Criminology*, Vol. 24, No. 1.

Barnett, R.E. (1977)."Restitution: A New Paradigm of Criminal Justice." In *Ethics: An International Journal of Social, Political and Legal Philosophy*, vol. 87, no. 1, pp. 279-301. Reprinted in *Perspectives on Crime Victims*. B. Galaway and J. Hudson (eds.). St. Louis: The C.V. Mosby Co., (1981) pp. 245-261.

Barnett, R.E. and Hagel III, J. (1977). *Assessing the Criminal: Restitution, Retribution and the Legal Process*. Cambridge: Ballinger Publishing Co.

Bartholomew, A.A. (1986). *Psychiatry, the Criminal Law and Corrections: An Exercise in Sciolism*. Bundalong, Australia: Wileman Publications.

Becker, H. (1963). *Outsiders: Studies in the Sociology of Deviance*. New York: Free Press of Glencoe.

Canada: Law Reform Commission (1974)."The Meaning of Guilt: Strict Liability." *Working Paper No. 2*. Ottawa: Information Canada.

Law Reform Commission (1974)."The Principles of Sentencing and Dispositions." *Working Papers No. 5* and *No. 6*. Ottawa: Information Canada.

Law Reform Commission (1974)."The Principles of Sentencing and Dispositions." *Working Paper No. 3*. Ottawa: Information Canada.

Commission on Sentencing (1988) Report. Ottawa: Ministry of Supply and Services. Government of Canada (1982). *The Criminal Law in Canadian Society*. Ottawa.

Chappell, D. (1973). *Evaluating the Effectiveness of Programs to Compensate Victims of Crime*. Paper presented to the First International Symposium on Victimology. Jerusalem.

Christie, N. (1977)."Conflicts as Property." *British Journal of Criminology*, Vol. 17, No. 1, pp. 1-19.

Christie. N. (1981). *Limits to Pain*. Oslo: Universitetsforlaget.

Clarke, R.V. (1981)."The Prospects of Controlling Crime." *Home Office Research Unit Research Bulletin*, no. 12, pp. 12-19. London: HMSO.

Elias, R. (1986). *The Politics of Victimization*. Oxford: Oxford University Press.

Fattah, E.A. (1976). *Fear of Punishment*. Ottawa: Law Reform Commission of Canada.

Fattah, E.A. (1982)."Making the Punishment Fit the Crime: The Case of Imprisonment – Problems Inherent in the Use of Imprisonment as a Retributive Sanction." *Canadian Journal of Criminology*, vol. 24, no. 1, pp. 1-12.

Fattah, E.A. (1988). *The Impact of Crime Prevention on Victim Compensation*. Report prepared for the Canadian Department of Justice in Ottawa (mimeographed), 105 pages.

Fattah, E.A. (1988). *On Victims, Parole and the Sentencing Commission*. Brief submitted to the House of Commons Standing Committee on Justice and the Solicitor General (March).

Fattah, E.A. (1989)."Victims and Victimology: The Facts and the Rhetoric." *International Review of Victimology*, vol. 1, no. 1, pp. 43-46.

Ferri, E. (1917). *Criminal Sociology*. Boston: Little, Brown and Company.

Finland: Institute of Legal Policy (1983). *The Penal Law of Finland* (translated by Matti Joutsen). Helsinki.

Floud, J. and Young, W. (1981). *Dangerousness and Criminal Justice*. London: Heinemann.

Fredriksson, G. (1962). *Kriminalstatisken och Kriminologin*. Doctoral dissertation, University of Uppsala.

Gallaway, B. (1988). "Restitution as Innovation or Unfulfilled Promise?" *Federal Probation* (Sept.), pp. 3-14.

Greve, V. (1992). "On Negligence." In this volume.

Gross, H.A. (1992). *A Theory of Criminal Justice.* New York: Oxford University Press.

Hall, J. (1982). *Law, Social Science and Criminal Theory.* Littleton, CO: Fred B. Rothman.

Hart, H.L.A. (1968). *Punishment and Responsibility: Essays in the Philosophy of Law.* Oxford: Clarendon Press.

Hough, M. and Mayhew, P. (1983). "The British Crime Survey." *Home Office Research Study No. 76.* London: HMSO.

Hulsman, L. (1986). "Critical Criminology and the Concept of Crime." In H. Bianchi and R. Swaanigen (eds.) *Abolitionism: Towards a Non-Repressive Approach to Crime.* Amsterdam: Free University Press.

Jobson, K.B. (1977). "Dismantling the System." *Canadian Journal of Criminology and Corrections,* vol. 19, no. 3, pp. 254-272.

Joutsen, M. (1987). *The Role of the Victim of Crime in European Criminal Justice Systems.* Helsinki: Institute for Crime Prevention and Control.

Joutsen, M. and Shapland, J. (1989). *Changing Victim Policy: The UN Victim Declaration and Recent Developments in Europe – A Report on an Ad Hoc Working Group Meeting.* Helsinki: Institute for Crime Prevention and Control.

Kuhn, T. (1970). *The Structure of Scientific Revolutions,* second edition. Chicago: University of Chicago Press.

Lahti, R. (1983). "Finland: National Report." *Revue Internationale de Droit Pénal.* 54, pp. 249-262.

Lahti, R. (1987). "Scandinavian Criminal Policy: Trends and Interactions." In *Kansainoikeus – Ius Gentium,* vol. 4, 1-2, pp. 128-148.

Lahti, R. (1990a). "The Utilization of Criminological Research in Finnish Criminal Law Reform." In R. Lahti and K. Nuotio (eds.) *Towards a Total Reform of Finnish Law.* Helsinki: Publications of the Department of Criminal Law and Judicial Procedure, University of Helsinki, pp. 39-54.

Lahti, R. (1990b). "Recodifying the Finnish Criminal Code of 1889: A Scandinavian Way to Make the Criminal Law More Efficient, Just and Humane." In R. Lahti and K. Nuotio (eds.) *Towards a Total Reform of Finnish Law.* Helsinki, pp. 55-85.

Lamer, A. (1978). "Criminal Justice: A Total Look." *Canadian Journal of Criminology,* vol. 20, no. 2, pp. 126-141.

Lappi-Seppälä, T. (1992). "Penal Policy and Sentencing Theory in Finland." In R. Lahti, K. Nuotio and P. Minkkinen (eds.) *Criminal Policy and Sentencing in Transition: Finnish and Comparative Perspectives.* Helsinki: Department of Criminal Law and Judicial Procedure, University of Helsinki, pp. 3-48.

Morris, N. and Hawkins, G. (1969). *The Honest Politician's Guide to Crime Control.* Chicago: University of Chicago Press.

Morris, N. (1973). *The Law Is a Busybody.* Copyright by the New York Times Company, reprinted by the World Correctional Service Center.

Nuutila, Ari-Matti (1990). "On the Principle of Guilt in Finnish Criminal Justice: Intentionality, Knowledge and Motivation Factors as Preconditions for Criminal Liability." In R. Lahti and K. Nuotio (eds.) *Towards a Total Reform of Finnish Criminal Law.* Helsinki, pp. 101-157.

Orloski, R.J. (1977). *Criminal Law: An Indictment.* Chicago: Nelson Hall.

Parker, G. (1977). *An Introduction to Criminal Law.* Toronto: Methuen.

Ranish, D.R. and Shichor, D. (1985). "The Victim's Role in the Penal Process." *Federal Probation,* vol. 49 (1), March, pp. 50-57.

Saleilles, R. (1929). *The Individualization of Punishment* (translated from French). Montclair, NJ: Patterson Smith (reprint, 1965).

Sevón, K. (1990). "Legality, Efficiency and Legitimacy: Some Comments on the Legitimacy Problems of Modern Criminal Law." In R. Lahti and K. Nuotio (eds.) *Towards a Total Reform of Finnish Criminal Law.* Helsinki, pp. 181-222.

Sparks, R.F. (1981). "Surveys of Victimization: An Optimistic Assessment." In *Crime and Justice: An Annual Review of Research,* M. Tonry and N. Morris (eds.), vol. 3, pp. 1-60.

Straus, M. A. (1976). "Sexual Inequality, Cultural Norms and Wife-Beating." *Victimology: An International Journal,* vol. 1, no. 1, pp. 54-70.

Sykes, G.M. (1971). "The Pains of Imprisonment." In L. Radzinowiez and Wolfgang (eds.) *Crime and Justice, Volume 3, The Criminal in Confinement.* New York: Basic Books.

Törnudd, P. (1975). "Towards Crime Statistics Based on Damages." In Aspelin, E. et al. (eds.) *Some Developments in Nordic Criminal Policy and Criminology.* Scandinavian Research Council for Criminology.

Wootton, B. (1959). *Social Science and Social Pathology.* London: Allen and Unwin.

Wootton, B. (1960). "Diminished Responsibility: A Layman's View." *The Law Quarterly Review,* vol. 76 (April), pp. 224-239.

Wootton, B. (1978). *Crime and Penal Policy.* London: Allen and Unwin.

Young, J. (1988). "Radical Criminology In Britain: The Emergence of a Competing Paradigm." In P. Rock (ed.) *A History of British Criminology,* pp. 159-183. Oxford: Clarendon Press.

PART II

Victims Are Double Losers in Punitive Justice Systems: Injury/Harm and No Redress or Indemnification

Chapter III
From a Handful of Dollars to Tea and Sympathy: The Sad History of Victim Assistance

In J.J.M. van Dijk, Ron G.H. van Kaam and Jo-Anne Wemmers (eds.)
Caring for Crime Victims: Selected Proceedings of the 9th International Symposium on Victimology, pp. 187-206. Monsey, NY: Criminal Justice Press.

Introduction

The history of the decline and reemergence of victims of crime is too well known. Suffice it to say that the real decline began when a branch of public law, the criminal law, developed. When certain types of harmful actions came to be defined as crimes, they were no longer considered offences against the victim but were commonly regarded as offences against the sovereign and, later, the state. Under the penal law, the commission of a harmful, injurious, hurtful act created not an obligation to restore the victim but a debt to society. Once the wrongdoer was punished, the debt was paid and the victim was left out in the cold – without redress, compensation, assistance or even recognition. Victims, in other words, became the forgotten persons. They lost their case and their cause to the state. They lost their voice and their choice. Surely, they were often used, and continue to be used, by the prosecutors to buttress the state's case and are abused if they refuse to cooperate or testify. But in all industrialized societies with so-called modern penal codes, victims were relegated to the background, to the shadows. They were no longer masters of their own conflict nor their destiny. They lost their legal status and even the right to speak or intervene (unless of course they chose to take the usually fruitless route of the *partie civile* recognized in a few jurisdictions). They lost whatever decision-making power they had to the state's representative: the prosecutor. They were no longer consulted (or even advised) as to what should or would be done, and their wishes, if they dared to express them, were simply ignored.

The plight was even worse in Anglo-Saxon justice systems, where the practice of plea bargaining is quite common. Victims were completely excluded from the process. And the new fads of victim-impact statements and the right of allocution have done little or nothing to alleviate the problem. When private wrongs were converted into public offences, victim rights were usurped with the promise that the criminal justice system would protect their rights and alleviate their plight. Instead, the situation of victims only became worse. Their rightful dues – the composition, the *weregild* – were expropriated by the state and became penal fines, and the protection victims were supposed to get in return never materialized. As a result of ridiculously low clearance rates and of high attrition in the justice process, only a tiny fraction of all those who commit criminal offences face charges before the courts, and even a smaller minority end up being punished. Estimates range from as low as one per cent to the optimistic percentage of ten per cent. A system that promises crime victims that it will punish their victimizers and fails to deliver more than nine times out of ten is surely a system in crisis (see Fattah, 1997b). It is a system that offers the victim no protection no satisfaction, no relief and no redress.

Victim Support: The Balance Sheet

To remedy the situation, to do justice to the victims and to alleviate their plight, many changes were introduced in the last three decades. Victim compensation schemes, victim assistance programs and other victim services have been in existence for over a quarter of a century. The time has come to examine the balance sheet and to assess the effectiveness, impact and success of these initiatives in improving the sad lot of crime victims. To what extent have they achieved their avowed goals, their enunciated objectives? Have they been successful in doing what they were supposed to do, and with good results?

Evaluations of victim programs, victim services and other victim initiatives, rather than highlighting positive achievements, generally point to a negative balance sheet. For political and ideological reasons, the new policies and initiatives, despite the great fanfare that accompanied their introduction, targeted only a few categories of victims. The vast majority of crime victims remained without help, assistance, care or compensation.

The conclusions of the experts who have studied the programs and services are definitely discouraging and hardly inspire much confidence in the programs or much optimism about their future. State compensation programs for crime victims, introduced in the mid sixties, created a great deal of expectations that were never met. The programs were described as political palliatives (Burns, 1980), political placebos (Chappell, 1972) and band-aid measures, even as a symbolic gesture.

Victim support, write Maguire and Pointing (1988), remains essentially a grassroots, low-budget enterprise that relies upon the good will and hard work of volunteers. Shapland et al. (1985) maintain that the major projects aimed at fulfilling victims' needs were set up without regard to or even investigation into victims' expressed needs. Rock (1990) insists that victims' interests were never the motivating or mobilizing force behind the new initiatives to help victims. Mawby and Gill (1987) detected a right-wing, law-and-order focus among victim support scheme volunteers. They expressed concerns that crime victims might become "the victims of political expediency" (p. 228). Elias (1992) affirms that victims' services really serve official needs, not victims' needs.

State Compensation to Victims of Crime

To see whether these negative appraisals are justified, let us take as an example monetary compensation to crime victims, which, in the case of property victimization – by far the most common type of victimization – is the most pressing need and the foremost objective of the victims. State compensation programs that started in New Zealand in the early 1960s are now in place in many countries. They have been assessed by Burns (1980), Miers (1978), Doerner (1978) and Elias (1983a, 1983b), among others. The evaluations suggest that the amounts victims get from the schemes are, for the most part, token amounts and that the programs in reality fulfil no more than a symbolic function. A very tiny proportion of victims end up by receiving compensation and for those who do it is, more often than not, too little and too late. Ironically, one researcher (Elias, 1983a, 1983b) found that victims who apply for and go through the process of compensation (even those who end up receiving some funds) are less satisfied than those who do not apply. Elias's conclusions describe well victims' frustration and disenchantment:

> "Respondents were dissatisfied with delays, inconveniences, poor information, inability to participate and the restrictive eligibility requirements. These sentiments, coupled with the large number of award applications that were denied, produced strongly negative attitudes among victims toward victim compensation. Unfortunately for victim compensation's advocates, victims having applied to the compensation programs were more discontent than those who had not, thus causing one to wonder whether attitudes would not have been better overall if victim compensation had never existed," (1983a:245-246).

Cozijn's (1984) findings on the Netherlands are very similar to those of Elias on the United States. While paying lip service to the victims' cause, politicians show no genuine commitment to the schemes, are reluctant to allocate sufficient funds to them and allow them to operate only within a strictly preset budget. In recent years, several governments decided to transfer the financial burden of victim compensation to offenders through a levy called a "victim fine surcharge" imposed on those who are sentenced to a fine even if the sentence is for a so-called victimless crime. Politicians who are quick to seize upon and exploit the popular cause of crime victims are the same ones who refuse to make adequate allocations to the schemes, to earmark the fines collected by the criminal justice system to victim compensation or to enlarge the categories of victims eligible for indemnification. Miers (1983, 1990), quoted by Maguire and Shapland (1997), argued that state compensation is essentially a symbolic act by governments to show their concern for victims, but with little real intention of following it through with hard cash.

Over the years I have repeatedly proposed a universal state insurance system for crime victims similar to traffic accident insurance, labour accident insurance, unemployment insurance, etc., but the idea was always summarily rejected as a utopian dream. So while almost all other risks are covered in the welfare state by some form of insurance or another, the risk of becoming a victim of crime is not. This leads in practise to flagrant injustices. In Canada, for example, if someone is killed, injured or disabled as a result of a car accident, plane crash, ski lift mishap, medical malpractice, pharmaceutical error, etc. he or she or their heirs can receive millions of dollars in compensation. If the death or injury resulted from a criminal act, the maximum award available from the criminal injuries compensation scheme can be as low as $20,000. And because state compensation schemes are strictly and explicitly limited to victims of violent or sex crimes, the vast majority of victims end up receiving no compensation whatsoever for the losses they have suffered. In the United States, Karmen (1996:332) reports that the rate of compensation in a particular state in a given year, calculated as the proportion of crimes actually compensated compared to all reported crimes that are potentially eligible for compensation, was as low as one per cent in Michigan, and averaged out at nineteen per cent. Most victims of property crime, who are excluded from state compensation schemes, do not have and cannot afford private insurance. In four out of five cases of these property crimes, the culprit is neither identified nor caught. And the few who are arrested, charged and convicted are, more often than not, poor or so insolvent that nothing can be obtained from them through a civil judgment. And to add insult to injury, in most countries, the collection of criminal fines continues to have priority over the payment of civil damages or of restitution/compensation orders.

Victims of violence for whom the schemes are designed do not fare much better. The conditions of eligibility for state compensation are such that only a small fraction do qualify. In almost all systems, eligibility is contingent upon reporting the offence to the police and the victim's willingness to cooperate with the criminal justice system. Moreover, many schemes have a means test ensuring that compensation is given only to the poorest of the poor. Most exclude violence among family members, whereas a good part of all violence occurs in domestic settings. Most schemes also exclude (or drastically reduce the awards to) victims who provoked or otherwise contributed to their own victimization. One sure way of making the majority of victims of violence ineligible for state compensation is to set a high minimum limit for compensation below which victims do not qualify. In the United Kingdom, for example, the lower limit was set at £1,000 despite the recommendations made by victims groups to remove it. The burden of proof is upon the victim, and it is easy to imagine how difficult it can be to prove that the injury resulted from a criminal attack when the attacker has run away and there are no witnesses. With the exception of sexual victimization, most schemes do not provide funds to compensate the victim's emotional pain and suffering.

It is not surprising that many victims are deterred from applying due to the lengthy bureaucratic procedures and the investigative process. According to Maguire and Shapland (1997), compensation procedures in the Netherlands are very bureaucratic, require the participation of lawyers and ensure delays of over two years before awards are made. The findings of van Dijk (1989) affirm that the great dissatisfaction with the operation of the schemes is such that victim support associations are not recommending them to victims. More distressing still is that many victims are simply unaware of the existence of the schemes. As in many jurisdictions, the budget is determined in advance and cannot be exceeded; the more applications the program receives, the lower are the awards. And as the schemes are poorly funded in the first place, successful applicants usually end up receiving ridiculously low amounts as compensation for their victimization. It is easy to understand, therefore, why it is that in some countries there is a deliberate attempt not to publicize these state compensation schemes.

Smith and Hillenbrand (1997) examined three ways that victims may be repaid for the financial harm inflicted on them: restitution, victim-offender reconciliation programs and compensation. They found that only a small minority of victims benefit from these programs. Among the reasons they give for this sad reality is the lack of awareness about the programs, the inability or unwillingness of defendants to pay restitution, an insufficiency of state fund to compensate victims and limits on which victims are eligible for compensation.

If this brief description of state compensation schemes to victims of crime is accurate, and I believe it is, then it is fair to say that their primary function is not really to financially help victims or alleviate their distress but to assuage society's conscience and appease the guilt we feel about the plight of the victim. The sad conclusion that state compensation is not really meant to serve the interests of crime victims is supported by Rock's (1990) revelations about the history and politics of victim compensation in England and Wales. Having traced and analyzed the history of state compensation programs to victims of violence, Rock concluded that victims' interests were never the motivating or mobilizing force behind these initiatives. He writes:

> "Criminal injuries compensation was supposed to mollify the reactionary victim-vigilante, and reparation was a device to divert offenders from custody. In both instances, victims were the creatures of penal imperatives, invested with the characters needed to get on with the business of reforming prisons. Compensation and reparation did not have much of a foundation in the declared or observed requirements of victims themselves: they were bestowed on victims in order to achieve particular ends," (p. 408).

The same observation was made by Törnudd (1996). He reports that the Finnish State Committee, which, in 1972, proposed a law granting victims the right to demand compensation from state funds, explicitly motivated its proposal with "the need to lessen the aggressive feelings of the general public towards offenders," (p. 127).

Victim Assistance Programs

If this is true for victim compensation, how is it with other victim support schemes? In Canada, victim assistance programs have been set up within many police departments in large cities. As with compensation schemes, the guiding influences do not seem to be compassionate or humanitarian consideration for victims, but the administrative goals of the agency. The Calgary Victim Services Program, one of the first of its kind in Canada (started in 1977), is just one example of many. The program is described in a pamphlet published by the Solicitor General Department in Ottawa. The document makes no secret of the fact that the objective of the program "is to develop a good working relationship with victims of crime in order to encourage their future co-operation with the police in crime prevention." This statement speaks volumes about the real motives behind the service. It explains why there is a distinct preference to house these programs in police departments or public prosecutors' offices rather than in the community (Fattah, 1992).

As most of these programs are dominated by police ideology, they tend to share the traditional biases of the police. Distinctions are thus made between innocent and guilty victims, good and bad victims, honourable and dirty-handed victims, deserving victims and non-deserving victims. Victim assistance programs in Canada and in many other countries follow a standard model. They have a hired coordinator, but the services are provided exclusively or predominantly by volunteers. As the volunteers have no training or expertise in psychology or counselling, they are instructed to refrain from acting as psychologists or counsellors. They might be able to provide some practical assistance to the victim: driving, cleaning, shopping, helping with the children and so forth, but in most cases the only thing volunteers provide is emotional support, tea and sympathy.

The Need for Solid Empirical Research

While action to affirm victims' rights and to improve their lot has been in full swing on many fronts, animated by political and ideological considerations, research has been lagging behind and in many instances totally lacking. Several areas, pivotal to the theory and practice of victim assistance, have hardly been investigated and are in dire need of solid empirical research. One cannot help but wonder why it is that when the area of victim services is flourishing, research on the effects of victimization and on the impact of victim assistance is hard to come by. And yet, it seems obvious that individualized care, individualized assistance and personalized treatment or counselling require a profound knowledge of the differential impact of victimization and the differential needs of crime victims. Clearly this is an area that offers golden and endless opportunities for original research.

The indisputable fact that crime victims constitute a highly diverse and heterogeneous group means that the impact of victimization and the consequences of the victimizing event will be extremely different from one victim group to another and from one individual victim to the other. Lurigio and Resick (1990) insist that because reactions to crime and other deleterious experiences are often quite varied, it is essential to study individual differences in response to criminal victimization. They state that variability in victim recovery can be a function of victim characteristics and predispositions, the nature of the incident, victims' perceptions and interpretations of the occurrence, and events that occur in the aftermath of the crime. Lurigio and Resick (1990) place great emphasis on the individual correlates of post-crime distress and recovery.

Sociocultural factors and attitudes can be of great importance as well, and play a significant role in speeding up or delaying the recovery process. In our society, there is a tendency to stress – even overblow – the negative effects of victimization, whereas in other cultures only the positive effects are emphasized. Even physical injuries resulting from victimization do not carry the same weight everywhere, and their impact therefore is bound to be greater or lesser according to a host of variables. It is undeniable that psychological wounds heal faster and better in some cultures than in others.

Research is necessary to identify the characteristics of the cultures that facilitate and accelerate the healing process and those of the cultures that hinder or delay the victim's recovery. Why are coping mechanisms and strategies better developed in certain cultures than in others? What role does the social network have? It is well known that the network is stronger and more cohesive in certain cultures than in others (Fattah, 1997a). Cross-cultural research of this type is lacking and urgently needed, but it is not by any means the only kind. There is a need to know how the effects of victimization vary, not only by type of victim but also by type of offender and type of crime. A large number of variables – socio-demographic, psychological, cultural, social, situational – need to be examined in order to find out how and to what extent they shape, mould or influence the effects of different types of victimization. We need to know, for example, whether the effects of criminal victimization are similar to or different from those of victimization by other sources, such as accidents, negligence, natural disasters, abuse of power, etc. Is victimization by intimates or friends more or less traumatic than victimization by strangers? Is face-to-face victimization more or less traumatic than perfidious victimization? Is victimization by the state or by a state agency (such as the police) more or less traumatizing than victimization by an ordinary criminal? Is collective victimization more or less traumatizing than individual victimization? In what way do the traumatic effects differ in cases of provoked victimization when compared to cases of unprovoked victimization? What role does ethnicity or culture play? Do members of Canada's First Nations, for example, suffer more or less when victimized than do other Canadians?

These are just a few examples of dozens of questions that remain unanswered. And there are many others related to victim needs. The diversity and heterogeneity of the victim population mean that the needs of the victims will greatly differ. The needs of victims of violence could be quite different from those of property crime victims. The needs of child victims are no doubt different from those of adult or elderly victims, and so on. Obviously, the differential needs will have to be studied and assessed if the services offered are to be tailored to the specific needs of each victim group, not to say each individual victim.

One important and interesting question that has not received much attention is the effect of repeat victimization. Do repeat victimizations have or produce a cumulative effect that gets stronger with each subsequent victimization? Or do they have a desensitizing effect, thus gradually losing their traumatic effect the more the victimized individual gets used to them? Do those who are victimized frequently suffer more or less than those who are rarely victimized or are victimized only once? Are the effects of victimization similar to those of the prison experience: highly traumatizing the first time around and becoming milder and milder with every subsequent experience? Or to put it differently, do recidivist victims suffer more or less than the one-timers? Do recidivist victims need more or less support than first-timers?

Another area that is conspicuous by its absence in victimization research is that of the positive effects of victimization. The conventional wisdom of course is that victimization has only negative and traumatic effects. The discourse on victims has focused entirely on the devastating impact victimization has on the victim. Very little has been said or written on the positive effects victimization might have. One lesson learned early in the social sciences is that nothing is totally functional or totally dysfunctional; nothing has only negative or positive effects. Human experiences can be negative in some ways and positive in others, functional in some respects and dysfunctional in others.

Victimization is a great teacher. As the popular saying goes, "people learn from experience" or "these negative events have turned him into a much stronger person." Victimization awakens people's defensive instincts and forces them to be alert, cautious and more careful and prudent than they were. They become less negligent, less reckless and less nonchalant than before.

Victimization forces people to reassess their lives – to sort out the important from the trivial, the vital from the inconsequential. It usually has a strong impact on the victim's relationships with others. It can destroy the victim's marriage or it can save and strengthen it. Victimization is a powerful test of the marriage because of the strong strain it places on the marital relationship. We have heard about countless marriages that were destroyed as a result of rape or sexual assault of the wife. But victimization, like other traumatic experiences (for example, the loss of a beloved child), can draw the couple closer together and consolidate the bond that ties them to each other. Gerard Vader, a Dutch journalist who wrote an interesting book about his experience as a hostage on a train hijacked by Moluccan nationalists in Indonesia in the 1960s, affirms that the hostage experience saved his faltering marriage. It remains to be seen whether similar positive effects will be reported by the hostages held captive in the house of the Japanese ambassador in Lima, Peru, for several weeks in 1997.

The Mark of Abel

Crime victims, regardless of the type of victimization they suffer, need different types of support and varying kinds of assistance. They need practical services, such as fixing the lock, replacing the window or driving the kids to school. They need information and advice, particularly on how to avoid future victimization. They might need referral to other services or legal assistance. They need a great deal of emotional support. None of these types of services is problematic, and the more of them that are made available to the victim after the event the better. It is the other kind of well-intentioned support – counselling, therapy, treatment – that can pose real problems and that may produce negative and undesirable side effects.

While preparing my paper I came across the July 1997 issue of the *Mental Health Letter* published by the reputable Harvard Medical School. It contained a brief article by Dr. Robert A. Hahn (1995), which contained a statement that bears great relevance to the discipline of victimology and the field of victim assistance. Speaking of harmful effects, using the Latin word *nocebo*, Dr. Hahn wrote: "Nocebo effects are different in different cultures because societies teach their members which illnesses exist, which symptoms indicate the illnesses, how they are acquired and how they are treated. These categories may promote as well as describe illness, causing the pathologies they are meant to heal," (p. 8).

Reading Dr. Hahn's statement immediately brought to my mind some of the dangers I outlined in the early history of the victim movement (Fattah, 1986). I wondered then, as I do now, whether the outpouring sympathy for crime victims was doing more harm than good, whether it was hurting victims rather than facilitating and speeding their recovery. The amplification of the negative effects of victimization and the pathologizing of the normal reactions it evokes might have been done with the best of intentions. But by doing so, victim advocates portrayed and communicated to crime victims (actual and potential) a specific pattern of suffering that almost forces them to feel and behave in a certain manner.

Victims feel compelled to conform to this pattern of suffering because otherwise they might not be or be seen as normal or typical victims. Thus by trying hard to highlight the intense suffering, some victims might go through and draw attention to their plight, and by trying to help them cope with the negative effects of victimization, victim advocates might inadvertently be creating undue suffering.

To better understand the dangers, let me share with you the story of a twenty-five-year-old woman from Nova Scotia, Canada, who as a child had been a victim of incest and who last month was denied custody of her five-year-old son, allegedly because she has not received psychological therapy to deal with her childhood victimization. The woman's words as she was interviewed by the Canadian press (*The Globe and Mail*, 1997) are very telling. They illustrate what I mean when saying that we force victims into specific patterns of suffering, inculcating in their minds that they cannot cope on their own and that their recovery hinges on getting the appropriate psychological or psychiatric treatment. Here is what the victim said:

> "They are classifying me as this person who can't get anywhere in life because this happened, that no one can overcome something that terrible. But they don't know me. I didn't give up on life because this happened to me. It made me the person I am now," (p. A3).

Then she added:

> "I don't believe I need help, okay? Not at the present time. Maybe when I am 50 it might bother me or even when I am 29. But right now my life is going in a positive direction, and it's not something that even affects me," (p. A3).

One cannot help but say: good for you! And then wonder how many other victims gave up on life because they believed what they were told: that the trauma of victimization lasts a lifetime, that they will forever suffer from what they endured in their early childhood. There is an important lesson to be learned from the experience of the Nova Scotia victim. It tells us to exercise a great deal of caution before labelling victims with the "mark of Abel."

Potential Nocebo Effects of Intervention

Telling victims of incest, rape, sexual assault or other types of victimization that the effects are disastrous, nefarious, too serious, too traumatic, long lasting, etc. and telling them that they cannot cope on their own without the help of psychiatrists, psychologists, sex therapists, social workers and so forth can easily become a self-fulfilling prophecy. It can delay the process of natural healing as well as the process of self-recovery. It can be particularly damaging in the case of impressionable young children. For example, in many cases of incest or child sexual abuse, the children are too young to understand the wrongfulness of the behaviour or to realize the seriousness of what happened. It is the parents, the child welfare workers, the therapists and the criminal justice personnel (police, prosecutors, etc.) who, through their questions, attitudes and behaviour, communicate to the child that something really awful has been done to them. By so doing, these professionals can themselves create what may be a long-lasting trauma. In other words, the help and assistance they are trying to give the child victim can produce more trauma than the trauma of the victimization itself.

Surprisingly, the message victims often get from those trying to help them is the opposite of the one usually offered by physicians and psychiatrists to their patients. In their attempts to aid and hasten a patient's recovery, those well-trained professionals usually take a reassuring stance, trying to minimize the seriousness of the ailment while emphasizing the potential for recovery. They try to foster in the patient an aura of optimism rather than distress, pessimism or despair. This positive, supportive attitude is in sharp contrast to the one exhibited *vis-à-vis* crime victims.

Even seemingly innocent, harmless slogans, such as 'justice for victims" or "victims deserve better" may prove detrimental to victims interests and well-being. Such slogans are invariably interpreted as a call for more and harsher punishment for the victimizers. As such, they tend to create among victims expectations that may not be easily fulfilled, such as the promise of harsh punishment – death, long prison sentences, denial of parole – which too often cannot be met in practice. This is a sure recipe for producing angry, bitter, resentful and frustrated victims. Fomenting victims' vindictiveness and hailing revenge as the ultimate goal of justice inevitably leave a host of unhappy, unsatisfied victims who feel betrayed whenever the goal has not been attained and every time punishment falls short of expectations. Those who knowingly or unwittingly fuel the vindictiveness of victims might be doing them a disservice, because this emotion does not facilitate closure and delays the healing process.

Well-intentioned assistance practices may also hurt crime victims in other ways. There is a widespread yet misguided belief that every well-intentioned reform is bound to yield good results and should therefore be enthusiastically (and unquestioningly) endorsed. Social scientists should know better. They are fully aware of the potentially disastrous consequences of doing good. Those who want examples need only look at the noble attempts to assimilate North America's First Nations and Native Americans or the Aborigines in Australia, to save their souls and secure them a place in heaven. Criminologists are painfully aware of the countless intervention programs and techniques aimed at treating, helping and rehabilitating young offenders that ended up producing the opposite results: intensifying delinquent activities and prolonging a delinquent career. The field of victim assistance is no different. Intervention with victims (victim therapy), though widely regarded as being in their best interest and as necessary, beneficial and commendable, can also have adverse, unanticipated ill effects. This is perhaps the saddest aspect of victim support, the possibility that those who are genuinely trying to help victims may inadvertently end up hurting them. And no discussion of victim assistance and services would be complete without pointing out the dangers inherent in such assistance. Space limitations do not allow a detailed accounting of those dangers, but a couple of examples will suffice to illustrate the point.

Actual and Potential Dangers of Victim Therapy

One good example of a possible danger is the so-called repressed memory syndrome. In the process of helping "victims" believed to have suppressed all recollection of early sexual abuse, overzealous therapists implant false memories in the minds of troubled persons already suffering psychological and psychosomatic symptoms, as well as social inadequacies. Women who have no recollection of sexual victimization, but who were complaining about marital problems, eating disorders, anxiety, depression or low self-esteem, seek help, only to be told that they must have been sexually abused. Memories of abuse are extracted during lengthy and intensive therapy sessions. Those whom the therapist believes were abused find themselves in a double-bind, no-win situation. Either they have to go along with the therapist's suggestions and admit to abuse that never happened or risk being declared as being in denial by the therapist.

There seems to be little dispute among psychologists and psychiatrists that repressed memory is not a memory that was simply forgotten but one that was intentionally repressed from consciousness. They maintain that repression is an unconscious mechanism of defence that allows the mind to bury a severely traumatic or frightening event that happened in early childhood. As Ofshe and Watters (1995) correctly point out,

> "The properties of robust repression are dramatically different from those of accepted memory-related mental processes, such as ordinary forgetting, intentional avoidance of

> a subject and traumatic amnesia. While sharing certain superficial features with these phenomena, repression implies something distinct from each... Repression is an all-or-none phenomenon – now you see it, now you don't. Repression will cause the knowledge of the event to disappear entirely from awareness, perhaps only minutes after it happened... Simple failure or perfect recall or recall of only gross characteristics of distant events is not repression, as the mechanism appears in recovered memory therapy," (pp. 12-13).

One has to wonder why it is that the mind of a baby or a very young child with no understanding or realization of the horrific nature of sexual abuse would unconsciously repress the memory of an event whose traumatizing nature is not comprehended!

Psychologist Elizabeth Loftus, in an interview in *The Vancouver Sun* (Mullens, 1992), maintains that memory can be easily influenced by suggestion. She is greatly concerned that suggestive questioning and probing by therapists about sexual abuse may become a relentless search for specific memories and may lead to recollections of events that never happened. Loftus relates how numerous people had come to her saying, "My therapist is convinced I have been abused, but I have no memories. Can you help me find memories?" Loftus's circumspect attitude is in marked contrast to that of non-psychologists. Ellen Bass and Laura Davis, who in their 1992 book *The Courage to Heal* claim that if a woman feels she was abused but has no memories, she probably was! One has to wonder, once more, about all the lives that have been destroyed by false memories: the lives of those who became convinced that they had been sexually abused when in reality they had not, the lives of their close family members and the lives of those individuals who were accused on the basis of these false memories – regardless of whether they were charged, convicted or acquitted. If it is true that repressed memory, as claimed by many (e.g. Crews, 1995; Loftus and Ketcham, 1991, 1994; Ofshe and Watters, 1995; Showalter, 1997), is often a false memory or a figment of therapists' imaginations, then the therapists who carelessly, inadvertently or unwittingly implant such false memories in their troubled patients are guilty of one of the worst crimes that a human being can commit against another.

There is, however, a glimmer of hope that the end of this extremely dangerous practice might be in sight. In October 1997, *The London Daily Telegraph* reported on a ban imposed on members of Britain's Royal College of Psychiatrists that disallows them to use any method to recover memories of child abuse. Those who violate the ban are threatened with a series of sanctions. Although the report that led to the ban will not be published until next year, the new guidelines make it clear that the ban was imposed because of concern that the techniques employed to "recover memory" can give rise to strongly held false memories and can lead to false accusations (*The Vancouver Sun,* 1997).

The same over-zealousness is also responsible for blinding parents, police, child welfare workers and prosecutors to the harm they are doing to children believed to have been molested, through repeated uninhibited interrogations: sexualization through the use of so-called anatomically correct dolls, withdrawal of love and affection until the child admits what they suspect had happened, and so forth.

In the zealous pursuit of physical evidence to support suspicions or allegations of sexual abuse and satanic rituals, children's bodies have been violated through digital, instrument, vaginal and anal penetration. Children have had their most private parts examined and filmed, with the slides repeatedly shown in public sessions in United States courts. The revelations made by the Eberles (1993) are not only shocking and revolting but also eye-opening and should be required reading for anyone genuinely interested in the well-being of children and society. The extent of the harm done to children, though for good cause, can only be fully comprehended when keeping in mind that in many cases no sexual abuse had in fact taken place, that the process causing the harm to the child was based on nothing more than an unfounded suspicion. One has to wonder whether the interests and the well-being of children are being sacrificed in an attempt to satisfy the urge to punish and whether the victims are being used as tools to achieve administrative and ideological goals.

Another questionable practice is to instill fear and suspicion in the minds of children through so-called street-proofing techniques aimed at guarding against potential victimization. This practice is questionable because quite often the objective risk of victimization does not in any way justify the powerful psychological fear that can become a permanent trait of a child's personality. The same is also true of attempts to alert children to the possibility of sexual abuse by family members, which could in the long run backfire by creating a whole generation of people fearful to touch or be touched, to receive and to return affection.

Many of the dangers of the questionable and potentially harmful practices outlined above can be traced to the fact that the methods and the techniques are not based on solid empirical evidence or hard scientific facts. They stem from the popular tendency to pathologize natural symptoms and perfectly normal reactions and to fit them under new illness categories, such as post-traumatic stress disorder, that quickly find their way to the diagnostic manuals.

The mere talk of victim therapies creates the impression and fosters the belief that victims cannot cope on their own or solely with the help of their family or social network, that intervention of some kind (psychiatric or psychological treatment, counseling, etc.) is absolutely essential for restoring a victim's well-being and curing the effects of victimization. This belief is not different from the one that dominated criminology until a few years ago, when it was generally felt that delinquents and criminals are unable on their own to change their attitudes and behaviour, that they are in desperate need of treatment or rehabilitation. Empirical research conducted to assess the effects of formal intervention with delinquents and criminals revealed negative rather than positive results. It showed that the intervention - the ensuing labeling, stigmatization and self-identification with the label- can produce the opposite results of what they were supposed to achieve, and can lead to the continuation rather than the cessation of delinquent activities.

Although the effects of psychological and psychiatric intervention with victims have not yet been carefully studied, there are indications that such intervention is ineffective. A decade ago, Davis (1987) observed that crisis intervention programs for victims had grown rapidly in the absence of hard data demonstrating their effectiveness. He examined the effects of services on victims' psychological and material adjustment. Although substantial recovery occurred for all victims in the first three months post-crime, there was no evidence that recovery was any greater for victims who received services than for those who did not. Davis and Henley (1990) reviewed research findings and found little indication that counseling of any sort is effective in reducing post-crime trauma. They regretted the fact that much money is being spent on crisis intervention services for victims in the absence of knowledge as to which forms of treatment work and which do not. There are also reasons to believe that intervention if not done properly, can delay rather than accelerate the natural healing process and can prolong rather than shorten the trauma of victimization.

Bisson and Deahl (1994) reviewed the available evidence on the effectiveness of psychological debriefing (PD), the most widely advocated measure for preventing post-traumatic stress. The studies reviewed suffered from methodological flaws. They were, however, able to conclude that, at best, PD affords some protection against later sequelae and, at worst, makes no difference. The data also suggested that the presence or absence of other factors, for example, adequate social support, are likely to affect the psychological outcome of individuals involved in traumatic events more than the presence or absence of PD.

Bisson and Deahl stress that when individuals have an adequate support network and do not suffer from specific vulnerability factors, PD may be redundant. In view of the considerable resources that will be required if PD or any other professional psychological intervention is to be made available to a large number of individuals, Bisson and Deahl feel it is essential that the efficacy of PD be adequately evaluated. Such evaluation would indicate whether or not it should be routinely offered to everyone involved in traumatic events, restricted to high-risk individuals or abandoned altogether. An evaluation might also indicate who should deliver PD, when and what form it should take. The possibility that psychological debriefing following traumatic events might have adverse side effects is one of the important conclusions of Carlier et al. (1995), who conducted a longitudinal follow-up study of two groups that suffered a traumatic event in an attempt to assess the long-term effects of debriefing on the one group that was debriefed.

The Potential Healing Functions of Self-Blame

The criminological experience gained over many decades should serve as a warning to those interested in victims' mental health. It amply demonstrates that conventional wisdom and ideological considerations can be a disastrous foundation for social intervention. For example, on the basis of advice given by feminist groups and other victim groups, it became a standard practice in victim assistance to assure victims that nothing they could have done would have prevented the crime from happening. Victims were urged to rid themselves of any feelings of guilt and to refrain from blaming themselves. They were repeatedly assured that they were the innocent prey of predators who pick their victims at random or of mentally unstable individuals who have no control over their predatory instincts or their aggressive urges and behaviour.

Countering and erasing "self-blame" became not only a standard practice, but the cornerstone of victim counselling. This conventional wisdom was immediately accepted with little or no questioning. No one cared to search for the manifest or latent functions of the phenomenon of victim self-blame nor to find out whether it is a psychological defence mechanism that has healing functions for a victim's psyche. Only now are we gradually starting to understand the role self-blame plays in the coping process (see Frieze et al., 1987; see also Rosenbaum, 1980). We know that victims' greatest fear is that the victimization will reoccur, that they will be re-victimized. This is why one of the first things victims try to do in their attempt to cope is to find out what they did or did not do that might have contributed to their victimization. By assuming some responsibility for what happened, they desperately try to regain some control over their destiny, to convince themselves that, had they behaved differently, they could have prevented their victimization. They want to believe that by changing their attitude, their behaviour or this or that aspect of their lifestyle, they will reduce the chances of future victimization. In addition to helping victims regain some control over their future, self-blame seems to have other beneficial functions. One of the most traumatizing aspects of victimization is the inability to find a satisfactory answer to the victim's most pressing question: "Why me?" Therefore there is little doubt that victims who are able to attribute the victimizing event, at least partially, to their aggressive, provoking, reckless, imprudent, careless or negligent behaviour suffer less and cope better than those who believe that their victimization was an unjust blow in an unlucky destiny or a freak act of a deranged, sick or abnormal individual.

The realization that the process of self-blame has useful psychological functions is of great importance and has profound implications for the practice of victim assistance. Those involved in victim therapy should give some thought to whether, by discouraging self-blame and absolving victims of any responsibility for the victimization, they are in fact enhancing the chances of re-victimization by dissuading victims from changing any of the victimogenic factors that might have promoted or facilitated the victimization.

This is to say that for many victims the lack of assistance might be better than misguided, badly delivered or ideologically tainted assistance. The fact that victim services and victim assistance programs are for the most part a do-good, humanitarian and charitable endeavour or are public relations enterprises is a good reason for carefully monitoring their actions and assessing their results.

Conclusion

At this Ninth International Symposium on Victimology the primary task should be to candidly tackle the most fundamental question of all: Are victims of crime better off now than they were three or four decades ago?

Few, undoubtedly, are. But for the vast majority of crime victims things have changed little, if at all, and some are definitely much worse off than ever before. Victims of property crimes, together with victims of abuse of political and economic power (by far the most numerous) have hardly been touched by the so-called new initiatives or the much-heralded reform. When I was recently victimized by a non-violent property crime on a train trip from Amsterdam to Brussels, I could only rely on the help and assistance of my colleagues Tony

Peters and Ivo Aertsen. Everywhere else I turned I encountered apathy, indifference, impatience or outright hostility. And when I tried to have my American Express Travellers Cheques replaced, I was treated like a swindler who was trying to defraud the company. The only thing my interrogators, or shall I say my tormentors, were interested in knowing was my first language or my mother's tongue – a clear example of how negative ethnic stereotypes can affect victims' efforts to cope with the effects of victimization. Since I, like most victims, did not have insurance, I got absolutely no compensation despite the significant financial loss I suffered. I even had to pay to have my passport and plane tickets replaced. Not only was I not eligible for financial compensation, I was not even offered tea or sympathy!

But the victimization was beneficial in many ways. I am now more cautious and alert than I have ever been, and this is bound to reduce my chances of being re-victimized. As a result of my victimization, I can better relate to the pain, suffering, resentment and anxiety victims endure, to their stress and distress, to their fears and their hopes, to their shaken faith and shattered expectations. In my lectures and in victimological meetings like this one, I can admit with pride that I am a VICTIM and can refer to and rely on my first-hand experience of victimization. As traumatic as the experience might have been, I am a stronger, more prudent and more knowledgeable individual. I have accepted my share of responsibility for what happened but have refused to let the victimization incident and its consequences spoil my life or poison my existence. And, like the Nova Scotian victim, I reject and refuse to wear the "mark of Abel." Luckily, nature has endowed human beings with an amazing healing capacity. Tragedies and traumatic experiences of every kind all end up being forgotten or simply turned into unpleasant memories. This is the strength of the human psyche, and it is on those strengths that we should capitalize in our endeavours to help and support victims of all kinds.

References

Bass, E. and L. Davis (1988). *The Courage to Heal: A Guide for Women Survivors of Child Sexual Abuse* (third edition). New York: HarperCollins Publishers.

Bisson, L.L. and M.P. Deahl (1994). "Psychological Debriefing and Prevention of Post-Traumatic Stress – More Research is Needed." *British Journal of Psychiatry*, (165):717-720.

Burns, P. (1980). *Criminal Injuries Compensation: Social Remedy or Political Palliative for Victims of Crime.* Toronto: Butterworths.

Carlier, I.V.E. et al. (1995). "Het Lange-Termijn Effect van Debriefen: Een Vervolgonderzoek bij de Amsterdamse

Politie Naar Aanleiding van de Bijlmerramp." *Intern Rapport.* Amsterdam: Academic Medical Centre, University of Amsterdam.

Chappell, D. (1972). "Providing for the Victim of Crime: Political Placebos or Progressive Programs?" *Adelaide Law Review,* (4):294-306.

Cozijn, C. (1984). *Schadefonds Geweldsmisdrijven* (Criminal Injuries Compensation). The Hague, Netherlands: Dutch Ministry of Justice.

Crews, F., H.P. Blum, M. Cavell, M. Eagle and F. Crews (1995). *The Memory Wars: Freud's Legacy in Dispute.* New York: A New York Review Book.

Davis, R.C. (1987). "Studying the Effects of Services for Victims in Crisis." *Crime & Delinquency,* 33(4):520-531.

– and M. Henley (1990). "Victim Service Programs." In: A.J. Lurigio, W.S. Skogan and R.C. Davis (eds.) *Victims of Crime: Problems, Policies and Programs.* Newbury Park, CA: Sage Publications.

Doerner, W. (1978). "A Quasi-Experimental Analysis of Selected Victim Compensation Programs." *Canadian Journal of Criminology,* 20(3):239-251.

Eberle, P. and S. Eberle (1993). *The Abuse of Innocence: The McMartin Pre-School Trial.* Buffalo, NY: Prometheus Books.

Elias, R. (1992). "Community Control, Criminal Justice and Victim Services." In: E.A Fattah (ed.) *Towards a Critical Victimology.* London, UK and New York, NY: Macmillan and St. Martin's Press.

– (1983a). *Victims of the System: Crime Victims and Compensation in American Politics and Criminal Justice.* New Brunswick, NJ: Transaction Books.

– (1983b). "The Symbolic Politics of Victim Compensation." *Victimology,* 8(12):213-224.

Fattah, E.A (1986). "On Some Visible and Hidden Dangers of Victim Movements." In E.A Fattah (ed.) *From Crime Policy to Victim Policy.* London: Macmillan.

– (1992a). "The United Nations Declaration of Basic Principles of Justice for Victims of Crime and Abuse of Power: A Constructive Critique." In: E.A Fattah (ed.), *Towards a Critical Victimology.* London: Macmillan.

– (1997a). "Toward a Victim Policy Aimed at Healing, Not Suffering." In: R.C. Davis, AJ. Lurigio and W.G. Skogan (eds.) *Victims of Crime* (second edition). Thousand Oaks, CA: Sage.

– (1997b). *Some Reflections on the Paradigm of Restorative Justice and Its Viability for Juvenile Justice.* Paper presented at the International Conference on Restorative Justice for Juveniles, Leuven, Belgium, May.

Frieze, I.S., M.S. Greenberg and S. Hymer (1987). "Describing the Crime Victim: Psychological Reactions to Victimization." *Professional Psychology, Research and Practice,* 18(4):299-315.

Hahn, R.A. (1997). "What Is a Nocebo?" *The Harvard Mental Health Letter,* 14(1):8.

Karmen, A (1996). *Crime Victims* (third edition). Belmont, CA: Wadsworth.

Loftus, E. and K. Ketcham (1991). *Witness for the Defense: The Accused, the Eyewitness and the Expert Who Puts Memory on Trial.* New York: St. Martin's.

– and K. Ketcham (1994). *The Myth of Repressed Memory: False Memories and Allegations of Sexual Abuse.* New York: St. Martin's.

Lurigio. AJ. and P.A. Resick (1990). "Healing the Psychological Wounds of Criminal Victimization: Predicting

Postcrime Distress and Recovery." In AJ. Lurigio, R.C. Davis and W.G. Skogan (eds.) *Victims of Crime: Problems, Policies and Programs.* Newbury Park, CA: Sage Publications.

Maguire, M. and J. Pointing (1988). *Victims of Crime: A New Deal?* Milton Keynes, UK: Open University Press.

– and J. Shapland (1997). "Provisions for Victims in an International Context." In: R.C. Davis, A.J. Lurigio and W.G. Skogan (eds.) *Victims of Crime* (second edition). London: Sage.

Mawby, R.I. and M.L. Gill (1987). *Crime Victims: Needs, Services and the Voluntary Sector.* London: Tavistock Publications.

Miers, D. (1978). *Response to Victimization.* Oxford: Milton Trading Estate.

– (1983). "Compensation to Victims of Crime." *Victimology,* (8):204-212.

– (1990). *Compensation for Criminal Injuries.* London: Butterworths.

Mullens, A (1992). Interview with Elizabeth Loftus, *The Vancouver Sun,* Nov. 28, p. A11.

Ofshe, R. and E. Watters (1995). "Making Monsters." In: NJ Pallone and J. Hennessy (eds.), *Fraud and Fallible Judgement: Varieties of Deception in the Social and Behavioural Sciences.* New Brunswick, NJ: Transaction Books.

Rock, P. (1990). *Helping Crime Victims: The Home Office and the Rise of Victim Support in England and Wales.* Oxford: Clarendon Press.

Rosenbaum, D.P. (1980). *Victim Blame as a Strategy for Coping with Criminal Victimization: An Analysis of Victim, Community and Police Reactions.* Ann Arbor, MI: University Microfilms International.

Shapland, J., J. Wilmore and P. Duff (1985). *Victims in the Criminal Justice System.* London: Gower.

Showalter, E. (1997). *Histories: Hysterical Epidemics and Modern Culture.* New York: Columbia University Press.

Smith, B.E. and S.W. Hillenbrand (1997). "Making Victims Whole Again: Restitution, VORP and Compensation." In R.C. Davis, AJ. Lurigio and W.S. Skogan (eds.), *Victims of Crime* (second edition). London: Sage.

The Globe and Mail (1997). "Incest Victims Can't Escape Past. Canadian Press Release." July 7, p. A3.

The Vancouver Sun (1997). October 10, p. A14.

Törnudd, P. (1996). *Facts, Values and Visions: Essays in Criminology and Crime Policy.* Helsinki, Finland: National Research Institute of Legal Policy.

van Dijk, J.J.M. (1989). "Recent Developments in the Criminal Policies Concerning Victims in the Netherlands." In *Changing Victim Policy: The United Nations Victim Declaration and Recent Developments in Europe* (Heuni Publication #16). Helsinki, Finland: Helsinki Institute for Crime Prevention and Control.

Chapter IV
A Critical Assessment *of* Two Justice Paradigms

Contrasting the Restorative and Retributive Justice Models

In Fattah, E.A. and Peters, T. (eds.)
Support for Crime Victims in a Comparative Perspective, pp. 99-110.
Leuven, Belgium: Leuven University Press.

In this article I will try to show that victim-centred remedies to criminal victimization are far superior to offender-centred punitive measures. After discussing the bankruptcy of the present system of punishment, I will proceed to show that the positive and constructive approaches of mediation, conciliation, restitution and compensation are better alternatives to the negative and destructive system of punishment.

The Bankruptcy of the Present System of Punishment

One hardly needs to present any evidence to show the bankruptcy of the present system of punishment, to show that it is hurting, not helping, that it is doing more harm than good. Still, it might not be a bad idea to highlight what is fundamentally wrong with the current obsession with punishing offenders, transgressors and wrongdoers.

1. Punishment is ineffective

Historical and empirical evidence provides irrefutable proof that the system of punishment has not worked in the past, is not working at present and will not work in the future. The record prison population in many countries and the overcrowding of prisons are ample proof of the failure of the present system. Anyone who might have any doubt needs only to look at the United States, which sends more people per capita to prison than any other Western country and whose crime problem has not shown much improvement over the years. Or one can look at China, which executes offenders by the thousands in a futile attempt to stem the tide of crime.

2. Punishment Achieves Nothing

None of the desirable goals of modern penal policy is achieved by punishment. In other words, punishment does not serve any useful purpose. Punishment does not deter, does not rehabilitate, does not educate, does not undo what has been done, does not heal the injury, does not compensate the loss, does not restore the victim or redress the harm he/she has suffered.

Instead, punishment breeds anger, hostility, resentment, antagonism. "Violence breeds violence" is a well-known and well-proven saying. People have naively thought that they can put offenders in cage-like cells, treat them like animals and then expect them to come out and behave responsibly like reasonable human beings. To expect a negative experience like imprisonment to produce such a positive transformation is beyond comprehension! Offenders come out from prison more angry, more hostile and more resentful than when they went in. Is it any wonder that recidivism rates are as high as they are?

3. Punishment Is Costly

The system of punishment is a very costly system in human, social and material terms. The financial costs have been escalating year after year, not only as a result of inflation and the growing prison population, but also as a result of changing sentencing practices and the uncritical acceptance of fashionable, though questionable, policies such as that of "just deserts," with its emphasis on minimum sentences, mandatory sentences, presumptive sentences, etc. So much money is being wasted at present on punishing offenders that hardly any is left to compensate their victims or to feed their innocent families. But the financial costs pale when compared with the human and social costs of punishment. The waste in human and social potential is simply enormous. Offenders sent to prison are reduced to and are treated as social waste, social junk, human garbage! They are cut off from their families, from their jobs (if they happen to have one) and from the rest of society. In prison they become dependent, despondent, unproductive and disheartened, and once released they are too difficult to retrieve.

4. Punishment Is Never Personal or Individual

Imprisonment is neither a personal nor individual punishment. It extends far beyond the punished offender. By removing the offender from his family and his social network the children are punished, the wives, the relatives, the friends are punished. All are punished for something they took no part in and had no way to stop.

5. Punishment Is Degrading, Humiliating and Stigmatizing

Incarceration, confinement, detention and other forms of deprivation of liberty are degrading and humiliating experiences. Prisoners lose their identity – they become numbers. They lose their dignity, their pride, their humanity.

Imprisonment is also a traumatizing experience that puts the permanent tag of "ex-con" on those who are put in prison and makes it extremely difficult for them to reintegrate into society or to turn their lives around.

6. Punishment Treats Human Beings as a Means to an End

Whether punishment is inflicted as a means of deterrence, that is, to make an example out of the criminal so that others might not follow in his steps, or as a means of satisfying the victim or protecting society, it always uses human beings as a means to an end – they are sacrificed to achieve some other goal, in the same way human sacrifices were made to appease the gods – like the virgin who used to be thrown in the river Nile to stop it from flooding its banks or into a volcano to stop it from erupting. Punishment might have some cathartic effects on the general public, but has no redeeming effects on the person being punished.

7. Punishment Looks at the Past

Retributive punishment looks at the past, at what the offender has done and does not aim at the future. It tries to dispense an amount of suffering that is supposedly equal to the suffering that the offender has caused to his victim. This task, needless to say, is an arbitrary one – because no law since the talion law (*lex talionis*) has succeeded in making the punishment fit the crime. In view of the extremely subjective and relative effects of victimization, it is utterly impossible to come up with a dosage of imprisonment that corresponds, even remotely, to the victim's suffering.

8. Punishment Perpetuates Rather than Settles the Conflict

For obvious reasons, punishment of the offender neither settles the conflict nor puts an end to the dispute. If anything, it widens the gap that separates the doer and the sufferer, it generates further animosity and antagonism and often engulfs the parties in bitter, never-ending hostilities. It forces others to join in and to take sides, thus contributing to the widening and perpetuation of the conflict.

9. Punitive Penal Sanctions Amount to Punishing the Victim

Whether one believes in biological, psychological or sociological theories of criminality, whether one believes in the bad seed or bad environment, whether one believes that criminals are born or society-made, it is impossible to find a valid rationale or a reasonable justification for punishment.

The interchangeability of the roles of victim and victimizer and the fact that crime is often a reaction to victimization, a means of self-help or of obtaining justice, mean that offenders, like those whom they harm or hurt, are victims in the true sense of the word. But instead of helping them, society turns around and punishes them. Society does not want to accept its failures. It rejects them and puts them away – out of sight and out of mind. But every inmate comes out sooner or later, and if they come out worse than when going in, which is often the case, the chances of recidivism are greater than ever.

Critics of the punishment model are gaining ground; Barnett (1977), for one, insists that the paradigm of punishment is in a "crisis period." This, he believes, is as much because of its practical drawbacks as the uncertainty of its moral status. He further suggests that the alleged absolute justice of repaying evil with evil is in reality an empty sophism since Christian moralists have always preached that an evil is to be put right only by doing good. Barnett concludes by admitting his inability to find any theory which justifies the deliberate, forceful imposition of punishment within or without a system of criminal justice.

The Urgent Need for a Viable Alternative

By summarizing very briefly what is terribly wrong with the present system of punishment, I hope to have succeeded in pointing out the urgent need for a viable alternative. We blame offenders, particularly recidivists, for not learning from their mistakes. But we can be accused of the same shortcoming – because if we were clever enough to learn from our mistakes, we would not have let the punishment system continue for as long as it had.

With the twenty-first century fast approaching, it seems unthinkable that we would continue with a system that has not yielded one positive result, has not achieved one single goal of the goals assigned to it. So where should we look for an alternative?

There is substantial historical and anthropological evidence showing that in every society studied, social evolution dictated that the primitive and destructive responses of revenge, vengeance and retaliation be abandoned in favour of the positive and constructive means of conciliation and compensation.

The emergence of the criminal law had as a result that victims lost their legal status and were transformed from full parties to peripheral witnesses. Prior to this unfortunate development, all harmful, injurious actions were civil torts that led not to a retributive or atoning punishment but to some form of redress, the payment of a specific amount called "*weregild*," or composition.

All conflicts, whether serious or minor, were settled by financial, civil and peaceful means, to the satisfaction of all parties involved. This peaceful, civilized way of putting an end to human disputes gave way to barbaric, savage and cruel punishments, once the erroneous idea that crime is an offence against the king or the sovereign, gained acceptance. Victims were excluded from the process and their dues were usurped by the institution of criminal fines.

Luckily, victims have been rediscovered and there are commendable efforts aimed at restoring their rights. These rights have to figure prominently in the new system of justice. To understand the paradigm upon which the new system is based, two questions have to be answered: (a) What do victims get from the present punitive, retributive justice system? (b) What do the victims want: vengeance or redress?

(a) A punitive, retributive system of justice offers nothing to the victim of crime, except maybe for the very few whose vindictive sentiments are satisfied by nothing other than seeing the offender suffer. Whatever satisfaction vengeance may provide, it is usually ephemeral and short-lived. More important still is that the criminal law not be used to promote revenge and retaliation or to offer blood to those who are bloodthirsty. This is the main rationale behind abolishing the death penalty in so many countries. The primary aims of the criminal law should be to restore peace, heal the injury and redress the harm; to achieve conciliation, to settle human conflicts, not perpetuate them; to bring the two founding parties closer together instead of setting them apart. One has to keep in mind that a very high percentage of violent crime is committed between people who are related to each other by some family or other personal relationship. This fact alone shows how essential it is to have a conflict-resolving mechanism that settles the dispute, prevents further violence while maintaining those vital relationships intact. The system of punishment does exactly the opposite. It breaks the ties, disrupts the harmony and generates a great deal of hostility and antagonism. This hostility and antagonism render any future reconciliation either very difficult or virtually impossible.

(b) The second question is: What do victims want from the justice system: vengeance or redress? And the answer is an easy one. Studies by Sessar (1992) and by Pfeiffer (1993) in Germany, by Waller and Okihiro (1978) in Canada, and by many others show unequivocally that victims are not as vindictive or as bloodthirsty as the advocates of the punishment model would want us to believe. Their primary concern is to have redress: to have the stolen goods returned, the broken windows fixed, the vandalized car repaired, the destroyed bike replaced, etc.

Their expectations and their demands are realistic, not moralistic.

They have down-to-earth goals, quite different ones from the divine and metaphysical goals pursued by a theocratic criminal justice system, such as expiation, atonement or retribution. Victims see the offence committed against them as creating a direct obligation for redress, not as creating a debt to society or to divinity that can only be settled by an expiatory punishment.

In its attempt to achieve divine, metaphysical and abstract goals, the criminal justice system ignores the basic needs of the victims, it leaves their wishes unfulfilled and their desires unmet. This is particularly true of the primary need for compensation.

Because the vast majority of victims of property crime cannot afford and have no insurance, because three-quarters of crimes are property crimes and because state compensation programs are strictly limited to violent crime, the majority of victims do not get any compensation for whatever loss they have suffered. In punitive systems there are two losers. The victim loses his property, the offender loses his liberty. And it has been estimated in Canada that the costs of putting a burglar in a federal penitentiary for two years are enough to compensate the average loss of five hundred victims of burglary! This is the extreme irony of a system that puts the suffering of the offender ahead of the satisfaction of the victim.

The Superiority of Restorative Justice Systems to Punitive, Retributive Justice Systems

Positive, Constructive

When restorative justice systems are contrasted to punitive, retributive systems, they prove to be superior in every respect.

Whereas the punishment system is negative and destructive, as already explained, restorative justice by means of mediation, reconciliation, restitution and compensation is positive and constructive. Not only does it avoid the humiliation, degradation and stigmatization of punishment, but it also spares the offender and his family the pain, suffering and indignity of punishment. More important still, mediation and conciliation appeal to what is good and positive in human beings rather than to their base instincts as punishment does. They appeal to the noble sentiments of forgiveness, compassion, fraternity, etc. In a nutshell, restorative justice is more humane than punitive justice and has none of the negative side effects of the latter.

More Economical

The restorative justice model is also far more economical than the punishment model. Mention has already been made of how costly punishment is. Not only this, but punishment and victim compensation are functionally incompatible. The lack of work in prison and the extremely low wages paid to the lucky few inmates who are put to work make it impossible for the offender to pay restitution to the victim. And if the offender is sentenced to a fine rather than to prison, fines take precedence over restitution. And with the inadequate financial means of most offenders, they are usually unable to pay either.

More Effective

If the primary purpose of social intervention is to restore the peace, redress the harm, heal the injury and stop the repetition of the offence, then it is easy to understand how and why the restorative system (based on mediation, reconciliation, restitution and compensation) succeeds where the punishment system fails.

Mediation and reconciliation bring the two parties together, face to face, and ensure that they see each other as human beings in a state of distress. When faced with the victim, it becomes impossible for the victimizer to deny the victim's existence or the injury or harm he has caused her. He can no longer depersonalize, de-individuate, objectify or reify the victim. He can no longer avoid post-victimization cognitive dissonance. The confrontation between the offender and the victim in a mediation situation is the surest and most effective means of sensitizing him to the victim's plight, of countering and reversing the mental process of desensitization that he has gone through in order to avoid guilt feelings or bad conscience (Fattah, 1991a).

The mediation process, when done properly, can be very effective in awakening and activating any positive emotions the offender might have lying beneath his cruel and indifferent façade. Emotions such as pity, sympathy, empathy, compassion, commiseration, can all be brought to the surface and reinforced.

On the side of the victim, the mediation situation can also have salutary effects. The feared, strong, cruel and unemotional victimizer is bared to his weak and often helpless being, a being that evokes more pity than fear, more compassion than anger. Distorted but long-held stereotypes disappear when checked against the real offender. Both parties end up by gaining a realistic view of one another and reconciliation becomes possible.

The Return to the Original Notion of Crime as a Human Conflict

Another advantage of the restorative justice model over the punitive model is that it corrects the popular and widely-held misconception that crime is an offence against society and that the criminal has a debt to pay to society. This is a fallacious notion. How could it be that an act that hurts, injures or harms a human being, an act that might thoroughly affect the person's life and disrupt their existence, be considered not an offence against that individual but against society, the king or the queen? How is it that such a personal offence does not create an obligation to the victim but a debt to society? And how is it that when the wrongdoer is sentenced to a fine, the money goes not to the victim but to the state? At least ninety per cent of the cases that come before the criminal courts end up in a sentence to a fine of varying amounts. It does not seem fair that if the source of injury, harm or loss happens to be an act defined as a criminal offence, the money paid by he who caused it goes to the king's coffers, whereas if the source happens to be a civil matter such as negligence, accident, medical malpractice, etc. then the damages are paid to the person who suffered. Why is it that parties in civil disputes are entitled to all the damages ordered by the courts, while victims of acts arbitrarily defined as crimes get nothing?

Necessary Conditions for Mediation to Become an Effective Penal Alternative

1. The Need for a Paradigm Shift

Unless there is a paradigm change, unless the punishment paradigm is replaced by the new paradigm, mediation will not and can never become an effective and viable penal alternative. Thomas Kuhn, who coined the term "paradigm shift," acknowledged that new paradigms encounter a great deal of resistance and hostility before successfully imposing themselves. New paradigms emerge when the old ones become outdated, outmoded and obsolete, when the old ones become anachronistic and are no longer in harmony or in tune with the times. This is a description that fits well the punishment-retribution paradigm, a paradigm that has survived but is a vestige from a bygone era, a paradigm that we inherited from the Middle Ages when the dominant law was canon law (Fattah, 1992).

2. Secularization of the Criminal Law

Although most of us believe in God and regularly practise our religion, we live in a secular society. There has been a separation between the state and the church. Yet this secularization is hardly noticeable when one looks at the criminal code and the criminal justice system. Notions that still dominate the criminal law, such as moral guilt, moral fault, malice, evil intent, wickedness, punishment, retribution, expiation, atonement, are all philosophical and theological notions (Fattah, 1992, 1993).

The task of the criminal court judge is not an easy one, because he/she is asked to administer justice, not according to earthly criteria such as "harm," "injury or "loss," but according to heavenly or divine criteria by making the punishment fit the crime or seeing that the offender gets his "just deserts." Contrary to the civil court judge, who simply needs to establish liability and assess the amount of damages that corresponds to the injury, harm or loss, the criminal court judge has to figure out how many days, months or years in prison would expiate or constitute just retribution for a sexual or physical assault, attempted murder, robbery and so on (Fattah, 1982).

It goes without saying that the system of mediation and compensation is a secular one and in order to operate the system of justice according to the new paradigm it is necessary to achieve the secularization of the criminal law.

3. Removing the Artificial Boundaries Between Criminal and Civil Law

As mentioned earlier, all harmful, injurious acts used to be civil torts that led to some material compensation. Criminal law emerged when those in power realized that it can be a profitable source of revenue, not only through fines, but also the confiscation of the estate of the accused. Acts that were singled out for inclusion in the criminal code were so chosen because of historical, political and religious reasons, and not because they were qualitatively or inherently different from those that remained under civil law. Any comparison between acts defined as criminal offences and civil torts would reveal that there is a great deal of overlap, that the demarcation line is ambiguous and arbitrarily drawn, and to reaffirm the arbitrariness of the division many European codes allow the victim to bring a civil suit (or instate themselves as a civil party) against the offender.

Mediation and reconciliation require that the artificial boundaries between the criminal and civil law be removed. Mediation, arbitration, compensation are recognized mechanisms of resolving civil disputes. Once they are accepted as true substitutes to punishment, criminal and civil conflicts will be dealt with in a very similar manner. And this can only be to the benefit of the victim – because having suffered from an act defined as a crime should not be a hindrance to compensation. Because ultimately for those who suffer physical injury, material harm or financial loss, it does not make a difference whether the act comes under the provisions of the criminal or the civil code.

4. Using Mediation as a Genuine Substitute to Punishment

Keen as they are to see an end to the system of punishment, criminologists and penologists have tried for several decades to come up with suitable and less costly alternatives. Over the years, many of these alternatives were implemented but failed to replace punishment or reduce its widespread use. The lack of success of the alternative measures is primarily due to the fact that they were not used as genuine substitutes to punishment but simply as supplements, complements or additions to it. What they did was not to reduce the prison population but to widen the net of social control. For mediation to succeed where those alternatives have failed requires that it be fully accepted and applied as a genuine substitute to punishment and that its use not be restricted but generalized. This means using mediation as a means of settling the conflict not only for petty offences or misdemeanours but for serious crimes as well, not only for property offences but also for offences against the person. This is exactly the view taken by the experimental project at the Catholic University in Leuven, Belgium. The initial results of the projects, undertaken in collaboration with the office of public prosecutor, are quite encouraging (personal communication from Professor Tony Peters, the project's director) and suggest that mediation is a viable alternative to punishment in cases of serious offences. Zehr and Umbreit (1982) provide evidence that mediation has wide applicability to the criminal process. They state that:

> "Negotiations and confrontation between victim and offender offer real possibilities for meeting victim needs, facilitating restitution, encouraging offender accountability and easing workloads for probation departments and courts," (1982:66).

5. Impartiality and Neutrality

Another requirement for the success of mediation is total neutrality and impartiality; mediation cannot, and will not, work if sides are taken or if a positive attitude is displayed toward the victim and a negative attitude is shown to the offender. Expressions of outrage, indignation and moral condemnation at the offender and his action are likely to create insurmountable obstacles in the way of an effective mediation process. They are impediments to the full understanding of the motives, the personality and the mode of thinking of the victimizer. To gain such understanding, those conducting the mediation process need to take a neutral and impartial stand, to be able to put themselves in the offender's shoes, and to be capable of analyzing his mental processes. This does not mean that they have to approve his actions or condone his behaviour or attitude, but that they have to abstain from assuming a moralizing posture or taking an exhortative stand.

One important step that could help achieve and maintain the ideals of neutrality and impartiality is a change in the present terminology; value-laden and pejorative terms, such as offender and victim, could be replaced by more neutral and value-free ones, such as those used in the civil courts: litigants, plaintiffs, complainant, defendant, etc. These terms do not imply value judgements, do not evoke positive or negative sentiments and are more conducive to the success of the mediation process than the emotionally-loaded designations of criminal and victim.

Conclusion

Last century, the French sociologist Émile Durkheim and the German jurist Jhering affirmed that the history of punishment is a history of constant abolition. Despite this, punishment is still widely practised. But in view of its manifest failure to achieve any of its supposed goals, the prospect that the twenty-first century will witness its replacement no longer seems unthinkable. The same social considerations which dictated that vengeance in primitive, pre-modern societies be replaced by the positive practices of conciliation, restitution and compensation suggest that the end of punishment might be closer than many people think. Already the new measures of electronic monitoring and other means of electronic control have shown how archaic imprisonment is. And the mounting concern being shown to crime victims suggests that the punishment system, as detrimental as it is to the interests of the victim, will have to give way to another system in which victim needs are met and victim wishes are respected. This is why mediation appears to be a viable alternative that is superior in every respect to vengeful, retributive punishments. The success of mediation, however, depends on certain conditions being met. These include a paradigm shift, the secularization of the criminal law, the removal of the artificial boundaries between the criminal law and the civil law. Mediation has also to be used, not as an "add up" punishment, but as a genuine substitute.

Last, but not least, those in charge of the mediation process need to maintain complete neutrality, impartiality and objectivity to ensure that mediation leads to a successful settlement of the dispute.

Replacing the retributive model by a restorative model will signal the dawning of a new era in human justice because, as the Friends World Committee for Consultation states in its brief to the United Nations, "...restorative justice respects the basic human needs of the victim, the offender and the community. The administration of justice, according to the restorative model, includes the active participation of people directly involved and affected by the criminal activity. Settlements provide redress to the victim and make it possible for the offender to fulfil agreed obligations."

References

Barnet, R.E. (1977). "Restitution, a New Paradigm of Criminal Justice." In *Ethics: An International Journal of Social, Political and Legal Philosophy*, vol. 87, no. 1, pp. 279-301.

Christie, N. (1977). "Conflicts as Property." *British Journal of Criminology*, vol. 17, no. 1, pp. 1-19.

Fattah, E.A. (1978). "Moving to the Right: A Return to Punishment?" In *Crime and Justice*, vol. 6, no. 2, pp. 79-92.

Fattah, E.A. (1982). "Making the Punishment Fit the Crime: The Case of Imprisonment – The Problems Inherent in the Use of Imprisonment as a Retributive Sanction." In *Canadian Journal of Criminology*, vol. 24, no. 1, pp. 1-12.

Fattah, E.A. (1991). "From Crime Policy to Victim Policy: The Need for a Fundamental Policy Change." *Annales Internationales de Criminologie*, vol. 26, nos. 1 & 2, pp. 43-58.

Fattah, E.A. (1991a). *Understanding Criminal Victimization*. Scarborough, ON: Prentice Hall Ltd.

Fattah, E.A. (1992). "Beyond Metaphysics: The Need for a New Paradigm – On Actual and Potential Contributions of Criminology and the Social Sciences to the Reform of the Criminal Law." In R. Lahti and K. Nuotio (eds.) *Criminal Law Theory in Transition*. Helsinki: Finnish Lawyers' Publishing Company, pp. 64-101.

Fattah, E.A. (1993). "From a Guilt Orientation to a Consequence Orientation: A Proposed New Paradigm for the Criminal Law in the 21st Century." In W. Küper and J. Welp (eds.) *Beiträge zur Rechtswissenschaft*. Heidelberg: C.F. Müller Jursitischer Verlag, pp. 771-792.

Marshall, T.F. (1984). *Reparation, Conciliation and Mediation*. London: Home Office Research and Planning Unit. Paper no. 27.

Pfeiffer, C. (1993). *Opferperspektiven: Wiedergutmachung und Strafe aus der Sicht der Bevölkerung*. Manuscript, 22 pages.

Sessar, K. (1992). *Wiedergutmachungen oder Strafen: Einstellungen in der Bevölkerung und der Justitz*. Pfaffenweiler.

Waller, I. and Okihiro, N. (1978). *Burglary: The Victim and the Public*. Toronto: University of Toronto Press.

Zehr, H. and Umbreit, M. (1982). "Victim-Offender Reconciliation: An Incarceration Substitute?" In *Federal Probation*, pp. 63-68.

Chapter V

From Crime Policy *to* Victim Policy

The Need for a Fundamental Policy Change

Originally published in 1991 in *Annales Internationales de Criminologie* (Paris), vol. 29, nos. 1 et 2, pp. 43-60.

RECENT YEARS HAVE witnessed great strides in applied victimology. During the 1980s legislation was passed, services were created, programs were set up, all aimed at helping crime victims and improving their unhappy lot. One of the most important developments was the formal approval of the UN Declaration of Basic Principles of Justice for Victims of Crime and Abuse of Power by the General Assembly on November 11, 1985 (1). In adopting it, the General Assembly of the United Nations stated that it was "Cognizant that millions of people throughout the world suffer harm as a result of crime and the abuse of power and that the rights of these victims have not been adequately recognized," (see Joutsen, 1987, p. 68). All this signals the dawning of the promised golden age of the victim.

What is remarkable about the developments of the last decade is the ease and smoothness with which the legislative changes were introduced and passed. Not only was there no opposition to the proposed initiatives but they were also not preceded by the usual impact studies to assess the effects they were likely to have on the criminal justice system and on the larger society. Even more surprising was the fact that the changes were introduced in the absence of clear empirical evidence indicating that they do represent what crime victims really want. It is therefore time to critically assess these victim initiatives and to see how successful they have been in alleviating the plight of the victims of crime.

This paper will attempt to show that, despite the fanfare with which the new measures were introduced, they have not tangibly improved the lot of crime victims. The paper will show that what is necessary to achieve this goal is a new criminal justice policy, a new penal and sentencing philosophy that places the emphasis not on punishment and retaliation but on reparation, mediation and conciliation. In most instances these two sets of goals (retributive/distributive) are functionally incompatible. Parallel to this change, there needs to be another fundamental change in the traditional views on crime. The offence should cease to be regarded as an affront to the state and be viewed as an offence against the individual victim, not as a violation of an abstract law but a violation of the rights of the victim.

The argument I am advancing is that if we genuinely care about crime victims and truly want to substantially improve their lot then we will need much more than hollow slogans (justice for victims), symbolic gestures (victim-impact statements), punitive measures (fine victim surcharge) and political palliatives and placebos (victim compensation schemes).

The Legal Status of Crime Victims

Protection of, and assistance to, victims will have to become part of the core values of society. Social commitment to victims will have to be deeply rooted in the general belief system. It is important, therefore, to establish the legal sources of the rights of victims. If action and policies are to be guided by more than just humanitarian concern for the victims and their plight, it is necessary to identify the legal as well as the social bases for both society's obligation and the offender's responsibility to the victim.

In the 1950s and the 1960s, when Margery Fry and others called for state compensation to victims of crime, there were serious attempts to determine the legal and philosophical foundations on which such compensation is to be based. Among the theories advanced at the time were the legal tort theory, the social contract theory, the utilitarian theory, and the social solidarity theory, to mention but a few. Current concern for and discussions of victims other rights have not been accompanied by any similar attempt. Probably the reason is that the emergence and enactment of the Victims Bills of Rights was the outcome of political and grassroots initiatives rather than legal or juridical initiatives.

Since in law rights originate from and are closely linked to the person's status, to establish the rights to which victims of crime are entitled it is necessary to define their legal status. This is all the more important since in many jurisdictions, at present, victims seem to have no legal status. Prior to the 1988 amendments made to the Criminal Code of Canada (see note 2), this was made abundantly clear by court rulings in Ontario and British Columbia. In November 1987, in a criminal case of dangerous driving resulting in the death of a sixteen-year-old youth, a Supreme Court judge in the province of British Columbia denied the prosecutor's request to submit a statement by the family of the victim. He quoted from a judgement of the High Court of Ontario in which the sentencing judge declared that "the principles of sentencing establish guidelines for judges and do not include consideration of the effects of the tragic death upon the survivors," (*The Vancouver Sun*, November 1987). This judicial statement suggests that the victim of crime (or his survivors in the case of death) does not enjoy any legal status and cannot, therefore, become legal party to the proceedings. It highlights the need to fundamentally change the way society looks upon crime and punishment if the victim is to become a full party in judicial proceedings and if she/he is to recover their lost status in the criminal process. In other words, what is urgently needed is a new paradigm of criminal justice. In this new paradigm, which in reality is a very old one, crime will no longer be viewed as a wrongful, sinful act that needs to be punished. It will be regarded as a harmful behaviour that needs to be redressed in the present and prevented in the future.

Victims were better off when there was no differentiation between civil law and criminal law, when all harmful actions were civil torts. Victims were the principal protagonists when prosecutions were private, handled not by the Crown but by the person who suffered or his representative. The reduction of the victim to an inconsequential figure coincided with the emergence of the public prosecutor (Galaway and Hudson, 1981). But the real decline started with the emergence of a criminal law, which viewed the criminal act not as an offence against the victim but as an offence against the sovereign and later the state. Gradually the victim, who used to be the central figure, in whose name and on whose behalf the proceedings were conducted, was reduced to the status of a witness used to buttress the Crown's case and abused if he refused to cooperate or to testify. Once the state monopolized the right to criminal prosecution and converted the "*weregild*," or the composition paid to the victim, into a fine destined for the king's coffers, the victim became the forgotten man, a legal non-entity.

The historical decline of the victim is traced by the Law Reform Commission of Canada (1974) to the emergence of the criminal law. The commission describes the process as follows:

> "In Anglo-Saxon England there was no criminal law as we know it. Disputes were dealt with by a process greatly resembling our civil law. When an individual felt that he had suffered damage because of another's wrongful conduct, he was permitted either to settle the matter by agreement or to proceed before a tribunal. Restitution was the order of the day and other sanctions, including imprisonment, were rarely used.
>
> "As the common law developed, criminal law became a distinct branch of law. Numerous antisocial acts were seen to be "offences against the state" or "crimes" rather than personal

> wrongs or torts. This tendency to characterize some wrongs as "crimes" was encouraged by the practice under which the lands and property of convicted persons were forfeited to the king or feudal lord; fines as well became payable to feudal lords and not to the victim. The natural practice of compensating the victim or his relatives was discouraged by making it an offence to conceal the commission of a felony or convert the crime into a source of profit. In time, fines and property that would have gone in satisfaction of the victim's claims were diverted to the state. Compounding an offence (that is, accepting an economic benefit in satisfaction of the wrong done without the consent of the court or in a manner that is contrary to the public interest) still remains a crime under the Canadian Criminal Code and discourages private settlement or restitution.
>
> "It would now seem that historical developments, however well intentioned, effectively removed the victim from sentencing policy and obscured the view that crime was social conflict," (1974:4-5).

This historical development leaves no doubt that it was political ruse by which the legitimate rights of the victims were usurped by the rulers to the latters' benefit. It is this usurpation that Christie (1977) refers to when he states that conflicts have been stolen from the parties directly involved and thereby have either disappeared or become other people's property. It is also a historical fact that with the passage of time the criminal law became a powerful tool of subjugation used by governments and by rulers to consolidate their grip over the population, and it is not a coincidence that many criminal codes begin with the section dealing with offences against the state.

At present, the administration of criminal justice emphasizes the roles played by professional, specialized third parties: judges, prosecutors, defence lawyers, experts and so on. While these third parties have assumed an increasingly important place in the criminal justice system, the victim's role has become largely peripheral and the victim has been treated by the system as largely irrelevant (see Galaway and Hudson, 1981:229). Christie (1978) believes that the root problem of the administration of justice is that conflicts have become the property of professionals rather than people. He adds that by taking over the ownership of disputes between people, professionals have taken the community's opportunity to learn from individual disputes and develop structures for improving the situation.

The Old and New Paradigms of Criminal Justice

Victims' current plight stems from the fact that crime is no longer regarded as a conflict between two individuals, two human beings, but as a conflict between the offender and society. Viewed as such, crime generates not an obligation to the victim but a debt to society, and once the criminal is punished the debt is paid. In this scenario, there is no place for the victim, no part for him to play. The recent report of the Canadian Sentencing Commission leads to the painful realization that despite all the current talk about victims of crime, their rights and their plight, this basic outlook has not changed. Instead of stating that the primary goal of sentencing is to repair the harm done to the victim by the offence and to prevent future harm, the Sentencing Commission (1987) regrettably declared that:

> "...the fundamental purpose of sentencing is to preserve the authority of, and promote respect for, the law through the imposition of just sanctions," (1987:151).

Such abstract goals are responsible for the depersonalization and dehumanization of the justice system, for the reification of both the offender and the victim. In an era meant to become the golden age of the victim, there seems to be a growing obsession with punishment, euphemistically called "just deserts." And yet having punishment as the central focus of the criminal justice system is neither morally legitimate nor practically effective. It can only act to the detriment of the victim. Dispute settlement, mediation, reconciliation, arbitration, reparation, are concepts foreign to a system centred on punishment, a system which regards the crime not as a human action but as a legal infraction. Such a system acts to intensify the conflict rather than settling it. And instead of bringing the feuding parties closer to one another, it widens the gap that separates them. The obsession with punishment leads to an unwarranted differentiation between criminal victimization and other types of victimization and results in grave injustices to those who offend and those who suffer.

In the new paradigm of criminal justice, the primary purpose of the criminal law would be to heal the injury, repair the harm, compensate the loss and prevent further victimization. This requires among other things a rethinking and a reexamination of the artificial boundaries which have been erected over the years between civil and criminal law, between civil and criminal courts, as well as the artificial distinction between crimes and torts. This artificial distinction, which seemingly is taken for granted, is detrimental to the victims and their interests. The greatest majority of criminal offences brought to trial end in a sentence to a fine. Civil cases end in the payment of damages. Thus the only actual difference in outcome between a civil and a criminal case is that in the former the damages are paid to the person who suffered the loss, whereas in the latter it is the state that benefits at the expense of the victim. And this is what has to change.

The band-aid remedies that were adopted by many countries in the past ten years ignore the roots of the present plight of crime victims. The philosophical, deontological and theological ideas and the political interests that led to the emergence of the notions of crime and punishment are responsible for the decline of the victim. The constructive practices of reparation, compensation and reconciliation gave way to punishments supposedly aimed at achieving expiation and atonement. Improving the victim's lot requires that the notion of crime be taken back to its sociological origins. Sociologically, crime is not a sin, it is not an immoral behaviour, it is a harmful, injurious act. Since crime is an inevitable feature of social life, it is only logical that it be considered in a secular, technological society as a social risk, a hazard of modern life, not very different from other risks to which people are daily exposed. The way society responds to other social risks to minimize their occurrence and their effects should guide the action against crime. Crime is as much a fact of life as are natural disasters, traffic accidents, disease and death. But while other social risks are covered, in the welfare state, by some form of insurance or another, the risk of becoming a victim of crime is not adequately covered. Victim compensation schemes have done little to remedy or to improve this situation. Insufficient funding, inadequate information and stringent eligibility requirements have meant that the overwhelming majority of victims are excluded from the realm of compensation (see note 3). Because the funds allocated to these programs are severely limited, more publicity and more applications can only result in lower awards and a higher rate of rejection. As to restitution by the offender, it remains, for obvious reasons, a seldom used and largely ineffective means of redress. The only potential restitution has is to be used instead of, and not in addition to, incarceration. In the present punitive climate, this is not a very attractive proposition.

The reluctance of governments to go beyond symbolic gestures, political palliatives and placebos to improve the plight of crime victims is quite evident in victim legislation introduced in several countries.

In 1987, for example, the Canadian government, following the steps of some American states, introduced in the federal Parliament a bill (see note no. 2) aimed, among other things, at imposing a victim fine surcharge not exceeding fifteen per cent of any fine that is imposed on the offender, or where no fine is imposed for the offence, ten thousand dollars. Instead of returning the fines to their original and legitimate owners by placing them in a fund earmarked for victim compensation or using them to finance a comprehensive insurance scheme for crime victims, the new legislation is a clear attempt to finance the present compensation programs by imposing an additional penalty on the offender. The fine surcharge concept is neither practical nor fair. Most offenders, particularly those charged with violent crimes, are unable to pay whatever fines they are sentenced to and have to spend additional time in prison for default. What the fine surcharge really does is to make an already bad situation much worse. The idea is also unfair because it penalizes all offenders and not only those who should be responsible for compensation. Most victimless crimes are punished by a fine. People convicted of these offences will be paying extra to make up for the stinginess of the government. Drug offenders and non-violent offenders would be charged what should have been paid by those who commit crimes of violence.

Victims Needs and Victims Services

The question of how crime victims are currently treated and how they should be treated by criminal justice personnel is an administrative issue. It has to do with the attitudes, the policies, the practices of the system and the interactions between those working in it and their clientele. Needless to say, all users of the system have to be treated with courtesy, sensitivity, understanding, compassion as well as respect for their dignity. This should be the case regardless of their role or characteristics, whether complainants or suspects, victims or offenders, young or old, male or female, rich or poor, white or black. Improving the general attitudes of those in the system to its users is both essential and beneficial. The training of criminal justice personnel should be designed to sensitize them to the needs and plight of their clients. Special training is necessary for those who will be called upon to deal with special categories or specific types of clients. Special training should also be required for those whose activities dictate that they intervene in certain conflict situations such as family violence.

What are the needs of crime victims and how could these needs be met? (see note 4). These are research issues. Some of the needs may be obvious, others are less evident. There are general needs and there are needs that are specific to certain categories or types of victims. Once the needs are properly identified, the question is: What existing services should cater to those needs? What services have to be created or strengthened to adequately satisfy them? This requires full assessments of existing services. Then political decisions will have to be made. Implementation of the UN declaration's provisions in this area is problematic because of the financial costs involved. As commitments by politicians do not usually match their rhetoric, it would be rather naive to expect, especially in times of economic restraint, that there will be massive infusion of funds into victim services. This, however, is the area where society can show the extent of its real commitment to victims.

Before embarking on the creation of large-scale victim services, it is also necessary to assess some of the dangers involved (see note 5). Social services in the welfare state, whether run by professionals or volunteers, have a tendency to develop dependency among their clients and even to extract those clients from their social networks. In the long run, these networks, composed of relatives, neighbours, friends, peers and so on, are weakened as their members are freed from their social obligations. The professionalization of victim services presents yet another danger. The personalized care of the victim's social network is replaced by the depersonalized care of the state. The victim, who within his family, neighbourhood or small community is treated as a person and who in such a setting feels and acts as an individual, is converted into a "client" or a "recipient of services" (see note 6). He/she has to suffer the dehumanization of being transformed from a person to a number. The psychological support and regeneration the victim feels when cared for by family or friends is replaced by the confusion and humiliation of having been placed within the hands of strangers who have to deal daily with dozens of other victims.

In addition to the dangers outlined above, there are the general dangers of intervention. In providing the care, help and support victims need, caution has to be exercised to avoid causing greater harm to the victim. Intensive and/or excessive intervention can delay the natural healing process. It can prolong the agony and the trauma resulting from the offence, create undue anxieties about the crime situation and the risks of victimization and nurture attitudes of mistrust or distrust among actual and potential victims. There are reasons to suspect that there might be a link between the new interventionist strategies and techniques with victims and the growing pains of victimization. This raises the question of whether the heightened fear of victimization, reported in recent years, is in any way related to the increasing attention and publicity being given to crime victims. Do policies of intervention prolong rather than shorten the traumatic effects of victimization? These are all questions worthy of serious exploration. The zeal to help and assist crime victims should not blind us to the potential dangers of our action (see Fattah, 1986).

The consistent talk about victim services in recent years has already created or heightened expectations among crime victims. Such expectations, if not met, can only lead to various levels of dissatisfaction and frustration with the criminal justice system and the greater society. The history of victim services, as brief as it may be, is one of unfulfilled promises and unmet expectations. There is ample empirical evidence of the inadequacy of the services and the frustrations that ensue. In England, Shapland (1986) detected a mismatch between victim expectations of the system and the system's assumptions about victim needs. Consequently she warns that public statements about the worth of victims, which are later shown to be hollow, may rebound on any who set up such ineffective schemes. This is confirmed by her finding that by the end of police and court processes there was a significant decline in a victim's satisfaction with the police handling of the case and also a decline in attribution of positive qualities to the police generally. In the U.S., Elias (1983) found considerable disenchantment and even some evidence of greater discontent among applicants to victim compensation: delays, inconveniences, poor information, inability to participate, restrictive eligibility requirements, denial of awards in many cases, unrealistic ceilings and so on.

The Role of the Victim in the Criminal Justice Process

The United Nations declaration calls for "allowing the views and concerns of victims to be presented and considered at appropriate stages of the proceedings where their personal interests are affected..." This provision raises fundamental questions about the victims' legal standing and their role in the criminal justice process, whether they should have a say in bail hearings, plea-bargaining, sentencing, parole hearings or parole decision-making and so on, and what form such input should take (see note 7).

A brief review of the initiatives taken in recent years to ensure victims' participation in the justice process suggests that the changes have been hastily introduced without a full assessment of their potential effects, nor concern for whether or not they are compatible with existing policies and philosophies. The review also provides unmistakable clues to the real intentions behind victim legislation.

Thus a dispassionate analysis of the so-called Victims Bills of Rights inevitably leads to the conclusion that such a legislation is not meant to improve the lot of crime victims but to toughen an already harsh system of punishment. For example, California's attorney general George Deukmejian (who later became the state's governor) comments on California's Proposition 8, "the Victims Bill of Rights," leave no doubt as to the real objectives underlying the legislation. Writing in a voters' brochure, Deukmejian said:

> "There is absolutely no question that the passage of this proposition will result in more criminal convictions, more criminals being sentenced to state prison and more protection of the law-abiding citizenry," (quoted after Paltrow, 1982, p. 1).

The statement is very revealing of what seems to be the hidden agenda of those who are willing to exploit the noble cause of crime victims to bring about more punishment.

California's Proposition 8, the Victims Bill of Rights, is certainly one of the strongest attempts to formalize the victim's role in the judicial process. The bill gives the victims the right of allocution, that is the right to appear and be heard at felony sentencing hearings. A 1986 study by the McGeorge School of Law of the implementation of this right by state and local agencies revealed that less than three per cent of the eligible victims appeared at sentencing hearings. Another interesting finding is that the majority of judges and chief probation officers viewed allocution at sentencing as unnecessary, while the majority of district attorneys viewed it favourably and were more confident than judges that it affected sentencing.

Obviously, the overwhelming majority of crime victims are unwilling, for one reason or another, to exercise whatever rights they may be given. Thus one might question the practical value and returns of granting victims such rights, despite strong objections from many quarters (see note 8).

Victim-Impact Statements

Do victim-impact statements and victim allocution have on impact on sentencing? If they do not influence the sentence, then they are bound, at least in the long run, to alienate the victims who in good faith exercise this right believing that it will have an impact on the court's decision. In case they do have an impact, one might question their effects on the principles of fairness and equality. The tiny minority of offenders in whose cases the right is exercised will receive harsher sanctions than others who had committed identical offences. In other words, if victim-impact statements have no impact on sentencing, they can only heighten the victim's sense of irrelevance; if they do, they can only aggravate the problem of sentencing disparity.

Despite all these problems with victim-impact statements, at no time was there any serious challenge to the proposed Canadian legislation (Bill C-89) and only few voices were heard opposing the suggested procedural change.

In his testimony before the Legislative Committee of the Canadian House of Commons on Bill C-89 (*An Act to Amend the Criminal Code – Victims of*

Crime), a distinguished Ontario lawyer, Mr. Paul Calarco (February 9, 1988), criticized the bill for being seriously flawed and for its failure to recognize the right of an accused person to a fair trial and the right of that accused person to test the Crown's case. He also predicted that once passed the bill will lead to longer trials, more appeals, greater legal costs, both to an accused person and to the public in terms of Crown attorneys and legal aid costs, as well as a greater court backlog. He added that the bill may indeed lead to illegal sentences, depending of course on the constitutional challenges, and an improper deprivation of the liberty of the subject (*House of Commons*, issue no. 7, p. 5).

Addressing the specific issue of victim-impact statements, Mr. Calarco said:

> "Finally, the victim-impact statement is, in my respectful submission, completely inappropriate. The principles of sentencing do not look and should not look at how an individual offence has affected an individual complainant. If an individual complainant has perhaps been emotionally shattered by an experience, instead of perhaps a six-month sentence, are we to say that the devastating effect on that victim would bring the sentence up to twelve or eighteen months or more? Conversely, are we to say that if this complainant has forgiven the offender totally or not had any adverse effect from the offence, that offender should then receive a suspended sentence rather than the six months society says should be imposed?" (1988-7:9).

Calarco's statements before the House of Commons Legislative Committee echoed those made by other lawyers. Earl Levy, president of the Criminal Lawyers Association of Ontario, was quoted in *The Globe and Mail* (April 11, 1984) as saying "[Victim-impact statement] injects an air of emotionalism in the sentencing procedure... I feel there are enough problems now with the disparity of sentencing." Levy added that victim-impact statements will only compound that problem, because with human nature being what it is, judges are bound to be affected by this air of emotionalism. Another lawyer, Richard Peck, who at the time was chairing the criminal justice section of the Canadian Bar Association, declared to *The Vancouver Sun* (September 21, 1983, p. A3) that judges are expected to act dispassionately and that the justice system relies on impartial judges handing down sentences based on a well-tried set of criteria. He insisted that "there is no place for vengeance in a dispassionate, logical sentencing process" and that victims "should never directly influence the length of sentence."

The same article (Still, 1983) quoted another Vancouver lawyer, Michael Bolton, who deplored the fact that the government appeared to be responding to pressure groups (the victim lobby), and expressed the opinion that organized groups, though serving a useful function in helping to alleviate the anguish felt by many crime victims, should not be involved in procedural reforms.

Political considerations overrode legal objections, and the bill was passed with an astounding majority and very little change. Victim-impact statements became, despite the reservations articulated by legal practitioners, part of the criminal code of Canada. It is still too early to assess the impact of this procedural change and to establish whether any of the predictions made by those who argued against the statements did in fact materialize. A recent development in the United States is worth noting, namely the fact that some courts have ruled that victim-impact statements are unconstitutional in capital cases (Sharman, 1988). There is also some evidence suggesting that at least some of the provisions contained in victim legislation under the guise of helping the victim may backfire. For example, one of the California Bill of Rights (Proposition 8) provisions is "Truth in Evidence." Originally this provision was intended as a way of eliminating the exclusionary rule, a rule that renders illegally obtained evidence inadmissible in court. This particular section of the California bill stipulates that "relevant evidence shall not be excluded in any criminal proceedings." It turned out that such a provision is in fact a double- edged sword. Paltrow (1982) reports that under this new provision it became possible for lawyers in rape cases to have victims examined by psychiatrists or to question the victim about sexual activity she had engaged in shortly prior to the alleged rape.

There are several additional problems with victim-impact statements and the right of allocution. It has been pointed out (Neto, 1986, p.7) that victims' interests are usually well enough represented by prosecutors and that victim intervention would add little that is useful to most cases and would impose upon an already overburdened system irrelevant information and requests.

It is also suggested that allowing the victim to play a direct role in the sentencing process injects an emotional element in what is meant to be a dispassionate and logical process (see above). Mention is also made that lengthy trials would become even longer because the accused will have to be given the right to challenge the victim's statement and to require the Crown to prove it (see note 9).

And with the overcrowding of prisons a wide use of this right may worsen an already intolerable situation, since judges may mete out longer sentences or become reluctant to use alternatives to incarceration.

More important still is that if we allow the victim to play a direct role in sentencing and to ask for more punishment, then logically we will have to give the victim also the right to demand an acquittal or no punishment! Are we willing to substitute the victim's wish for what we currently believe is society's right? Or are we willing to follow the victim's desire only if the call is for more punishment? And what about the right to appeal? Should the victim be given the right to appeal if he/she is not satisfied with the sentence?

After reviewing the arguments for and against victim-impact statements, and after noting that many victims do not wish to be involved by giving evidence on the impact of offences on their lives, the Victorian Sentencing Committee (Australia) concluded that the case against the introduction of victim-impact statements is more compelling than the case for them. Consequently the committee (1988) recommended that victim-impact statements not be adopted in Victoria (p. 545).

According to popular estimates (Ranish and Shichor, 1985), about 90 % of the criminal cases in the U.S. are disposed of through plea bargaining. This means that victim's involvement in the plea bargaining phase is even more important than at the sentencing stage. The growing trend to resort to determinate sentences means that whatever input the victim might be allowed will have to be made at the stage of plea bargaining. The Canadian Sentencing Commission (1987) examined the issue and rejected the idea of victims becoming independent parties in plea negotiations. The commission believed that this would be inconsistent with the ultimate responsibility of the attorney general in each province for the prosecution of criminal code offences. The commission added that such concept could potentially precipitate an adversarial relationship between Crown council and victims and that such provision may render victims vulnerable to pressure from either the crown prosecutor or defence council respecting a plea bargain.

Ranish and Shichor (1985) conclude that the evidence is clear regarding the two procedures they examined: victims' appearance at sentencing hearing and before parole board panels have not had any dramatic impact on the way in which sentencing and parole decisions are rendered.

After examining victim recommendations and offender sentences in sexual assault cases in a metropolitan Ohio County during the years 1980 through 1983, Walsh (1986) concluded that requiring a victim-impact statement and recommendation as part of the presentence report is a mere genuflection to ritualistic legalism. Walsh further detected a marked disregard for the preferences of victims of incestuous sexual assault.

These are by no means the only criticisms made of the new victim initiatives. Another authority, Elias (1990), is critical of victim policy for its explicit or implicit assumption that defendants have too many rights and for emphasizing a contest between victim and offender rights as if the former have to be at the expense of the latter. Elias finds many of the resulting changes disturbing: mandatory and increased imprisonment, longer sentences and eliminating parole. These "reforms," he suggests, seem to be a new dose of historically unsuccessful, get-tough policies that probably don't satisfy victim needs, including not being victimized in the first place. Elias passes a harsh judgement on the new victim initiatives. He writes:

> "Yet for all the new initiatives, victims have gotten far less than promised. Rights have often been unenforced or unenforceable, participation sporadic or ill-advised, services precarious and underfunded, victim needs unsatisfied if not further jeopardized and victimization increased, if not in court, then certainly in the streets," (1990:242).

Conclusion

Many initiatives in the area of victims rights seem to have been introduced without any serious assessment of their likely impact on the criminal justice system and the larger society. *Post facto* evaluations, on the other hand, are available. The picture they paint of the impact such new initiatives have had is far from rosy and is clearly negative. This is neither a criticism nor an indictment of the principles underlying these new measures or some of the humanitarian intentions behind them. It is simply another reminder that within the current structure of our criminal justice system, band-aid measures are not likely to work or to have their desired effects. Some contribute to the further alienation of the victim while others heighten the victim's sense of irrelevance,

The reasons why many of these new initiatives do not work are not too difficult to comprehend. Some were conceived and set up for political and administrative purposes that had nothing to do with helping victims. This is particularly true of victim compensation schemes which have been called, and rightly so, political placebos (Chappell, 1973) or political palliatives (Burns, 1980). Many of these programs, though propagated as a means of alleviating the suffering of the victim, were actually designed to increase victim reporting to the police and to improve victim cooperation with the criminal justice system. The primary benefits were seen as enhancing victim participation and collaboration, thus increasing the efficiency and effectiveness of the system.

The same can be said of victim assistance programs. The major guiding influence is not compassionate or humanitarian considerations for victims, but the administrative goals of the agency. The Calgary Victim Services Program, one of the first of its kind in Canada (started in 1977), is just one example of many. The program is described in a document published by the Solicitor General Department in Ottawa. The document makes no secret of the fact that the objective of the program "is to develop a good working relationship with victims of crime in order to encourage their future cooperation with the police in crime prevention." This statement tells a great deal about victim service programs, which were set up by various police departments in Canada as in other countries. It explains the distinct preference to have these programs housed in police departments or in public prosecutors' offices rather than in the community. The hidden danger of many of these programs is that they allow the police to have more control over the victim and for long periods of time.

Last but not least, some of the new rules on victim participation in criminal justice and parole processes do not meet the evidentiary standards required by the fundamental principle of due process. They risk to heighten an already recognized disparity in sentencing and to inject an element of emotionality in what should otherwise be an impartial and unemotional process. Furthermore, as Ranish and Shichor (1985) point out, some of these initiatives are clearly designed to intimidate judges and parole board members and to influence these professionals in one specific policy direction – towards harsher punishment or denial of parole. The drastic results of such a policy to an already punitive justice system and an overcrowded prison system are not too difficult to figure out.

If victims of crime are to regain their lost status, if they are to have a real say in the justice system and to play a direct (not symbolic) role, then we will have to move from retribution to restitution, from a punitive justice to a distributive justice. In other words, what is needed is a new criminal justice paradigm, a fundamental change in criminal policy.

Footnotes

1. The history of the United Nations declaration and the dynamics involved are outlined by Joutsen (1987), pp. 55-69.

2. To remedy the situation, Bill C-89, "An Act to Amend the Criminal Code" (assented to on 21st July, 1988), added to Section 662 of the Canadian Criminal Code the following subsection, among others: "For the purpose of determining the sentence to be imposed on an offender or whether the offender should be discharged pursuant to section 662.1 in respect of any offence, the court may consider a statement, prepared in accordance with subsection (1.2), of a victim of the offence describing the harm done to, or loss suffered by, the victim arising from the commission of the offence." Another subsection defines the victim as "the person to whom harm is done or who suffers physical or emotional

loss as a result of the commission of the offence" and adds that where the victim is dead, ill or otherwise incapable of making the statement, the definition would include "the spouse or any relative of that person, anyone who has in law or in fact the custody of that person or is responsible for the care or support of that person or any dependent of that person."

3. For a detailed analysis of victim compensation programs in Canada, see Fattah (1988).

4. The greatest and primary need of crime victims seems to be the need for information. The Canadian Federal-Provincial Task Force on Justice for Victims of Crime (1983) concluded that "the most frequently expressed need by the great majority of victims interviewed is the need for information. To meet this need, it is not new services which are required, but a firm commitment on the part of the various criminal justice officials to let the victims know what is happening to 'their' case (p. 150)... the key words are concern, consideration and communication," (p. 152). The South Australian Committee of Inquiry on Victims of Crimes concluded that the primary needs of crime victims were for social support and information.

5. For a discussion of some of the visible and hidden dangers of victim movements, see Fattah (1986).

6. In her critical analysis of the bureaucratization and professionalization of the shelter movement, Morgan (1981) shows how the victim, in this instance the battered wife, is transformed into a program client. Morgan identifies other dangers as well. She explains, for example, how social control devices are masked under the cloak of modern professionalized services, how the requirements for evaluation and reporting can seriously compromise client confidentiality and how some clients get trapped as a result for welfare fraud, drug problems or parole violations. Morgan insists that the growth of the interventionist state has meant the growth of bureaucratic and professionalized forms penetrating into everyday life. She also quotes an early shelter organizer, Betsy Warrior, who warned against the "exploitation by well-off professionals and bureaucrats who fund themselves with the money obtained, rather than letting it benefit the people whom it was secured for."

7. Rossini (1987) points out that giving victims legal standing could allow them to initiate criminal proceedings, contest a prosecutor's decision by means of an appeal to the court, examine evidence in the course of a court trial and to make submissions regarding sentencing and parole. Referring to the disparity which characterizes the existing system of sentencing and parole, Grabosky (1985) suggests that to inject another element, particularly one so variable by virtue of its dependence upon the resiliency, vindictiveness or other personality attributes of a victim, is to invite further inconsistency, a situation which the criminal justice system could ill afford.

8. Evidence from the U.S., Australia and the U.K. suggests that where the right to appear is accorded to victims only a very small minority of victims take up the opportunity. Walker notes that Arizona, Connecticut and California already have laws giving the victim a voice in criminal proceedings. He suggests that the evidence indicates that in fact victims do not want an active role. He refers to judge Lois Forer of Philadelphia who routinely extends an invitation

to victims but only few bother to appear. And in Connecticut, where the victim's right to participate has become law, victims appear at only about three per cent of all sentencings. The percentage is strikingly similar to the one reported by Neto et al. (1986) for California.

9. Rossini (1987) highlights some of the problems associated with greater victim participation in the criminal justice process. She notes that there are many reasons why victims may choose to participate only occasionally which would make the criminal process arbitrary. The cost of separate legal representation for a victim would be prohibitive for the majority. Use of government funds for this purpose (e.g. through legal aid) would add enormous financial cost to the state. The alternative of using Crown prosecutors to act on a victim's behalf could lead to a conflict of interest, particularly where the issue in question is the prosecution of a lesser charge or a decision not to continue with the case. She also discusses the problem of determining at what stage the victim should appear (p. 16).

Bibliography

Australia. *Report of the Committee of Inquiry on Victims of Crime.* South Australia, 1981.

Australia. *Victims Past, Victims Future: A South Australian Police Perspective.* South Australia Police Department, 1986.

Australia. *Victorian Sentencing Committee: Final Report.* Melbourne: Government Printing Office, 1988.

Bassiouni, Ch. *Introduction to the United Nations Resolution and Declaration of Basic Principles of Justice for Victims of Crime and Abuse of Power.* Chicago: De Paul University, 1987.

Bassiouni, Ch. *International Protection of Victims.* Association Internationale de Droit Penal. Toulouse: Érès Publications, 1988.

Burns, P. *Criminal Injuries Compensation: Social Remedy or Political Palliative for Victims of Crime.* Toronto: Butterworths, 1980.

Canada, House of Commons. *Minutes of Proceedings and Evidence of the Legislative Committee on Bill C-89, an Act to Amend the Criminal Code (Victims of Crime).* Ottawa: House of Commons, 1988.

Canada. *Canadian Sentencing Commission: Final Report.* Ottawa: Ministry of Supply and Services, 1987.

Canada. *Canadian Federal-Provincial Task Force on Justice for Victims of Crime: Report.* Ottawa: Ministry of Supply and Services, 1983.

Canada. *Law Reform Commission of Canada: Restitution and Compensation – Fines, Working Papers* 5 and 6. Ottawa: Information Canada, 1974.

Chappell, D. "Providing for the Victim of Crime: Political Placebos or Progressive Programs?" *Adelaide Law Review,* vol. 4, no. 2, pp. 294-306, 1972.

Christie, N. "Conflicts as Property." *British Journal of Criminology,* vol. 17, no. 1, pp. 1-19.

Council of Europe. *The Position of the Victim in the Framework of Criminal Law and Procedure.* Strasbourg, 1985.

Damaska, M. *Some Remarks on the Status of the Victim in Continental and Anglo-American Administration of Justice,* paper presented at the Fifth International Symposium on Victimology, Zagreb, Yugoslavia, August, 1985.

Dolliver, J.-M. "Victims' Rights Constitutional Amendment: A Bad Idea Whose Time Should Not Come." *The Wayne Law Review,* 34 (1): 87-93, 1987.

Elias, R. *Victims of the System*. New Brunswick, NJ: Transaction Books, 1983.

Elias, R. "Community Control, Criminal Justice and Victim Services," in E. Fattah (ed.) *From Crime Policy to Victim Policy*. London: MacMillan, 1986.

Elias, R. "The Symbolic Politics of Victim Compensation." *Victimology*, vol. 8, no. 1-2, pp. 213-224, 1983

Elias, R. "Which Victim Movement?: The Politics of Victim Policy." In A.J. Lurigio, W.G. Skogan and R.C. Davis (eds.) *Victims of Crime: Problems, Policies and Programs*. Newbury Park, CA: Sage Publications, 1990.

Fattah, E.A. "On some visible and hidden dangers of victim movements." In E.A. Fattah (ed.) *From Crime Policy to Victim Policy: Reorienting the Justice System*. London: MacMillan, 1986.

Fattah, E.A. *The Impact of Crime Prevention and Offender Rehabilitation Programs on the Costs of Victim Compensation: A Methodological Approach*. Unpublished report prepared under contract with the Ministry of Justice in Ottawa, 1988.

Forer, L.G. *Criminals and Victims: A Trial Judge Reflects on Crime and Punishment*. New York: W.W. Norton and Company, 1980.

Galaway, B. and Hudson, J. *Perspectives on Crime Victims*. St. Louis: The C.V. Mosby Company, 1981.

Galaway, B. *Restitution as Innovation or Unfulfilled Promise, Federal Probation*, 51, pp. 3-14, 1988.

Gittler, J. "Expanding the Role of the Victim in a Criminal Action: An Overview of Issues and Problems." *Pepperdine Law Review*, vol. 11, pp. 117-182, 1984.

Grabosky, P.N. *Crime Victims in Australia*. Canberra: Australian Institute of Criminology, 1985.

Henderson, L.N. "The Wrongs of Victim's Rights." *Stanford Law Review*, vol. 37 (April), pp. 937-1021, 1985.

Joutsen, M. *The Role of the Victim of Crime in European Criminal Justice Systems*. Helsinki: Heuni, 1987.

MacDonald, W.F. "Expanding the Victim's Role in the Disposition Decision: Reform in Search of a Rationale." In Gallaway, B. and Hudson, J. (eds.) *Offender Restitution in Theory and Action*. Massacheusetts: Lexington Books, pp. 101-104, 1978.

Malarek, V. "Voice-for-Victim Trend Disturbs Lawyers." *The Globe and Mail*, April 11, 1984.

Marshall, T.F. "Reparation, Conciliation and Mediation." London: Home Office Research and Planning Unit, *Paper No. 27*, 1984.

McLeod, M. *Beyond the Law: An Examination of Policies and Procedures Governing the Nature of Victim Involvement at Parole*. Paper presented at the ASC meeting, Montreal, November, 1987.

Morgan, P. "From Battered Wife to Program Client: The State's Shaping of Social Problems." *Kapitalistate*, 9, pp. 17-39, 1981.

Neto, V. et al. *Victims Appearances at Sentencing Hearings Under the California Victims' Bill of Rights*. Sacramento: Center for Research, McGeorge School of Law, 1986.

Paltrow, S.J., "Opposite Effects: New Anti-Crime Law in California Is Helping Some Accused Felons." *The Wall Street Journal*, Nov. 26, 1982.

Ranish, D.R. and Shichor, D. "The Victim's Role in the Penal Process: Recent Developments in California." *Federal Probation*, vol. 49 (1), March, pp. 50-57, 1985.

Rossini, G. *Victims and the Criminal Justice System in South Australia*. Paper presented at the Third Annual Conference of the Australian and New Zealand Society of Criminology, 1987.

Rubel, H.C. "Victim Participation in Sentencing Proceedings." *Criminal Law Quarterly*, 28, pp. 226-250, 1986.

Shapland, J., Willmore, J. and Duff, P. *Victims in the Criminal Justice System*. London: Gower Publishing Company Limited, 1985.

Shapland, J. "Victims and the Criminal Justice System." In E.A. Fattah (ed.) *From Crime Policy to Victim Policy*. London: MacMillan, 1986.

Shapland, J. "Victim Assistance and the Criminal Justice System: The Victim's Perspective." In E.A. Fattah (ed.) *From Crime Policy to Victim Policy*. London: MacMillan, 1986,

Sharman, J.R. "Constitutional Law: Victim Impact Statements and the 8th Amendment." *Harvard Journal of Law and Public Policy*, 11 (spring), 583-593, 1988.

Talbert, P.A. "The Relevance of Victim Impact Statements to the Criminal Sentencing Decision." *UCLA Law Review*, 36, pp. 199-232, 1988.

Still, L. "Victim Say in Sentencing Just Vengeance: Lawyers." *The Vancouver Sun*, Sept. 21, 1983, p. A3.

United Nations. *Declaration of Basic Principles of Justice for Victims of Crime and Abuse of Power*. New York: United Nations Department of Public Information, 1985.

United States. *President's Task Force on Victims of Crime: Final Report*. Washington, DC: U.S. Government Printing Office, 1982.

Walker, S. *Sense and Nonsense About Crime: A Policy Guide*. Monterey, CA: Brooks/Cole Publishing Company, 1985.

Walsh, A. "Placebo Justice: Victim Recommendations and Offender Sentences in Sexual Assault Cases." *The Journal of Criminal Law and Criminology*, vol. 77, no. 4, pp. 1126-1141, 1986.

Welling, S.N. "Victim Participation in Plea Bargains." *Washington University Law Quarterly*, vol. 65, pp. 301-356, 1987.

Welling, S.N. "Victims in the Criminal Process: A Utilitarian Analysis of Victim Participation in the Charging Decision." *Arizona Law Review*, 30: 85-117, 1988.

PART III

The Search for an Alternative Paradigm and a Humane Criminal Policy

Chapter VI
The Dawning *of a* New Era *in* Social Reaction *to* Injurious *and* Harmful Actions

See my paper in *Archiwum Kryminologii*, pp. 20-42.

THE DARK TUNNEL of punishment has been a long and painful one. For centuries both lay persons and professionals have been desperately searching for some light at the end of the tunnel. Many like me have been dreaming of a new non-punitive era in criminal justice. The advent of restorative justice rekindled the hope that this new era is dawning upon us.

Restorative justice is by no means a new concept or an ingenious idea. Nor is it a radical or revolutionary method for solving conflicts or settling disputes. What it is: a rational, peaceful and constructive way of restoring harmony and order that were disrupted by the harmful or injurious act.

Restorative justice offers a great promise. It offers to move us, or rather to remove us, from the medieval system of punishment that has been in place for centuries to a new era of social reaction to harmful, injurious behaviours, to personal conflicts and disputes. It promises us a peaceful, constructive, less onerous, less costly, less wasteful, less painful way of dealing with those who offend. It offers justice without caging those responsible. It promotes forgiveness, not revenge. It restores harmony while ensuring redress to the victim. It promises to get us out of the big penal mess we are in right now.

I still remember with ever-growing nostalgia the 1960s and early 1970s when serious attempts were made aimed at the humanization of the criminal justice system. Unfortunately, those progressive penal policies were soon replaced by regressive changes during the conservative era of Ronald Reagan in the U.S.A., Margaret Thatcher in Britain, and Brian Mulroney in Canada. But the futility and the enormous costs of the new wave of repression were bound to call into question the rationality of those punitive policies. The search for less destructive and less costly alternatives became a priority. Inspired by how native and aboriginal communities deal with conflicts and harmful actions and how they repond to offences committed by some members of the group against other group members, there were demands for peaceful and reconciliatory means of conflict resolution. Critics of the system wanted to make justice work and to make offenders pay. Restorative justice proponents called for the socialization and humanization of justice, for the personalization and civilization of conflicts. Victims' advocates demanded that justice be made more sensitive to victims and more responsive to their needs and their wishes. Soon restorative justice became an attractive option. It is not difficult to understand and explain the irresistible appeal and the growing popularity of restorative justice. Restorative justice calls for restitution, not retribution; for redress, not revenge; for reconciliation, not retaliation; for reparation, not incarceration (Fattah, 2004).

The major appeal of restorative justice is that it reconciles the aims of those who demand recognition of and a voice for the victim and those who feel that punishment is an abuse of the state's power and a misuse of public funds. What draws people from different backgrounds and different ends of the political spectrum to restorative justice is its ability to satisfy those who are in favour of active victim participation in the justice process and those who believe that offenders need to be sensitized to the pain and suffering they had inflicted upon their victims, those who feel that redress to the victim should be the primary objective of the justice process and those who want to hold offenders accountable for their actions (Fattah, 2004).

Some Overlooked Benefits of Restorative Justice

(see Fattah, 2004)

The benefits of restorative justice and the clear advantages it has over the current punitive system of criminal justice have been explained over and over again in the ever-growing literature on restorative justice. They are well summarized in the preamble to the recommendations made to the Council of Europe by the Committee of Experts on Mediation in Penal Matters chaired by Christa Pelican with the active participation of Ivo Aertsen. Among other things, the committee (1999) stressed that mediation in penal matters is a flexible, comprehensive, problem-solving, participatory and viable alternative to traditional criminal proceedings, an alternative that satisfies a strongly felt need to enhance active personal participation of the victim, the offender and others who may have been affected, as parties, by the offence. The committee also noted that mediation enhances the involvement of the community and recognizes the legitimate interest of victims in having a stronger voice in dealing with the consequences of their victimization, as well as their need to communicate with the offender to obtain an apology and reparation. The committee also emphasized that mediation encourages offenders' sense of responsibility and offers them practical opportunities to make amends which may further their reintegration and rehabilitation. It also has the potential of increasing the awareness of the important role of the individual and the community in preventing and handling crime and resolving its associated conflicts, thus encouraging more constructive and less repressive criminal justice outcomes.

All of those arguments are well known to those with an interest in restorative justice. I personally have discussed them at some length in my writings on the topic (Fattah, 1993; 1995; 1998; 1999; 2000). So is there anything that has not been said or remains to be said about the positives of restorative justice? Are there some hidden benefits that have been somehow overlooked and have not been thoroughly discussed in the fast-growing literature on this exciting and promising model of justice? I will briefly discuss eleven of the less often discussed or overlooked benefits of restorative justice.

1. Restorative justice avoids the inherent arbitrariness of retributive punishment and the enormous disparities in its application.

Arbitrariness is a structural, innate and irremediable defect in retributive systems. To maintain that a given number of days, months or years in prison is a fair and equitable punishment for offences such as assault, rape and robbery or else it strikes me as the height of arbitrariness (see Chapter II). It is rather difficult to understand how intelligent people – lawyers, scholars, academics and others – could believe and maintain that pain can be measured and dispensed according to some kind of mathematical formula. How could they believe it is possible to create some kind of equation that would make a prison sentence fit a crime that has caused physical or psychological injury, material harm or loss? That a seriously flawed concept and a fundamentally defective sentencing model like "just deserts" could be accepted and implemented for so long is a mystery. When Professor Graeme Newman of the School of Criminal Justice at Albany suggested many years back, at a meeting of the American Society of Criminology, that carefully measured electrical shocks be used to inflict a just dosage of pain on criminals, those attending the meeting simply laughed at him. And yet his suggestion makes more sense than the arbitrary use of imprisonment as a retributive sanction. Surprisingly, sentencing models that adopt a very similar punishment philosophy, such as the "just deserts" model, are not greeted with laughter and, more surprisingly, they are even taken seriously by some scholars and policy-makers. Except in a purely theological perspective, retribution is not, and can never be, an instrument of justice. To speak, therefore, of retributive justice is a contradiction in terms. And as it is impossible to establish a fair equation between the punishment and the crime, between the pain to be inflicted upon the offender and the pain caused by the offence to the victim and his/her family and associates, we should stop associating justice with retribution, as is often done when the popular term "retributive justice" is used. We should also remove the word "just" from the sentencing model that is erroneously called "just deserts" and call it instead the "arbitrary deserts" model.

2. By settling conflicts through a process and outcomes somewhat similar to that of civil courts, restorative justice offers a remedy to the arbitrary distinctions between civil and criminal conflicts.

Punitive/retributive justice is based on an erroneous premise, the premise that crime is a unique, distinct or exceptional category of behaviour. It is also based on a false dichotomy between the so-called crimes and civil wrongs. Both the premise and the dichotomy are fallacious. A comparison between acts made punishable by the penal law or criminal statutes and similar behaviours that are left unregulated or are regulated by non-criminal rules or by administrative bodies reveals that there is no qualitative difference between criminal and non- criminal behaviour. In fact, for every behaviour defined as criminal and sanctioned by law, there are identical or similar types of behaviour that are neither illegal nor punishable (see Fattah, 1997). If crime is not qualitatively different from civil torts or civil wrongs, then there is no valid reason to accept redress to the injured or harmed party in the latter and to insist on sanctions of a completely different nature for the former. One also has to wonder why it is that in the case of civil torts the damages ordered by the court go to the victim, whereas in criminal offences the penal fine goes to the public treasury. Surprisingly, many of those who oppose the notion of restorative justice and continue to demand retribution, even for non-violent crimes, have no problem accepting administrative or civil remedies for various types of corporate, white-collar and professional crimes, and voice no objection to the civil regulation of corporate wrongdoing.

3. Restorative justice avoids the vagaries and inherent injustice of punitive systems.

The enormous and inevitable disparities in the application of retributive punishments make a mockery out of what is supposed to be a fair and equitable justice system. No sentencing guidelines, no sentencing model has ever or will ever be able to remedy even partially the flagrant punishment disparities. Whether the disparities are a direct outcome of structural flaws in the system, whether they are the result of attitudinal differences, systemic discrimination or whether they are due to misguided reforms (such as victim-impact statements and the right of allocution), the end result is the same. Offenders who commit similar or identical crimes end up receiving enormously different punishments. The disparity in sentencing has become even greater with the introduction of what could only be described as lunatic laws, such as "three strikes and you're out," which make a travesty out of what is supposed to be a fair and equitable justice system. In the American states that introduced those laws, such as the state of California, a person with two felony convictions who commits an act of shoplifting could be sent to prison for life. Another found guilty of a serious crime, such as forcible rape, and who receives the average penalty for rape, is sentenced to five years.

4. Restorative justice avoids or at least minimizes the inherent bias of punitive justice.

Punitive justice is not only arbitrary but is inherently discriminatory as well. It is manifestly biased, and it is this bias that explains why the vast majority, the bulk of those incarcerated, are the powerless, the poor, the have-nots, the members of racial, ethnic and religious minorities. Take, for example, the advanced and generally progressive country like Canada. Despite enlightened attempts by the government in 1996 to alleviate just one aspect of the manifest bias against members of Canada's First Nations, by changing the criminal code requiring sentencing judges to look for alternatives to imprisonment "with particular attention to the circumstances of aboriginal offenders," members of Canada's First Nations continue to be overwhelmingly overrepresented in Canada's penal institutions. On April 17, 2012 an editorial in *The Vancouver Sun* (p. A14) stated that:

> "Aboriginal over-representation is a long-standing and growing problem. For example, in 1988 aboriginals accounted for 10% of federal inmates (those serving two years or more), while making up just two per cent of the population. By 1999, the percentage of aboriginal inmates in federal custody had increased to 12 per cent, and by 2005, aboriginals accounted for 17 per cent of the federal inmate population. And aboriginal over-representation is more dramatic

> still in provincial reformatories… Reports over the years have pointed to institutional bias within the criminal justice system itself – specifically to evidence that courts are more inclined to deny bail and to impose more and longer prison terms on aboriginals than on similarly situated non-aboriginals."

But punitive justice discriminates in so many other tangible and intangible ways. Having abolished the death penalty, incarceration is now the most severe sanction meted out by the criminal courts. Despite the fact that it is the most unjust and most unfair sanction there is, there is an overreliance on imprisonment as a means of punishing offenders, and every alternative proposed over the decades to reduce its use has failed. The principles of retribution, of just deserts, of proportionality all require making the punishment fit the crime. When the sentence to be meted out is imprisonment, all three principles require a dose of deprivation of freedom that equals the harm or injury done to the victim. In this context I always find it interesting to quote Gilbert and Sullivan, who in their operetta *The Mikado* refer to this eternal dilemma in a light-hearted verse:

> My goal is all sublime
> I shall achieve in time
> To make the punishment fit the crime!

The pains of imprisonment vary greatly from one offender to another, so how on earth could individual judges in their wisdom come up with a length of incarceration that corresponds to an assault, rape or robbery?

The system of punishment in every country on earth that practises it is characterized by the enormous disparities and unwarranted and unexplainable variations in sentencing from judge to judge and from court to court. What is disconcerting is that the variations do not follow any discernible pattern that would help explain their existence. Attempts to remedy the enormous disparities in sentencing, such as fixed sentences, minimum sentences, presumptive sentences, etc. make a mockery of the principle of proportionality. The so-called principle of just deserts requires that the amount of pain the offender is made to suffer is equal to the pain he had inflicted upon his victim. But is pain quantifiable? Do we have an accurate means of measuring an accurate dosage of pain? Rather than the infliction of pain, there must be some way or resolving conflicts and settling disputes where there is some gain for the person or persons who suffered at the hand of the harm doer. This is precisely one of the primary objectives of restorative justice.

5. Restorative justice would put an end to the unfair and shameful practice of plea bargaining.

Plea bargaining is an unfair and shameful, though popular, justice practice, more common in Anglo-Saxon systems than the justice systems of continental Europe. In the United States, for instance, 90 per cent of all the cases in which offenders are charged end up with a plea bargain (Ranish & Shichor, 1985).

The offender, or more frequently his lawyer, makes an agreement with the prosecutor (sometimes with the blessing of the judge) by which he/she accepts to plead guilty to a lesser charge in exchange for a milder sentence. For obvious reasons, victims are excluded from the negotiation process that leads to the guilty plea. They get surprised, frustrated and resentful when they discover that the charges laid by the prosecutor or the Crown attorney bear no or little resemblance to the actual offence committed against them. And when the mild sentence resulting from the bargain is finally pronounced, they become infuriated and feel betrayed by the criminal justice system, by society and by society's representative, the prosecutor. This sense of betrayal is an inevitable characteristic of punitive justice systems, because they promise victims more than they can deliver and create expectations that can never be fulfilled in practice.

6. Restorative justice encourages and enhances victim reporting.

Legalistic interventions usurp the victim's decision-making powers. The current system of criminal justice gives victims no say and no choice. It snatches the conflict from its legitimate owner, the victim, and hands it to the public prosecutor (Christie, 1977). By so doing it discourages in many instances victim reporting of the offence. Victims who, for one reason or another, do not want the offender punished (either by a prison sentence or a penal fine) are naturally reluctant to go to the police with their complaints. The same is true of victims who are related, in some way or another, to their victimizers. Knowing that the arrest and subsequent punishment of the offender will sever the bond or will strain the relationship beyond repair, they simply refrain from reporting their victimization to law enforcement bodies. Replacing punishment with a non-punitive conflict resolution mechanism would render those victims less reluctant to report. Restorative justice alternatives also promote the reporting of victimization by members of disadvantaged social groups that dislike, distrust or try to avoid the police. Speaking of the promise of restorative justice in the case of wife-battering, Presser and Gaarder (2000, p. 186) suggest that restorative justice has the potential to increase victims' likelihood of reporting the abuse. This is because it offers an array of flexible interventions, which can be particularly appealing to women, such as members of social, ethnic and religious minorities, who distrust the criminal justice system.

7. Restorative justice minimizes the chances of retaliation and the risks of repeat victimization.

This is without doubt one of the most positive aspects of restorative justice. Conflict resolution and dispute settlement are undoubtedly the most effective means to ensure that the violence will not flare up again, that the emotions that fuel the aggression are held in check. Most acts of violence are retaliatory in nature and a very high percentage are committed between people who are related to one another by some family relationship or other personal ties. Unless reconciliation is achieved, the seeds of violence will always remain. Restorative justice aims at restoring the peace and harmony disrupted by the offence, at revitalizing the bonds and ties that were severed by the criminal act. And contrary to the retributive system that feeds on vindictiveness and the thirst for revenge, restorative justice promotes forgiveness, understanding and restitution. It gives the victim and the offender a chance to meet face to face to reach a mutual understanding of one another, to put the past behind them and to come to a fair and just agreement about the future. Restorative justice makes wounds heal and is thus beneficial to the coping process, to the psychological well-being and the satisfaction of the victim.

8. Restorative justice is the most appropriate response to gang violence.

Conflicts and wars between rival gangs are the urban equivalent to the old family feuds that were quite prevalent in rural societies and led to interminable killings and counter-killings. This is yet an important area where restorative justice can succeed where punishment abysmally fails. There is a great deal of anecdotal and historical evidence showing that the most effective, perhaps the only, way to settle blood feuds in agrarian societies like

Albania, Sardinia, Sicily, Macedonia, Egypt, etc. is mediation, reconciliation and compensation. Opponents of restorative justice claim that these types of long-standing conflicts and blood feuds no longer exist in modern, industrialized, urbanized societies .They fail to recognize various types of conflict, common in urban centres, that have replaced those traditional blood feuds. Among those are youth gang wars, drug dealers' turf struggles, blood battles between organized crime factions, settlement of accounts between members of rival groups, such as motorcycle gangs, etc. Add to this the racial, ethnic and religious conflicts like those between Catholics and Protestants in Ireland; Arabs and Jews in the Middle East; Muslims and Copts in Egypt; supremacist groups and new immigrants; not to mention the ideological conflicts like those between pro-life and pro-choice groups; or between environmentalists and loggers or pipeline advocates, etc., etc. The only remedy and the most effective solution to violent acts emanating from those conflicts and similar ones is mediation and reconciliation. This is because the attitude that is basically responsible for the violence, and for the conflict in the first place, is intolerance. Punishment and penal sanctions, whether imprisonment or the death penalty, do not change this attitude. If anything, they are apt to perpetuate and intensify the conflict and to escalate the level of violence. Restorative justice designates the prevention of repeat victimization as one of the primary goals of the process of mediation and reconciliation and as a strategic priority of victim services. (Fattah, 2000).

Restorative justice acknowledges that what victims desperately want, even before redress, is the freedom from fear from the threat of future victimization. This is why when victims ask for or seek imprisonment for the offender, it is not, as erroneously believed or as retributivists claim, to satisfy their thirst for revenge, but to seek some assurances about the threat of future victimization, a threat that disappears when reconciliation is achieved.

9. Restorative justice personalizes the response.

Philosophers who tried to find an acceptable ethical or moral justification for punishment always insisted that for punishment to be just it has to be personal, meaning that it is inflicted on the guilty person and no one else. But retributive sanctions punish not only the guilty but the innocent as well, thus contravening one of the fundamental principles of justice. Punishment can never be made personal, because its effects inevitably extend to others who have done no wrong. The worst example is undoubtedly the death penalty. But the same is also true of incarceration. A prison sentence is a punishment not only for the offender, but also for the family, the friends and for everyone who cares about or relies upon the offender. If he is an employer, it penalizes the employees; if he is a worker, the incarceration can cause disruption in his work place and so forth.

10. Restorative justice offers some remedy to victims whose offenders have not been identified, arrested, convicted and punished.

The attrition in the legal process means that only a very tiny fraction of those who offend are punished! This is because a large number of offences, even serious offences, are never reported for one reason or another. Others are reported but no action is taken. Add to this that the clearance rate, particularly in property offences, is extremely low. In many cases no charges are laid, and even when charges are laid a number of cases end up in acquittal. All this means that more than nine out of ten victims get no satisfaction and no redress from the punitive justice system. This is not the case with restorative justice models that provide compensation as well as other help and assistance to those victims whose offenders are not known and have not been caught. Restorative justice is not to be pigeonholed as a diversion or a mediation practice. Restorative justice is much more than just victim-offender mediation. It is about helping victims overcome the economic consequences and the traumatic effects of victimization, regardless of whether the offender has been identified and arrested or not.

11. Restorative justice is the most appropriate model for cases of undisputed harm.

In the vast majority of criminal cases that reach the court the harm is not disputed. This inevitably raises the question of the criminal justice system's role in cases of undisputed harm. It may be argued that when the basic facts of the case are being disputed there is a need for a neutral, impartial mechanism, an adversarial system to establish what really happened, who is at fault and what is the extent of the harm or injury that has been caused. But when the harm is undisputed, why should the system impose its own judgement on the parties rather than letting them reach their own agreement about the best, the fairest and most acceptable way of repairing the harm? Why should the system be allowed to substitute its judgement for that of the victim? Japan is a good case in point because in more than ninety-five per cent of the cases with a known offender, there is a freely obtained confession. How can the involvement of a formal adversarial justice system be rationalized or justified? How can the enormous expenditures of the system be justified? To maintain that the unilateral determination of punishment is a process of doing justice simply defies logic and rationality. How can such an authoritarian, non-participatory process be preferable to restorative justice practices, be it mediation, sentencing circles, group/community conferencing or anything else?

On Some of the Dangers and Limitations of the Restorative Justice Paradigm

A. Dangers to and of the Restorative Justice Paradigm

In a paper I published some years ago (Fattah, 2004), I tried to draw attention to some of the dangers that restorative justice faces and some of the dangers it poses.

1. The danger of hasty and faulty implementation

The history of criminal justice is replete with good ideas that failed and good intentions that never achieved their potential. Unless we proceed carefully and measure our actions circumspectly, the fate of this promising paradigm may not be better than many of those that have preceded it. How many excellent ideas were introduced over the years into the justice system only to fade and die, sometimes a quick death and other times a slow one? Hopes were raised only to be shattered and the great promises never materialized. Those innovative ideas that failed testify to the system's resistance to change, its reluctance to accept and accommodate new concepts and new models. This should be a warning particularly to those who naively believe that the only hope for restorative justice is to be implemented within or through the existing system of criminal justice.

2. The danger of failing to gain and secure the support, the involvement and the active participation of the community

Restorative justice is community justice. It has no chance of succeeding or replacing the existing punitive system unless it is fully endorsed by the community and unless members of that community are actively involved in the resolution of conflicts and the settlement of disputes. Without strong community support and without intensive and extensive community involvement there is a real danger of replacing a state-run bureaucracy and a state-controlled system with yet another bureaucracy and another system under state control. This is precisely what is happening in some countries where mediation is now a bureaucracy run and controlled by state prosecutors.

3. The danger of widening the net of social control

Because the danger of net-widening is ever-present and too well known, there is no real need to dwell upon it in any great detail. Suffice it, therefore, to draw attention to the early warnings offered by some of those who assessed the pioneering experiments in restorative justice like Dittenhoffer & Ericson (1982, 1992:341), who wrote:

> "Interests distinct from those of correctional reformers have particularly given credence to the theme that VORP is destined to become part of the widening net of social control, similar to many previous reforms which have enhanced the discretion of various officials in different ways."

Like many other innovative programs (community service is just one example) in the past, there is a real danger that restorative practices will become an add-on to punishment rather than genuinely replacing it to become the sole or primary mode of social reaction to harmful, injurious behaviours.

4. The danger of restorative justice being co-opted by the existing agencies of the criminal justice system it replaces

As Davis (1992) warned in the early days of restorative justice, vested interests in the present system will do everything to marginalize new ideas which threaten their basic assumptions or their very existence. If attempts at marginalization happen to fail, they will try to co-opt the new programs. This should lead to increasing caution about the dangers of compromise and to rejection of any strategy based on the naive belief that the only way of implementing restorative justice is through pilot projects or small-scale experiments conducted within the system. Those who believe that this is the way to go should only look at mediation programs in different countries that had to close down because of lack of referrals from prosecutors.

5. The danger that restorative justice may develop into an offender- or victim-centred justice alternative rather than having both victim and offender as its central focus

In his insightful analysis of the history of victim initiatives, Paul Rock (1990:408) explained how many of those initiatives were not really meant to help victims but were designed to serve other purposes or some ulterior motives. He said:

> "...criminal injuries compensation was supposed to mollify the reactionary victim-vigilante, and reparation was a device to divert offenders from custody. In both instances, victims were the creatures of penal imperatives, invested with the characters needed to get on with the business of reforming prisons. Compensation and reparation did not have much of a foundation in the declared or observed requirements of victims themselves: they were bestowed on victims in order to achieve particular ends."

When restorative justice practices started in Canada and the United States, spearheaded by the Mennonite Church, redress to the victim prevailed over every other consideration. Although the programs initially called themselves VORP (victim-offender reconciliation programs), their foremost objective was to ensure restitution by the offender to the victim and to see to it that the offender fulfils the obligations agreed upon in the mediation agreement. Not surprisingly they were sarcastically described as collection agencies for the victim. That the programs deviated from their original objectives was highlighted in one of the early evaluations of the programs by Dittenhoffer and Ericson (1982), who stated that:

> "This investigation has revealed the manner in which the programme actually does operate, only partially obtaining its goals and departing substantially from the picture painted by most descriptions of the programme."

As the goal of reconciliation became secondary to that of restitution and as it proved to be an elusive goal, the programs had no choice but to change their name from "victim-offender reconciliation programs" to "victim-offender mediation programs." If there is a lesson to be learnt from those early restorative justice initiatives, it should be the realization of how essential and how important it is to maintain a fair and equitable balance between the interests of the victim and the interests of the offender. Those pioneering efforts show how vital it is, for the credibility and effectiveness of the programs, not to tilt the scale or to favour one party over the other. Those early experiments should also teach us to stick to the defined objectives and not to let administrative or pragmatic considerations alter what the programs are set up to achieve.

6. The danger that restorative justice will become a victim of its own success

Nothing can be more dangerous than success, particularly rapid success. The speed with which restorative justice programs, projects and experiments are being implemented is a constant reminder of the initial success and the instant explosion of diversion programs six decades ago. It should give us a reason to pause and reflect on how long the interest can last. How long can the enthusiasm be sustained before it begins to wane? How long can the state of euphoria be maintained? All this leads to the question: Could restorative justice become a victim of its own success? The alliance formed around and is currently promoting restorative justice inevitably raises suspicion about the interests and the motives of the diverse groups that seem to be united in their support of the new model. Restorative justice seems to make strange bedfellows. Both those on the left and the right of the political spectrum seem to find some things they like in restorative justice. For those leaning to the left, it is seen as a more humane, less destructive alternative to destructive and debilitating punishments. It is regarded as a way of socializing, decentralizing, deprofessionalizing and deformalizing justice. To those on the right, restorative justice is appealing because it has the potential for reducing state expenditures of the criminal justice system and is guaranteed to shift the financial burden of victim compensation from the state to the offenders. What is difficult to figure out are the real motives behind the wholehearted endorsement of police forces like the RCMP. Be this as it may, it remains to be seen what negative (or positive) influence the diversity of interests, of motives, of ideologies will have on restorative justice. One cannot but fear that different groups will try to gain control of restorative justice programs, claim them as their own creation and try to gear them in directions that fit their own agenda, interests and purposes. This calls for enhanced vigilance and more alertness as well as strong defences to resist any such takeover attempts.

B. On Some Limitations of the Restorative Justice Model

Restorative justice, despite its vast potential, is not the most appropriate mode of intervention in every single instance of harm-doing. It is not feasible or even advisable in every situation or in all circumstances. It has certain limitations. Some of those limitations may be due to lack of mental competency of one of the parties, lack of consent or unwillingness to participate for one reason or another. There are also cases where there are multiple victims or several injured parties (and cases where there are multiple offenders), some of whom are willing to participate while others are not. Those few limitations are such that they do not affect restorative justice's viability as a general model of justice. Space constraints allow only a very succinct enumeration of the most important of those limitations.

1. Restorative justice is not to be recommended in the cases of severely deranged offenders.

Their serious mental handicap will be a major hindrance when it comes to giving free informed consent to the practice, to participating meaningfully in mediation sessions, agreeing to the terms and complying with the conditions of the restorative agreement. The same problem arises in the case of child victims who are much too young to understand the practices, the objectives or to participate in the sessions. Like in other legal situations, child victims may be represented by their parents or guardians. However, the ideal of having the harm-doer confronted by the primary victim and sensitizing him to their suffering may not be easy to achieve in such scenarios. On the side of the child victim, the major objectives of coping, healing, forgiving and moving forward may not be easy or possible to achieve when a meaningful interaction is not possible due to the age, the mental state or the limited understanding of the person who suffered.

2. While restorative justice is possible and feasible in the case of violent, dangerous offenders, it needs to be combined with certain treatment or containment measures that would ensure that the dangerousness of the offender is neutralized.

The practical problem in some of those cases is how to secure the free, willing participation of the person who has been seriously victimized. In the current climate where revenge and retaliation are promoted as justice and where harsh sanctions are erroneously portrayed as doing justice to the victim, it is not surprising that some of the victims of serious offences may show a stubborn unwillingness to meet face to face with their victimizers.

3. One of the basic features of restorative justice is that it is a peaceful, voluntary and non-coercive mode of resolving conflicts and settling disputes.

This volitional aspect raises certain issues and imposes certain limitations on the generalizability of restorative justice as the sole available mode of intervention. A question we hear from supporters of restorative justice is: If there is no qualitative difference between crimes and civil torts, why is it that mandatory mediation and arbitration are allowed in civil and labour disputes but are shunned when it comes to violations of this or that criminal code disposition?

4. In some cases the same act may claim several victims, may injure or harm more than one person.

How to proceed when some accept and are willing to participate while others refuse? In other cases there may be two or more harm-doers. What to do when some are willing and others are unwilling to participate in the restorative justice process?

5. Then there is of course the issue of victimless crimes or crimes without victims.

As I repeatedly argued in the past, such actions that are simply deemed to be immoral, deviant, objectionable or not acceptable by some group or another have no place in the criminal code and should not be criminal offences in the first place. Aside from those behaviours there are others that cause harm in a general, diffuse, non-specific way. They are not directed at a concrete person or body, for example – bribery, corruption or tax evasion, to name but a few. Although those harmful actions may not lend themselves to common restorative practices such as mediation or arbitration, they still can be dealt with effectively by restorative remedies and in current practice they are dealt with by fines, restitution, community service and so forth.

A Proposed Strategy for Action

Obstacles on the Road to a General Institutionalized System of Restorative Justice and How to Overcome Them

There are several obstacles in the way of having the restorative justice paradigm, despite its obvious advantages and benefits, widely accepted and institutionally implemented. It requires a long and persistent but winnable struggle against deeply entrenched religious beliefs, philosophical views, ideological ideas and cultural attitudes. It also requires the vehement denunciation of the vested interests of the punishment machine, the lucrative prison industry that stands to realize obscene profits as a result of the new fad of private prisons or prisons for profit. The real and enormous costs of custodial sanctions that are usually kept secret from taxpayers need to be widely publicized and severely scrutinized (see Gopnik, 2012).

The transition from punitive justice to restorative justice will obviously require some fundamental changes. It will require a switch from the theological notions of expiation and penitence to the social notion of restitution. The name "penitentiary" will have to be abandoned! Shifting to the new paradigm will require moving from the abstract (retribution) to the concrete (restoration); from the infliction of harm (punishment) to the reduction and prevention of harm (reconciliation). It will also require a move from the politics of exclusion to policies of inclusion; from segregation to reintegration; from costly incarceration to effective reparation.

Restorative justice forces us to abandon what is commonly called a "philosophy of punishment" in favour of a "philosophy of justice" and "sociology of justice." It may very well be that certain religions dictate that those who do harm be punished. However, the social sciences, particularly criminology, psychology and sociology, offer substantive evidence to show that punishment is not only ineffective as a deterrent but is also unjust by any definition. Human behaviour, and this applies to criminal and delinquent behaviour, is motivated behaviour that has causes. Whether one believes in theories that claim that the causes of crime are genetic and that criminals are born or adheres to the theories that maintain that criminals are socially and environmentally made, punishing them seems to be unjust and unfair. Another philosophical/metaphysical concept underlying the notion of punishment and retribution is the abstract yet popular notion of "free will," which is utterly contradicted by the findings of behavioural sciences which prove that criminal and deviant behaviour are the product of factors and variables and not the free volition of the actor. Believing in free will is the negation of the notion of causality, a negation no social or behavioural scientist would accept.

One important strategy for restorative justice proponents is to get the powerful victim movement/lobby on the side of restorative justice and make it attractive for politicians to jump, as they always do, on the bandwagon. It should be obvious to any rational thinking person that retributive punishment does the victim more harm than good. Except for the few victims who were taught from an early age that retaliation is an appropriate (or the appropriate) reaction to harm-doing, retributive punishment clearly does nothing to alleviate the suffering of or to redress the harm done to the victim. And as if to add insult to injury, custodial punishments deny offenders the possibility to work and pay restitution, while state funds that could have been used to compensate the victim are wasted on keeping wrongdoers behind bars. We need to explain to those injured or harmed by crime and their lobby, if any explanation is needed, that the abstract goals of retributive punishment are antagonistic to the real interests of the victim and that their advocates' demands for more and harsher sanctions are detrimental to their recovery, restoration and well-being.

Punitive justice is detrimental to the victim in other ways as well. Punishment can only be applied to those offenders who are identified, caught, charged and successfully prosecuted. Victims of unknown, uncaught or acquitted offenders get no redress and no relief whatsoever from punitive justice. State compensation programs are strictly limited to victims of violence with onerous eligibility requirements and many restrictions, and for the lucky few who qualify and are ultimately awarded, more often than not, it is too little and too late (Fattah,1999b). Is it any wonder that victims who go through the cumbersome process and end up being compensated are less satisfied and more frustrated than those victims who do not take the trouble to apply for compensation in the first place? Restorative justice, on the other hand, does not require the identification of those who are responsible. The only proof required is the injury and harm done to the victim. A good example is the Claims Conference for Jewish Victims of Nazi Persecution that awards compensation and restitution to victims of Nazi atrocities and their heirs as well as help them recover confiscated and unclaimed Jewish property.

There is an urgent need to widely and publicly debate and compare the economies of punitive justice to those of restorative justice, the economies of the infliction of pain versus those of restoring the harmony. Contrary to the goals and objectives of the current punitive system of justice, which have never been clearly defined or articulated anyway, we need to publicize in great detail the major goals and tremendous benefits of a non-punitive system of restorative justice.

One of the basic issues that need to be widely and publicly debated is that of retribution. Is retribution an ethical and acceptable justice goal in modern civilized secular society? Is retribution acceptable at any price, regardless of the human, material and social costs it requires? In an age when there is growing recognition that the conflict is the victim's property (Christie, 1977), that the offence is primarily against the victim and only secondarily against the state, when it comes to a choice between punishment and retribution versus reconciliation and restitution – who should decide? Is it not logical that victims be given the right to choose their preferred mode of dispute resolution?

Conclusion

Tracing the origins of restorative justice to the practices of conflict resolution of aboriginal or indigenous people in precolonial societies does not mean that restorative justice is a simple means of doing justice. In fact restorative justice, if true in name and spirit, is a complex model that is not easy to implement in the highly urbanized, highly technological modern-day society. The enormous diversity of types, practices and modalities described in the literature as "restorative" attests to such complexity. And naturally there is no agreement as to what qualifies and what does not qualify as a restorative practice. Be this as it may, there are still some things on which there is wide agreement. This is, for example, the case with mediation. Mediation is not restorative justice per se. It is simply a technique, a modality of reaching some agreement between the parties and achieving restorative ends.

So what are the chances of having our current criminal justice system replaced by a general, comprehensive system of restorative justice? A dose of realism is in order. When it comes to law and justice, traditions are very powerful and long-lasting. Social reaction to harmful and injurious acts is very resistant to change but, like everything else, it slowly and inevitably does. It would be both naive and wrong to believe that any type of punishment is permanent or immutable. After centuries of fierce resistance, we have witnessed the change with regard to what seemed to be eternal practices such as lynching, the death penalty, corporal punishments and torture to name but a few. Although torture, unfortunately, is making a comeback in the United States as documented by Larry Siems in his excellent publication *The Torture Report* (2011), this is, in my personal opinion, just a setback that is unlikely to persist. Regardless of what excuses or justifications may be used to legitimize it, torture is and will always be morally repugnant and universally condemned. And the same fate inevitably awaits inhumane and barbaric practices such as imprisonment because the difference between punishment and torture is simply a difference in degree. In fact for many the deprivation of liberty can be as torturous as or even more torturous than physical or psychological pain. In this context it may be relevant to quote what Charles Dickens wrote after visiting the Eastern State Penitentiary in Philadelphia, widely regarded as a model prison, which at the time was the most expensive public building ever constructed in the U.S.A. (Gopnik, 2012), where every prisoner was kept in silent, separate confinement:

> "I believe that very few men are capable of estimating the immense amount of torture and agony which this dreadful punishment, prolonged for years, inflicts upon the sufferers... I

> hold this slow and daily tampering with the mysteries of the brain to be immeasurably worse than any torture of the body; and because its ghastly signs and tokens are not so palpable to the eye and sense of touch as scars upon the flesh, because its wounds are not upon the surface, and it extorts few cries that human ears can hear, therefore I the more denounce it as a secret punishment which slumbering humanity is not roused up to stay."

Yes! There is nothing moral or ethical about the deliberate infliction of pain and suffering on a fellow human being or even an animal. This is why I find it surprising that eminent scholars like M. Tonry (2006:22) still believe that prospects for restorative justice are not too great in jurisdictions with highly moralistic attitudes towards crime because restorative justice is seen as not proportionate enough to the harm or injury caused by the wrongdoer. Tonry cites England, the U.S., Sweden and the Netherlands as examples. Contrary to Tonry's belief, I would have thought that cultures with high moral attitudes would be more likely to come to the conclusion that the archaic, antiquated and primitive practice of punishment is highly immoral and deeply inhumane, and thus would be the first to try to replace it with a less reprehensible mode of social reaction and a more morally acceptable model like restorative justice.

A Look Into the Future

Social change in the twenty-first century promises to be the most radical and most sweeping ever! Globalization, mass communication, the powerful and far-reaching social media, are bound to produce upheavals undreamed of a few decades ago. We have seen some of their impact in the Jasmine Revolution, in the ouster of despots and dictators. We are witnessing the deep crisis of the capitalist system and the imminent threat of the crumbling of the economy of entire nations. We are witnessing the demise of dictatorships and the transition from totalitarianism to democracy, from tyranny to participatory government. The dawning of a new era in politics and governance highlights the urgent need for a new paradigm for criminal law and criminal justice. Retributive justice, even if it entails death, is not a commensurate response to acts of genocide, ethnic cleansing, mass extermination, use of weapons of mass destruction and many other forms of crimes against humanity. No one could argue that executing a dictator or a tyrant is a just, equal and proportionate response to the killing of millions or thousands of his subjects. Clearly, another type of justice is needed against those ousted dictators and despots and others responsible for horrendous acts of repression and genocide. South Africa's adoption of transitional justice and its truth commission provide a good example to follow. It clearly showed that there is a different and better way than easy punishment to deal with those who have committed indescribable atrocities and crimes. The model of transitional justice is both timely and vital, as the number of countries that will achieve freedom from tyranny and oppression is bound to increase year by year.

By calling for a new justice paradigm, for a general institutionalized restorative justice system that replaces the archaic punitive system we have now, am I being overly optimistic? Am I asking for utopia or lost paradise? Maybe it is my inner hope to leave the earth on an optimistic and promising note or maybe I am crying in the wilderness. Maybe I am dreaming the impossible dream. I keep attending restorative justice conferences hopelessly waiting for someone to join me, saying,"YES, it is possible. YES, it is doable." Because if there is any hope for a brighter future for human justice, it lies in the hands and rests on the shoulders of young people who can be the agents of real change. It is up to the young generation to make what may now seem an impossible dream become a future reality because they are masters not only of their own destiny but the destiny of many generations to come. If they have the will and determination, they will have the ability to reduce the pain and suffering that is being inflicted on millions of people in the name of a "pseudo" justice. They have the ability to change society to the better and to make the world a peaceful, harmonious place for their children and grandchildren.

References

1977 Christie, N. "Conflicts as Property," *British Journal of Criminology*, vol. 17, no. 1, pp. 1-19.

2000 Council of Europe. *Mediation in Penal Matters: Recommendation No. R (99) and Explanatory Memorandum.* Strasbourg: Council of Europe.

2003 Davis, Angela. *Are Prisons Obsolete?* Seven Stories Press.

1992 Davis, G. *Making Amends: Mediation and Reparation in Criminal Justice.* London: Routledge.

1992 Dittenhoffer, T. and Ericson, R. "The Victim/Offender Reconciliation Programme: A message to the Correctional Reformers." In E.A. Fattah (ed.) *Towards a Critical Victimology.* London: Macmillan & New York: St. Martin's Press, pp. 311-346.

2011 Drucker, Ernest. *A Plague of Prisons: The Epidemiology of Mass Incarceration in America.* The New Press.

Fattah, E.A.

1978 "Moving to the Right: A Return to Punishment?" *Crime and Justice*, 6:2, pp. 79-92.

1982a "Making the Punishment Fit the Crime: The Case of Imprisonment. Problems Inherent in the Use of Imprisonment as a Retributive Sanction." *Canadian Journal of Criminology*, 24:1, pp. 1-12.

1982b "Public Opposition to Prison Alternatives and Community Corrections: A Strategy for Action." *Canadian Journal of Criminology*, 24:4, pp. 371-85.

1992 "Beyond Metaphysics: The Need for a New Paradigm – On Actual and Potential Contributions of Criminology and the Social Sciences to the Reform of the Criminal Law." In R. Lahti and K. Nuotio (eds.) *Criminal Law Theory in Transition*. Helsinki: Finnish Lawyers Publishing Co.

1993 "From a Guilt Orientation to a Consequence Orientation." In F. Denker et. al. (eds.) *Beiträge zur Rechtswissenschaft*. Heidelberg: C.F. Muller.

1995 "Restorative and Retributive Justice Models: A Comparison," in H-H. Kühne (ed.) *Festschrift für Koichi Miyazawa*. Baden-Baden: Nomos Verlagsgesellschaft, pp. 305-15.

1997a "From Crime Policy to Victim Policy: The Need for a Fundamental Policy Change." In M. McShane and F. Williams III (eds.) *Victims of Crime and the Victimization Process*. New York: Garland Publishing, pp. 75-92.

1997b "Towards a Victim Policy Aimed at Healing, Not Suffering." In R.C. Davis, A.J. Lurigio and W.G. Skogan (eds.) *Victims of Crime* (second edition). Thousand Oaks, CA: Sage Publications, pp. 257-72.

1997 *Criminology: Past, Present and Future, a Critical Overview* (1997). London: Macmillan; New York: St. Martin's Press.

1998a "Restorative and Retributive Justice Models: A Comparison," in Fattah, E.A. and Peters, T. (eds.) *Support for Crime Victims in a Comparative Perspective*. Leuven, Belgium: Leuven University Press, pp. 99-110.

1998b "Some Reflections on the Paradigm of Restorative Justice and Its Viability for Juvenile Justice." In Lode Walgrave (ed.) *Restorative Justice for Juveniles: Potentialities, Risks and Problems*. Leuven, Belgium: Leuven University Press, pp. 389-401.

1999a "Victim Redress and Victim-Offender Reconciliation in Theory and Practice: Some Personal Reflections." *The Hokkaigakuen Law Journal*, vol. XXXV, no. 1, pp. 155-82.

1999b "From a Handful of Dollars to Tea and Sympathy: The Sad History of Victim Assistance." In J.J.M. van Dijk, Ron G.H. van Kaam and Jo-Anne Wemmers (eds.) *Caring for Crime Victims: Selected Proceedings of the 9th International Symposium on Victimology*. Monsey, NY: Criminal Justice Press, pp. 187-206.

1999c *Mediation in Penal Matters*. Report for Correctional Services Canada. Ottawa, 44 pages.

2000a "Victim Redress and Victim-Offender Reconciliation in Theory and Practice: Some Personal Reflections." *Resource Material Series No. 56*. Fuchu/Tokyo: UNAFEI (Asia and Far East Institute for the Prevention of Crime and the Treatment of Offenders), pp. 87-101.

2000b "How Valid Are the Arguments Frequently Made Against Mediation and Restorative Justice?" In Hedda Giertsen (ed.) *Albanian and Norwegian Experiences with Mediation in Conflict*. Oslo: Department of Criminology, University of Oslo, pp. 25-36.

2002 "From Philosophical Abstraction to Restorative Action, From Senseless Retribution to Meaningful Restitution: Just Deserts and Restorative Justice Revisited." In H.J. Kerner and E. Weitekamp (eds.) *Restorative Justice, Theoretical Foundations*. Devon, UK: Willan Publishing, Culmcott House, pp. 308-21.

2004 "Gearing Justice Action to Victim Satisfaction, Contrasting Two Justice Philosophies: Retribution and Redress," in Hendrik Kaptein and Marijke Malsch (eds.) *Crime, Victims and Justice: Essays on Principles and Practice.* Burlington, VT: Ashgate Publishing Company.

2007 "Is punishment the appropriate response to gross human rights violations? Is a non-punitive justice system feasible?" In *Restorative Justice: Politics, Policies and Prospects.* E. van der Spuy, S. Parmentier, A. Dissel (eds.). Published under the auspices of the Faculty of Law, University of Cape Town (Juta and Company). Originally published in *Acta Juridica* (Cape Town), 2007, pp. 209-227.

2011 "Is Restorative Justice a Viable Option in Crimes of Violence?" Published in a special issue of *Keio University Law Journal* dedicated to the memory of Prof. Koichi Miyazawa. pp. 713-730.

End of Fattah's references

2012 Gopnik, Adam. "The Caging of America: Why Do We Lock Up So Many People?" *The New Yorker Magazine,* January 30, 2012.

2000 Presser, L. & Gaarder, E. "Can Restorative Justice Reduce Battering?: Some Preliminary Considerations." *Social Justice,* vol. 27, no. 1, pp. 175-195.

1992 Ranish, D. and Shichor, D. "The Victim's Role in the Penal Process: Recent Developments in California." In E.A. Fattah (ed.) *Towards A Critical Victimology.* London: Macmillan & New York: St. Martin's Press, pp. 222-237.

1990 Rock, P. *Helping Crime Victims: The Home Office and the Rise of Victim Support in England and Wales.* Oxford: Clarendon Press.

2011 Siems, L. *The Torture Report: What the Documents Say About America's Post-9/11 Torture Program.* New York: O/R Books.

1971 Sykes, G. M. "The Pains of Imprisonment," in L. Radzinowicz and M.E. Wolfgang (eds.) *Crime & Justice (vol. 3), The Criminal in Confinement.* New York: Basic Press.

2006 Tonry, M. "The prospects for institutionalization of restorative justice initiatives in Western countries." In Aertsen, I., Daems, T. and Robert, L. (eds.) *Institutionalizing Restorative Justice.* Devon, UK: Willan Publishing, pp. 1-24.

PART IV

Is a Non-Punitive Society a Utopian Dream?

Chapter VII
Is Punishment Obsolete? Ethical *and* Practical Problems *with the* Punishment Paradigm

Why does punishment fail? Why is punishment the wrong response to criminal offending?

> "...if you punish a man retributively you must injure him. If you are to reform him, you must improve him. And men are not improved by injuries."
>
> George Bernard Shaw, *The Crime of Imprisonment*
>
> "Indeed, we need to question and rethink the entire bases of the punishment system. Virtually all discussion of change begins and ends with the premise that punishment must take place. All of the existing institutions and structures – the criminal law, the criminal processing system, the prisons – are assumed. We allow ourselves only to entertain debates about rearrangements and reallocations within those powerfully constraining givens... The sterility of the debates and the disturbing ways they are played out in practice underscore the need to explore alternative visions. We need to step back to reconsider whether or not we should punish, not just to argue about how to punish."
>
> K.M. Harris, "Moving Into the New Millennium: Toward a Feminist Vision of Justice," in H.E. Pepinsky and R. Quinney (editors), *Criminology as Peacemaking*

FEW WOULD DISPUTE the claim that punishment is a failure both as a deterrent and as a rehabilitation tool. A robust attempt to get accurate recidivism rates to use in this chapter proved to be a frustrating endeavour! In its *Forum on Corrections Research* (volume 5, no. 3), Correctional Service Canada states the following:

> "What's the overall recidivism rate in Canada? It's a common question, but one that's difficult to answer. In this article, we try to explain why this question is so tough to answer and try to answer it as best we can."

Correctional Service's conclusion is even more telling. It reads:

> "We have presented many reasons why it is difficult to come up with one all-encompassing recidivism rate that pleases everyone. Recidivism is a critical issue in corrections, but it is also one of the most difficult issues to address in an easy-to-understand manner. We hope this article has answered some questions, although it has probably raised more questions than it has answered."

Rather than repeating some questionable figures and percentages from various official publications, it is much safer and more enlightening to try to examine some reasons that may explain why it is that punishment quite often fails.

In a Department of Justice document, *Transforming the Criminal Justice System* (modified on July 26, 2017), the Department cites some percentages regarding populations or groups who are vulnerable to offending:

- Up to 80% of federal offenders have past or current substance abuse issues.
- According to some studies, two-thirds of crimes are committed while under the influence of drugs or alcohol.
- Estimates of fetal alcohol spectrum disorder prevalence among correctional populations range from 10% to 23%, ten times higher than in the general population.
- Those suffering from mental illness are also greatly over-represented in the criminal justice system, suggesting a need for more tailored and nuanced reforms.

The department also gives some data to show how the indigenous population is over represented in the criminal justice system. It reports that in Canada, indigenous people are the most at risk of becoming involved with the criminal justice system. The degree of over-representation cannot be overstated.

- While indigenous adults make up about 4.1% of the Canadian population, in 2016 and 2017 they represented 30% of admissions to provincial/territorial custody and 27% of admissions to federal custody.
- 50% of youth admitted to custody in 2016 and 2017 were indigenous, despite making up only 8% of Canada's youth population.

In view of the make-up and the characteristics of the populations and groups mentioned above, one does not need to be a rocket scientist or a criminologist to realize why it is that punishment can neither be an effective deterrent nor a tool of rehabilitation for members of those vulnerable groups. One also should question the wisdom and the morality of inflicting pain and suffering on offenders belonging to those groups in view of the fact that they are, for obvious reasons, victims themselves, victims of their social, cultural and family environments.

And since the title chosen for the document by the Justice Department indicates that there is a need to transform (not just to change or reform) the criminal justice system, one is justified to ask about the extent and the nature of the transformation the Justice Department is alluding to. Because to call for a radical transformation as the document does is a clear indication that the time is ripe for abandoning the retribution paradigm in favour of another non-punitive paradigm, such as restorative justice.

Some Faulty Premises Underlying the Punishment Response

Just because an institution, a practice, a tradition, a belief has existed and survived for ages or centuries does not necessarily mean that it is right, sound or without fault. As popular as the belief that certain institutions are permanent, transcendental or immutable may be, it is belied by both history and reason. Religion is a good example. We look back at the religious beliefs of early humanity and wonder how gullible and naive people were to worship statues, animals, the sun, the rain, etc., thinking they were gods who are determining and shaping their destiny! Does anyone know or dare to speculate on what future generations will think of the beliefs that we hold sacred in current day and age? Is it at all possible to figure out what deity or deities people will be worshipping two centuries from now?

Is it possible or foreseeable that religions that have survived almost unchanged for millenia could be scientifically proven in the near or distant future to have been the inventions of an inquisitive mind nurtured by a fertile imagination? Is it conceivable that future centuries will be the stage for religions utterly different from the ones we have now? Slavery is another example of how inevitable social and cultural change is. It continued unchallenged for several centuries and yet today it is universally condemned as brutal and uncivilized and its modern forms are widely criminalized and harshly punished.

Is it then too daring and too foolhardy to predict that punishment, as we practise it today, is bound to have the same fate? Penal history tells us that private vengeance was the earliest response to harmful, injurious actions. Gradually, it evolved into group vengeance. With the emergence of organized society this in turn was formalized, institutionalized and turned into state vengeance. This state vengeance, or retributive punishment to use the popular euphemism, is taken as a given, and its moral and ethical foundation, as its social justification, is hardly subjected to a critical scrutiny. This is rather unfortunate because an objective critical analysis clearly shows that the punishment response is severely flawed and is based on several faulty premises and on a set of erroneous beliefs. Such analysis would also show that retribution is an anachronistic paradigm that in many respects is incompatible with the values and beliefs of twenty-first century society.

A. The Mistaken Belief that Criminal Behaviour Is a Unique or Distinct Type of Behaviour

One such premise is the erroneous belief that criminal behaviour is somehow unique or a distinct type of behaviour that needs to be punished by a specific class of criminal sanctions. If this premise is incorrect, and it is easy to show that it is, then punishment has no moral or rational justification. While the general public may be under the impression that crime is qualitatively distinct, criminologists have shown over the years, with examples at hand, that criminal behaviour is not qualitatively different from non-criminal behaviour. They showed that for every behaviour defined as criminal and sanctioned by the criminal code or by criminal statutes, there are identical or similar types of behaviour that are neither illegal nor punishable (Fattah, 1997:49).

Leslie Wilkins (1964:46) noted that "at some time or another, some form of society or another has defined almost all forms of behaviour that we now call criminal as desirable for the functioning of that form of society."

Surely there is no qualitative difference between crime and civil torts, and in many instances the same act is both a crime and a tort. And yet society's response to them is very different. It is also important to keep in mind that not all types of violent, aggressive or assaultive behaviours are made criminal by the law. Many forms of violence are condoned and tolerated to the extent that they become culturally legitimate. Until a few years ago, the Canadian criminal code (and many others) did not define forcible sexual intercourse with one's own wife as a crime. But the same act perpetrated on a woman who is not the man's wife did qualify as a serious crime punishable by imprisonment for life. Although the behaviour in the two cases is identical, in one case it is criminal, in the other it is not, depending on whether the two parties are bound by marriage or not. The same can be said of statutory rape and other sexual behaviours with minors, where an arbitrarily determined age, an age that changes over time and varies greatly from one society to another, is the deciding factor whether the behaviour is criminal or not, is punishable or not.

Until recently, use of the strap in school for misconduct, using violence to discipline or control the behaviour of inmates in penal institutions and flogging offenders guilty of certain crimes were all seen as legitimate forms of violence, and those on whom such punishments were inflicted were seen as deserving targets. Milder forms of violence within the family are not criminal in most jurisdictions. Children are considered legitimate targets for the use of physical force in the process of training and control, and for a long time husband-wife violence was regarded as legitimate by both the police and the courts.

It seems necessary to ask why it is that crime, delinquency and violence start and reach their peak in the teen years, why they are more prevalent among boys than among girls. The reason is not a mystery. For the most part, delinquent and violent acts are those of suppressed youth protesting the values and norms being imposed upon them by the older generation, and expressing their defiance of, and their revolt against, authority. After a few years, delinquency and violence decline because those youthful rebels no longer feel the need to assert their independence or to impose their own will. Forget about the explanations that point to the raging hormones and rising levels of testosterone. It is this misguided search for the elusive causes that has led criminology astray. So, if most of delinquent and violent acts committed by young offenders or juvenile delinquents are acts of rebellion, revolt or defiance, then responding to them by violence can only make a bad situation much worse.

B. The Mistaken Belief that Criminals Are Radically Different from Law-Abiding Citizens

Another faulty premise underlying the use of penal sanctions is the mistaken belief that criminals are radically different from law-abiding citizens, a belief that leads to the creation of a false dichotomy between criminals and non-criminals. When we are faced with horrendous and horrible acts committed by fellow humans, it is human nature to try to distance ourselves from the perpetrators of those acts. An easy way of doing this is to think of them as abnormal, as different, as suffering from some kind of pathology. It is comforting to see them as monsters, as depraved psychopathic individuals. Positivist criminology takes as its point of departure that criminals are fundamentally different from the rest of the population. Hence the primary goal of scientific inquiry is to identify those distinguishing characteristics that differentiate criminals from the rest of us. The well-established tendency of positivist criminology to "over-pathologize" offending and offenders and to focus on their supposedly abnormal personalities, deviant characters or irrational modes of thinking discounts the fact that most criminal behaviour is of a mundane, opportunistic and rational nature. The Japanese criminologist Hiroshi Tsutomi (1991:14) said it best when he wrote:

> "People commit crimes, not because they are pathological or wicked, but because they are normal."

It is very true that the vast majority of criminals are normal people driven by the same motives and impulses that drive all of us. Whatever difference there may be lies not in the goals being pursued but in the means to achieve those goals. The popular saying "the end justifies the means" is an effective technique of rationalization used by criminals and non-criminals alike. It is the justification used by individual terrorists and terrorist groups as well as by torturers, prison guards, some law enforcement officers, etc. Following the events of September 11 it was adopted by leaders of democratic countries such as the USA and Britain. Positivist criminology's assertion that "people who break the law are often psychologically atypical" or that "offenders are... atypical in personality" (Wilson and Herrnstein, 1985:173) is contradicted by the observations that anyone placed in certain situations, under certain conditions and subjected to certain pressures and constraints is capable of committing acts of extreme atrocity, cruelty, cupidity, dishonesty and so forth (Fattah, 1997: 128/129). The experiments of Milgram (1969) and of Zimbardo (1972) prove it. So does Nils Christie's (1952) study of Norwegian guards in German concentration camps during the Nazi occupation of Norway in the Second World War. The same was shown by Christopher Browning's (1992) study entitled *Ordinary Men: Reserve Police Battalion 101*, by the Mai Lai massacre in Vietnam, by the atrocities committed by the American soldiers in Abu Gharib prison in Iraq and in Guantanamo Bay in Cuba, to name but a few. Former U.S. president George W. Bush's frequent assertions that anyone who attacks the interests of the U.S.A. is evil has nothing to do with science and everything to do with religion. The studies of Milgram, Zimbardo, Christie and Browning, among others, are of extreme relevance to those who are trying to comprehend and deal with the atrocities and gross human rights violations committed by former totalitarian, dictatorial regimes. They help understand the behaviour of those responsible for those atrocities, particularly those who were obeying orders or were totally intoxicated by the powers they held over their helpless captives. The psychological processes of rationalization, neutralization, demonization, de-individuation and dehumanization of the victims shed much better light on the perpetrators' seemingly incomprehensible behaviours than any search for the abnormalities or peculiarities of their character and personality. They should be pivotal in any attempt to find the most appropriate ways of dealing with their crimes.

C. The Erroneous Belief That Incarceration Is Bound to Transform the Inmate into an Honest, Docile Person

Another faulty premise underlying the punishment response is the erroneous belief that incarceration with the degradation, humiliation and dehumanization that it entails is bound to transform the offender into a better and more honest or docile person upon release. That some continue to believe that the prison experience can be a positive experience is truly mind-boggling. The deprivation of freedom and the detention in crowded inhumane conditions can only breed hate, hostility and anger. It creates resentful, vindictive and vengeful individuals who cannot wait to get out to take their revenge against society. Is it any wonder that recidivism rates are so high? Isn't this the reason why both juvenile and adult institutions have been described as "schools of crime"?

D. The Erroneous Belief That Criminal Courts Can Dispense Fair, Just and Individualized Sanctions

As shown above, the faulty premises underlying the punishment response are many. Yet probably the most erroneous of all is the idea that courts of justice can mete out penal sanctions that are proportionate to the injury or the harm done, that they can "make the punishment fit the crime."

It is utterly ludicrous to think that imprisonment can be a fair, just and personal punishment that is commensurate with the wrong being punished (see Chapter I). The plain truth is that the punishments that are daily dispensed by the criminal justice system are blatantly arbitrary and unjust, and thus cannot be ethically condoned or morally defended. And while the requirements of efficacy, profitability and necessity do not withstand any empirical test, it is the condition of proportionality that can never be met by punitive sanctions, particularly imprisonment. Almost four decades ago, as may be seen in Chapter I (Fattah, 1982), I went to great length to explain how impossible it is to make a prison sentence proportional to the offence being punished. And yet imprisonment continues to be used as the primary means of retribution. This despite the fact that it is totally impossible to rationally or equitably determine what prison term is a fair expiation for an attack on property or to create an equitable balance between physical and sexual assaults and a given number of days, months or years in prison. Despite well-meaning attempts such as "the justice model," "the principle of commensurate deserts," "the presumptive sentence," the arbitrariness of such equation is both evident and inevitable. Yes, it is possible to grade various offences according to their objective and/or perceived seriousness. However, to come up with a prison term equivalent to theft or robbery, to assault or rape, is inevitably arbitrary, capricious and despotic. As the inherent problem of equating the amount of deprivation of liberty with the degree of moral guilt of the offender or with the extent of the harm done has never been solved, the capricious determination of the length of imprisonment is left either to the arbitrariness of legislators or the discretion of sentencing judges, with all the disparities and inequities that ensue. That we continue to accept and to apply a punishment that poses such insoluble ethical, fairness and equity problem is, sad to say, a clear indication that we are more committed to the justice principles of the eighteenth century than we are to the egalitarian and human rights principles of the twenty-first century (Fattah, 2002:315/6).

Suppose it is argued that punishment will be proportionate not to the seriousness of the offence but to the moral responsibility of the offender. Could this proposition serve as a basis for a more equitable system of punishment? The answer, needless to say, is a categorical *no*. This is because the degree of moral responsibility of the offender, which is unique for every accused, can never be quantified or measured. It is therefore a serious scientific error to advocate a sentencing system which supposedly will dispense varying dosages of punishment on the basis of an abstract notion (moral responsibility) that is neither susceptible to quantification nor measurement (Fattah 1992:78).

Nor is fairness and equity achieved when the determination of punishment is made solely on the basis of the nature and the seriousness of the offence being punished. It is neither fair nor equitable to give those found guilty of identical or similar crimes identical prison sentences. The same prison term does not entail the same amount of pain and suffering, does not involve identical deprivations and does not carry with it the same consequences to different offenders. The pains and consequences of imprisonment are far different even when offenders are kept in the same institution, in similar conditions, for the same length of time. As long as it remains impossible to measure the pains of imprisonment (Sykes 1971) and to weigh the sufferings and deprivations resulting from it for each individual offender, the use of incarceration as a retributive sanction will never be justified in a democratic and just society.

The inherent unfairness and arbitrariness of a sentencing system based on the questionable premise of just deserts were highlighted by Thomas Gabor (1998:85), who pointed out that:

> "A sentencing system based on desert might not be so objectionable were commensurate or proportional sentences readily quantifiable as justice-oriented sentencing guidelines suggest. These highly systematized schemes promote the illusion that there is a fairly precise penalty fitting each type of offence."

Is There a Viable Alternative to the Punishment Response?

This brings us back to the eternal question: If we do away with punishment, what is the alternative? This question is more telling about our criminal justice system than anything else. The primary problem with our criminal justice system and our criminal justice policy is the total lack of vision, the absence of innovation and the strong resistance to experimentation. While every other sector of public policy has undergone radical changes in the second half of the twentieth century, the criminal justice system continues with the archaic practices of medieval times! This begs the question: In what way is what we do with criminals today any different from what the courts did in the early twentieth century or even in the nineteenth century"?

One answer may be: at least we abolished the death penalty. Far from it! Capital punishment is still practised in many countries in the world, including the most populated country (China) and the most powerful country (the U.S.A.). Or one may say, well, we have succeeded in doing away with the abominable practice of torture. People are no longer being tortured to extract confessions or to force them to provide information. Surely the shocking pictures from Abu Gharib prison in Iraq or from Guantanamo Bay in Cuba could not have been so easily and so quickly forgotten. Yes, torture, which was believed to be the trademark of the inquisition, is back with vengeance. And its traumatic effects on the victims far exceed any effects caused by conventional individual crimes. Some years ago, Denmark took the initiative of establishing a centre for the treatment of torture victims. May be we should start promoting the creation of similar centres in other countries of the Western world because the number of victims now is surely higher than at any time in recent memory.

So What About Restorative Justice?

Showing the futility of punishment, its limitations, shortcomings, its costs and problems helps answer the question: Is restorative justice a viable option in crimes of violence? If punishment is a dismal failure, if it does not achieve any of its avowed goals, then any alternative cannot be worse than what we have now and will more likely be far better. Surely a justice paradigm that has healing, closure, redress and prevention as its primary goals is a huge progress over the punitive system that we have inherited from canon law.

Are Victims Better Off in a Restorative System of Justice?

Most people either forget or are unaware that victims are the primary losers in punitive justice systems. From the time personal conflicts were converted into public crimes, and the institution of restitution and composition (known as *weregild*) was replaced by a punitive punishment, victims' interests were sacrificed and they were assigned a peripheral role in the criminal justice process. The new system completely ignored their plight and usurped their rights. The compensation or the "*weregild*" that was meant as a means of redress, as a way of compensating them for the injury, the harm or the loss they have suffered, was replaced with a so-called penal fine that went to the king's coffers or to the public treasury. And for centuries the plight of victims went unnoticed, unrecognized and unremedied. Voices calling to address and redress victims' disenfranchisement were not heard until the second half of the twentieth century. Modest state compensation programs were set up in some countries but offered only symbolic recognition and continue to suffer from a chronic lack of funding and resources. Studies showed that only a very tiny minority of those victimized end up receiving any state compensation whatsoever. And for those who do, it is too little too late (Fattah, 1999). Even worse, the studies found that those who go through the state compensation process were less satisfied than those who never applied for compensation in the first place. And as if to add insult to injury, the victim movement that was supposed to defend the interests of victims, to claim their rights and to speak on their behalf, was moving in the wrong direction. Its main concern was to increase the severity of punishment and to raise the level of penal sanctions. Somehow victim advocates failed to realize that since funds and resources are strictly limited, increasing the costs of the expensive system of punishment leaves less and less for victim compensation.

References

Barnes, H.E. (1972). *The Story of Punishment: A Record of Man's Inhumanity to Man* (second edition, revised). Montclair, NJ: Patterson Smith.

Browning, C. (1992). *Ordinary Men: Reserve Police Battalion 101 and the Final Solution*. New York: HarperCollins Publishers.

Christie, N. (1952). *Fangevoktere i Konsentrasjonsleire. Nordisk Tidskrift for Kriminalvidenskap*, 41:439-58. (Also published as a book in 1972.)

Canada, Correctional Service (2015). *Forum on Corrections Research*, vol. 5, no. 3. Ottawa: Government of Canada.

Canada, Department of Justice (2017). *Transforming the Criminal Justice System*. Ottawa: Government of Canada.

Fattah, E.A. (1982). "Making the Punishment Fit the Crime: Problems Inherent in the Use of Imprisonment as a Retributive Sanction." *Canadian Journal of Criminology*, 24(1):1-12.

Fattah, E.A. (1988). *On Victims, Parole and the Sentencing Commission*. Brief submitted to the House of Commons Standing Committee on Justice and Solicitor General, March, 1988.

Fattah, E.A. (1992). "Beyond Metaphysics: The Need for a New Paradigm – On Actual and Potential Contributions of Criminology and the Social Sciences to the Reform of the Criminal Law." In R. Lahti and K. Nuotio (eds.) *Criminal Law Theory in Transition*. Helsinki: Finnish Lawyers Publishing Company.

Fattah, E.A. (1993). "From a Guilt Orientation to a Consequence Orientation: A Proposed New Paradigm for the Criminal Law in the 21st Century." In J. Welp and W. Küper (eds.) *Beiträge zur Rechtswissenschaft*. Heidelberg: C.F. Muller Juristischer Verlag.

Fattah, E.A. (1994). *The Interchangeable Roles of Victim and Victimizer* (Second Inkeri Anttila's Honour Lecture). Helsinki, Finland: Heuni. 26 pages.

Fattah, E.A. (1995). "Restorative and Retributive Justice Models: A Comparison." In H-H. Kühne (ed.) *Festschrift für Koichi Miyazawa*. Baden-Baden: Nomos Verlagsgesellschaft; reprinted in E.A. Fattah and T. Peters (eds.) *Support for Crime Victims in a Comparative Perspective* (1998). Leuven, Belgium: Leuven University Press.

Fattah, E.A. (1997). *Criminology: Past, Present and Future – A Critical Overview*. London: Macmillan; New York: St. Martin's Press.

Fattah, E.A. (1997). "Some Reflections on the Paradigm of Restorative Justice and Its Viability for Juvenile Justice." In L. Walgrave (ed.) *Restorative Justice for Juveniles: Potentialities, Risks and Problems for Research*. Leuven: Leuven University Press.

Fattah, E.A. (1999). "From a Handful of Dollars to Tea and Sympathy: The Sad History of Victim Assistance." In J.J.M. van Dijk, Ron G.H. van Kaam and Jo-Anne Wemmers (eds.) *Caring for Crime Victims: Selected Proceedings of the 9th International Symposium on Victimology*. Monsey, NY: Criminal Justice Press.

Fattah, E.A. (1999). *Mediation in Penal Matters*. Report for Correctional Services Canada, Ottawa.

Fattah, E.A. (1999). "Victim Redress and Victim-Offender Reconciliation in Theory and Practice: Some Personal Reflections." *Hokkaigakuen Law Journal*, 35(1): 155-82.

Fattah. E.A. (2000). "How Valid Are the Arguments Frequently Made Against Mediation and Restorative Justice?" In Hedda Giertsen (ed.) *Albanian and Norwegian Experiences with Mediation in Conflict*. Oslo: Institute of Criminology.

Fattah, E.A. (2001). "Preventing Repeat Victimization as the Ultimate Goal of Victim Services." *International Annals of Criminology*, volume 38:113-33.

Felson, R.B. and Steadman, H.J. (1983). "Situational Factors in Disputes Leading to Criminal Violence." *Criminology*, 21(1):59-74.

Gabor, T. (1998). "Looking Back or Moving Forward: Retributivism and the Canadian Sentencing Commission Proposals." In T.F. Hartnagel (ed.) *Canadian Crime Control Policy: Selected Readings*. Toronto: Harcourt, Brace & Company.

Goldhagen, D.J. (1996). *Hitler's Willing Executioners*. New York: Alfred A. Knopf, Inc.

Milgram, S. (1969). *Obedience to Authority: An Experimental View.* New York: Harper and Row.

Shaw, G. B. (1946). *The Crime of Imprisonment.* New York: The Philosophical Library.

Sykes, G.M. (1971). "The Pains of Imprisonment." In L. Radzinowicz and M.E. Wolfgang (eds.) *Crime and Justice (vol. 3): The Criminal in Confinement.* New York: Basic Books.

Tsutomi, H. (1991). *Reformulating Cloward and Ohlin's differential opportunity theory into rational choice perspective: Occupational orientation of Japanese institutionalized delinquents.* Paper presented at the American Society of Criminology annual meeting in San Francisco.

Waller, J. (2002). *Becoming Evil: How Ordinary People Commit Genocide and Mass Killing.* Oxford University Press.

Wilkins, L.T. (1964). *Social Deviance.* London: Tavistock Publications.

Wilson, J.Q. and Herrnstein, R.J. (1985). *Crime and Human Nature.* New York: Simon and Schuster.

Wootton, B. (1963). *Crime and the Criminal Law: Reflections of a Magistrate and Social Scientist.* London: Stevens and Sons.

Zimbardo, P.G. (1972). "Pathology of Punishment." *Trans-Action,* 9:4-8.

Zimbardo, P.G. (1978). "The psychology of evil: On the perversion of human potential." In L. Drames, P. Pliner and T. Alloway (eds.) *Aggression, Dominance, and Individual Spacing.* New York: Plenum.

Chapter VIII
Is Restorative Justice *a* Civilized, Viable, Feasible *and* Acceptable Paradigm?

> "The degree of civilization in a society can be judged by entering its prisons. A society should be judged not by how it treats its outstanding citizens but by how it treats its criminals."
> Fyodor Dostoyevsky
>
> "There is no reformation in degradation... A punishment that degrades the punished will degrade the man who inflicts the punishment, and will degrade the government that procures the infliction."
> Robert G. Ingersoll

Civilized?

According to the dictionary definition, "civilized" is an adjective that describes the very opposite of barbarity. Even a brief literature search would show that the adjectives "civilized" and "humane" are almost synonymous and are frequently used interchangeably. The title of this book claims that restorative justice is a civilized justice paradigm. So what exactly is the justification for such a bold claim? Actually, this claim, despite its apparent simplicity, raises a host of questions:

What differentiates a civilized society from an uncivilized society? What differentiates a civilized culture from an uncivilized culture? What criteria, what denominators could be used to judge whether a specific culture is civilized or uncivilized? Could society's degree of civilization be measured by the types of behaviour that it defines as criminal and subject to a formal social reaction? Or is it the type of reaction and response to those behaviours that better indicates the level of civilization of a given society?

It is a well-known fact that certain behaviours can be glorified in a given culture while denounced vehemently in others. What differentiates humane behaviour from cruel or savage behaviour? And, more specific to the subject of this book, what differentiates a civilized justice paradigm from an uncivilized justice paradigm? Should the response to uncivilized behaviours be uncivilized itself? And if so, what actually differentiates the punished from the punisher?

On what basis and what yardstick do we use to label brutal justice practices of the past as barbaric? Are medieval punishments, such as burning, maiming, branding, flogging, acceptable in today's civilized society? There seems to be wide agreement that torture is an uncivilized and inhumane practice. Yet the definition of what constitutes torture is subject to wide variations. And how about electric shocks, chemical castration, solitary confinement, etc. – will they be judged uncivilized some years down the road from now?

What parameters do we use when we judge less advanced cultures as backward and label them as uncivilized? Why do we consider and describe atavistic behaviour as primitive and unrefined?

These are all tough questions begging for answers.

Countless authors who have tackled such thorny questions have maintained that the process of civilization brings about, or at least leads to, a greater sensitivity to the pain and suffering of others. At face value this sounds perfectly true. But if this is true, how can we explain the utter disregard, the complete apathy and the total indifference exhibited *vis-à-vis* the pain and suffering endured, not just by the punished offender, but also and above all by his innocent family and social network? How can the rejection and condemnation of pain, suffering, humiliation, degradation and hardship be so selective and one-sided? How is it that the growing sensitivity to the pain and suffering of the victim translates itself into more and stronger demands for the infliction of pain on the offender instead of heightened sympathy and compassion for him?

Complex human nature has always been a popular topic of study among philosophers, psychologists, psychiatrists, novelists, film-makers, etc., etc. It is not surprising, therefore, that there are variable and sometimes utterly contradictory notions and views about the nature of human beings. This is more so because human nature does not have only one side but multiple sides. Human beings can be gentle, kind, and caring, but they also can be extremely cruel, insensitive, sadistic and outright uncaring.

This is clearly shown in the book I have been working on for some years now, entitled *The Monstrous Side of Human Nature: A Chronicle of Man's Inhumanity to Fellow Humans*. The book covers a long and very elaborate list of atrocious behaviours committed by human beings against fellow humans since history began. The acts range from earlier gruesome behaviours, such as cannibalism, sacrifice of humans (and animals), to modern-day acts of genocide, ethnic cleansing, as well as the annihilation, extermination and elimination of whole groups and entire populations. They range from slavery, human trafficking and exploitation to wars of different kinds: political, religious, ethnic, civil, etc. and the use of weapons of mass destruction, like the atomic bombs dropped on Japan in the final days of the Second World War. Included in the behaviours covered in the book are horrendous acts committed in the past such as the Inquisition and witch hunts to modern day ghastly acts of torture, brainwashing, indoctrination and forced religious conversion. Equally covered are dreadful acts directed at large groups or entire populations, such as blockades, sieges, embargos, as well as macabre acts targeting individuals, such as assassinations and homicides of different types. The long yet non-exhaustive table of contents also covers hideous acts such as kidnappings, rape, honour killings, disappearances, violence against helpless victims such as children, the elderly, the handicapped, as well as spine-chilling acts of oppression, repression and suppresssion by governments and those in power. Brutal sports such as bullfighting, boxing, wrestling (to name but a few) are also used to illustrate the basic point the book makes, namely that human beings have (and probably will always have) a monstrous side that thousands of years of evolution have not yet managed to totally eliminate!

One important point I have tried to drive home throughout my professional life is that the atrocities, the killings, the genocides, etc. that we witness or hear about every day are not the actions of isolated groups or small minorities. They are NOT the actions of some abnormal, pathological or deranged individuals. They are NOT the actions of a few "bad apples." Those were generalized and often glamorized behaviours, and are thus revealing of the spiteful and brutal side of human nature.

Is it any wonder that the theological view that dominated religious and philosophical thinking throughout the Middle Ages until the Age of Enlightenment (the eighteenth century) is that human beings are egoistic by nature and irremediably bad. Therefore they had to be severely contained and restrained by violent and non-violent means to protect them against their natural selfishness and aggression. In line with this concept of the human race, philosophers like Thomas Hobbes (1599-1679) claimed that absolutism in government is essential to prevent the war of each against all, to which natural selfishness inevitably leads. According to Hobbes, humans in the state of nature are inherently in a "war of all against all" and life in that state is ultimately "solitary, poor, nasty, brutish and short."

Is Punishment Civilized, Is Retribution a Civilized Paradigm?

As G.B. Shaw (1946) correctly said, retribution is a euphemism for vengeance. Having examined what the definition of civilized means, having traced the historical evolution of social reaction to harmful, injurious and undesirable behaviours, the question to ask is: Is punishment a civilized response to those behaviours? Responding to harm by inflicting further harm, responding to violence by more violence imposed and executed by the state does not strike me as fitting the definition of "civilized" discussed above.

Just as I was writing this chapter, I came across a remarkable 2019 book entitled *Solitary*, the unbelievable life story of a black American named Albert Woodfox, who served more than four decades in solitary confinement in a six-foot by nine-foot cell, twenty-three hours a day, in notorious Louisiana State Penitentiary, nicknamed Angola, all for a crime he did not commit! I would like to humbly ask the millions of people who are fervent supporters of long prison terms and those who are staunch advocates of life imprisonment a rather simple question: How civilized is it to have a fellow human being spend forty-three years in solitary confinement for a crime he did not commit? Someone may claim that it was a judicial error and judicial errors in a human justice system do happen. But how is it possible in an advanced country like the U.S.A., with a supposedly modern (and fair?) criminal justice system, that a judicial error like this could go uncorrected for that many years? And suppose Woodfox was guilty of killing the prison guard, the act he was punished for, would that have rendered this harrowing life experience more humane or more acceptable? Could it then have been judged "civilized" or deserved?

It may take decades, it may even take centuries, but I am utterly convinced that civilized justice is the way of the future. Society and culture are dynamic entities that are in perpetual change. Despite short or long periods of stagnation (and sometimes regression), progress is continuous and unstoppable. Social evolution is inevitable, even though there may be some slow or backward periods along the way.The essence of civilization is that values change over time and that what was acceptable or defensible in the past is no longer tolerated or acceptable in this day and age. But we have to continuously explain, maintain and sustain our questionable claim to being a civilized society in the same way that we have to explain, defend and sustain our claim to being a social democracy. We have to prove that our claim to being a civilized society rests not on rhetoric but on facts, rests not on principles but on practice. This means we have to objectively scrutinize and assess our current response to behaviours that we deem to be harmful or injurious to our well-being in the same way that we assess our response to actions made criminal because they are simply unacceptable on religious or cultural grounds.

As a diligent student of penal evolution, I am proud that in Canada we have abandoned a relic from the past by abolishing the death penalty. We also have abolished corporal punishments, although many would maintain that imprisonment and solitary confinement do qualify as corporal punishments. But even more distressing is the fact that we continue to make abundant use of deprivation of liberty as a punisment, maybe not as extensively as our neighbour to the south, but to the extent that our penal institutions are overcrowded, sometimes to a dangerous level.

To ascertain whether incarceration is a civilized response to criminal behaviour, let us see what some authors say about the use of imprisonment as a punishment. Here is what one of the greatest philosophers of the twentieth century, George Bernard Shaw, had to say about imprisonment:

> "...imprisonment is at once the most cruel of punishments and the one that those who inflict it without having ever experienced it cannot believe to be cruel," (1946:23).

Shaw continued, to claim that:

> "Modern imprisonment, that is, imprisonment practised as a punishment as well as a means of detention, is extremely cruel and mischievous, and therefore extremely wicked," (1946:117).

It is clear from these citations that Shaw considered imprisonment to be an uncivilized response to unacceptable behaviour. It is not an exaggeration to say that his view is shared by thousands and thousands of penal and social reformers who have been fighting as hard as they can to see the ghastly punishment of imprisonment come to an end.

More than a century ago, in 1906, another writer, Robert G. Ingersoll, in his book *Crimes Against Criminals,* wrote:

> "Only a few years ago there were more than two hundred offences in Great Britain punishable by death. The gallows tree bore fruit through all the year, and the hangman was the busiest official in the kingdom – but the criminals increased.
>
> "Crimes were committed to punish crimes, and crimes were committed to prevent crimes. The world has been filled with prisons and dungeons, with chains and whips, with crosses and gibbets, with thumbscrews and racks, with hangmen and headsmen – and yet these frightful means and instrumentalities and crimes have accomplished little for the preservation of property or life. It is safe to say that governments have committed far more crimes than they have prevented," (p. 11).

Viable?

Is Restorative Justice a Viable Alternative to the Punishment Response?

Having shown above that responding to harm with more harm, that responding to violence with further violence, that responding to pain by inflicting more pain, is not a civilized response, we need to show and prove that there is a viable alternative to the punishment response.

This brings us back to the eternal question: If we do away with punishment, what is the alternative? This question is more telling about our criminal justice system than anything else. The primary problem with our criminal justice system and our criminal justice policy is the total lack of vision, the absence of innovation and the strong resistance to experimentation. While every other sector of public policy has undergone radical changes in the second half of the twentieth century, the criminal justice system continues with the archaic practices of medieval times! This begs the question: In what way is what we do to criminals today any different from what the courts did in the early twentieth century or even in the nineteenth century?

One answer may be that at least we abolished the death penalty. Far from it! Capital punishment is still practised in many countries in the world, including the most populated country (China) and the most powerful country (the U.S.A.). Executions by the dozens are carried out frequently in advanced countries like Russia, as well as in smaller developing countries like Saudi Arabia, Iran, Sudan, Egypt, etc. And as if legal executions are not enough, extrajudicial executions are carried out in those countries and in many others with abominable regularity as documented and reported by Amnesty International.

Others may say, well, we have succeeded in doing away with the horribly inhumane practice of torture. People are no longer being tortured to extract confessions or to force them to provide information. Surely the shocking pictures from Abu Ghraib prison in Iraq or from Guantanamo Bay in Cuba could not have been so easily and so quickly forgotten. Yes, torture, which was believed to be the trademark of the Inquisition, is back with vengeance. Its traumatic effects on the victims far exceed any effects caused by conventional crimes committed against individuals. And if any proof of this is needed, one needs only to look at Larry Siems' *The Torture Report* (2011).

Some years ago, Denmark took the initiative of establishing a centre for the treatment of torture victims. Maybe we should start promoting the creation of similar centres in other countries of the Western world, because the number of victims now is surely higher than at any time in recent memory.

So Is Restorative Justice a Viable Option?

Showing the ethical and moral problems of punishment, its futility, its limitations and shortcomings, its costs and inherent problems helps answer the question: Is restorative justice a viable option in crimes of violence? If punishment is a dismal failure, if it does not achieve any of its avowed goals, then any alternative cannot be worse than what we have now and will more likely be far better. Surely a justice paradigm that has reconciliation, healing, closure, redress and prevention as its primary goals is a huge progress over the punitive system that was inherited from canon law and has destroyed millions of people throughout the ages.

Are Victims Better Off in a Restorative System of Justice?

Most people either forget or are unaware that victims are the primary losers in punitive justice systems (see Part II above). From the time personal conflicts were converted into public crimes, and the institution of restitution and composition (known as *weregild*) was replaced by a punitive punishment, victims' interests were sacrificed and they were assigned a peripheral role in the criminal justice process. The new system completely ignored their plight and usurped their rights. The composition, or the "*weregild,*" that was meant as a means of redress, as a way of compensating them for the injury, the harm or the loss they have suffered, was replaced with a so-called penal fine that went to the king's coffers or to the public treasury. And for centuries the plight of victims went unnoticed, unrecognized and unremedied. Voices calling to address and redress victims' disenfranchisement were not heard until the second half of the twentieth century. Modest state compensation programs were set up in some countries but offered only symbolic recognition and continue to suffer from a chronic lack of funding and resources. Studies showed that only a very tiny minority of those victimized end up receiving any state compensation whatsoever. And for those who do, it is too little too late. (see Chapter III). Even worse, the studies found that those who go through the state compensation process were less satisfied than those who never applied for compensation in the first place. And as if to add insult to injury, the victim movement that was supposed to promote and defend the interests of victims, to claim their rights and to speak on their behalf, was moving in the wrong direction. Its main concern was to increase the severity of punishment and to raise the level of penal sanctions. Somehow victim advocates failed to realize that since funds and resources are strictly limited, increasing the costs of the expensive system of punishment, leaves less and less for victim compensation (Fattah, 1999).

Restorative Justice as a Means of Preventing Future Victimization

Conflict resolution and dispute settlement are probably the surest way to ensure that violence will not flare up again, that the emotions that fuel the aggression are held in check. If this is true, and I sincerely believe it is, then the best way to prevent future victimization are restorative justice practices. Unless and until reconciliation is achieved, the seeds of violence will always be there. The motives for violence will continue to simmer until they get an opportunity to express themselves in renewed acts of hostility and violence. Restorative justice aims at restoring the peace and harmony disrupted by the offence, at revitalizing the bonds and the ties that were ruptured by the criminal act. And contrary to the punitive/retributive justice system that feeds on vindictiveness, and the thirst for revenge, restorative justice promotes forgiveness, reconciliation and restitution. It gives the victim and offender a chance to meet face to face, to reach a mutual understanding of one another, to put the past behind them and to reach a fair and just agreement about the future. Restorative justice promotes closure and facilitates healing, and is thus beneficial to the coping process, to the psychological well-being and the satisfaction of the victim, precisely the goals that victim organizations and victim services want to achieve. Punitive justice, as Nils Christie (1977) pointed out, steals the conflicts from their rightful owners: the victim and the offender. It takes over and reduces the main protagonists to mere spectators in a process that is more theatre than reality, a process in which restorative justice officials wear strange robes and speak a language that is almost incomprehensive to those whose conflicts are being judged.

Contrary to the punitive justice system that keeps victims and victimizers apart and stops or hinders any meaningful communication between them, restorative justice brings them face to face and promotes meaningful communication between them, thus allowing the victims to find the answer to their most pressing question: Why me? Victims, who by themselves or with the help of others, are able to find the answer to this haunting question seem to suffer less and to cope better than those who believe, or are led to believe, that their victimization was an unjust blow in an unlucky destiny or that it was a freak act of a deranged, sick or abnormal individual.

Restorative justice gives victims the opportunity to identify predisposing, vulnerability and other victimogenic factors that might have invited, initiated, triggered, promoted or facilitated their victimization. This enhanced awareness and this new understanding of why they were victimized, of why they were selected as victims, help them regain control of their lives, enables them to shed the denigrating label of victim, the debilitating "mark of Abel" and allow them to put an end to the state of victimhood in which they inevitably found themselves as a result of the victimization (Fattah, 2000).

Is Punishment the Right Answer to Torture and Gross Human Rights Violations?

Is punishment the right answer to torture? Definitely not, because it never reaches those who are responsible, those untouchables at the top. Contrary to the popular rhetoric about the bad apples, torture in most cases is not the initiative of individuals. More often than not it is a government policy. How just and how fair is it to punish those who were obeying orders or following policies when those who are really responsible are left unpunished? This is to say that punishment is never an appropriate response. Although the futility of punishment has been a proven fact for centuries, the horrific acts of recent years have exposed one of the fundamental shortcomings of the punishment response. Obviously punishment is not, and cannot be, a deterrent for so-called terrorists or for suicide bombers. Their actions prove that when the motives are strong or overwhelming people will sacrifice anything, even their lives!

Furthermore, no punishment yet invented could be an appropriate or proportionate response to the horrendous acts of genocide that seem to have become commonplace in recent years: in Bosnia, in Rwanda, in Sudan, etc., etc. How can the punishment of a handful of carefully selected offenders be an adequate retribution for the extermination of hundreds of thousands of victims? And what exactly is being achieved by incarcerating those individuals for varying terms of imprisonment? Surely, in the cases of genocide, as in the case of terrorist actions, punishment is no deterrent. In those cases punishment is nothing more than a symbolic gesture and a hollow one at that.

This is one thing the black leaders of South Africa, like Nelson Mandela and Desmond Tutu, realized once the apartheid rule came to an end. They could have arrested hundreds or even thousands of those who were responsible for the atrocities against black people and subjected them to all kinds of punishment. But what purpose would this have achieved? A temporary and short-lasting satisfaction of the vindictive instincts of an oppressed population? Instead, they wisely chose the moral high ground. They were fully aware that what had been done could not be undone, and rather than retaliating against some of those responsible (they obviously could not punish everyone who was) they decided to show forgiveness and opted for reconciliation through the establishment of the

Truth and Reconciliation Commission. The healing effects of this conciliatory approach were truly remarkable and will remain in the annals of history as a bold and highly successful experiment. One only needs to imagine what would have happened to the country if the thousands and thousands of those responsible for the atrocities of the apartheid regime were executed or sent to prison!

Is Punishment the Answer to Terrorist Acts?

As many acts of violence and acts labelled as terrorism are rooted in injustices that are unacknowledged or denied, punishing the perpetrators is simply to double the injustice. It can only enhance the chances of further and more serious violence. On August 7, 2004 psychiatrist Jerrold Post, who interviewed many potential and unsuccessful suicide bombers, was quoted in *The Globe and Mail* (p. A6) as maintaining that suicide bombing is gaining new converts. Asked why this is happening, he responded with a single word: "despair." He said suicide bombers are people who see no other solution for the forces they see arrayed against them and no other way of avenging their families' losses.

> "I think one has to look to the despair that they are experiencing... These are not deviant, psychologically disturbed individuals. Everyone of them I have talked to has made perfect sense."

Dr. Post's explanation illustrates the sheer lunacy (or shall I say the hypocrisy) of reintroducing the death penalty in some countries (such as the interim government in Iraq), as if those who are willing to sacrifice their lives or who are facing death every minute of the day will be deterred by the prospect of a death sentence! Isn't this another example of how irrational the reaction can be when frustration with a certain behaviour has reached a high level?

If violence, if terrorism, is the act of people who are driven to it by hopelessness and despair, by their unheeded cries for justice, is it conceivable that punishment will deter such hopeless and desperate individuals? It is precisely in those cases, as in most others, that restorative justice, with its emphasis on mediation, reconciliation and reparation, proves to be a much more appropriate and much more effective response.

When examining the viability of restorative justice in the cases of violence, one has to keep in mind that gratuitous violence is extremely rare, it is the exception, not the rule, and so are unmotivated and unprovoked violent acts. Moreover, violence that is sexually or financially motivated constitutes only a small fraction of all acts of violence, just ten per cent of all violence, if criminologists are to be believed. The vast majority of acts of violence are retaliatory in nature. Study after study has shown that retaliation is a key ingredient in violence (Felson and Steadman, 1983). In fact there are reasons to believe that revenge is the most prevalent motive for the use of force (Black, 1983; Marongiu and Newman, 1987). Researchers affirm that violence in most instances is an expression of a grievance, a response to an attack, injury or provocation. As Black (1983) points out, violence is a mode of conflict management resembling the modes used in traditional societies, which have little or no formal law.

If we analyze the most serious form of violence, namely homicide, we find that it is rarely predatory in nature. Relatively few homicides are committed for financial gain or for sexual gratification. In the vast majority of cases the killing is a reaction (or rather overreaction) to some form of victimization. When aggression is met with aggression, when violence is countered with violence, the roles are simply reversed. The initial aggressor becomes the victim and the initial victim ends up being the victimizer. Labels are applied, not on the basis of the original roles, but on the final outcome. The violent response, though defined as crime by the law, is perfectly legitimate in the eyes of the perpetrator who perceives violent retaliation as an act of justice, as a rightful reprisal.

All this is to show that individuals defined and labelled as "criminal" are not fundamentally different from those considered to be law-abiding citizens. It shows that offender and victim populations are not mutually exclusive but are homogenous and overlapping (Fattah, 1994). By ignoring offenders' history of victimization, a false dichotomy between offenders and victims is made. And by ignoring the dynamics of violent behaviour and the rapidly changing nature of potentially violent situations, a predator-prey model is created. The model reinforces the popular dichotomy between the active aggressor and the passive sufferer, the guilty offender and the innocent victim, the evil Cains and the good Abels; the former deserve our condemnation and the latter our sympathy and commiseration (Fattah, 1994). So deeply entrenched is the belief in the predator-prey (the active doer, passive sufferer) model of criminal victimization that any attempt to introduce the characteristics or the behaviour of the victim as an explanatory variable is invariably greeted with a great deal of hostility and antagonism. The dynamic concepts of provocation and victim-precipitation are often singled out for particular criticism and summarily dismissed as irresponsible attempts to blame the victim!

Feasible?

Is a Non-Punitive Justice System Possible? A Scandinavian Example

The year 2019 marks the sixty-fifth anniversary of a remarkable achievement that never got the acclaim or the publicity it deserves! In 1954, a new criminal code, specifically drafted by Professor Verner Goldschmid for the former Danish colony, the large Arctic island of Greenland, was promulgated. Inspired by the old traditions of the people of Greenland, this unique criminal code is non-punishment-oriented, which sets it apart from other retribution-focused Western criminal codes, including that of Denmark itself. Here is how this unique code is described by one commentator (Schechter 1983:70):

> "...the unique Greenland Criminal Code attempts to graft traditional Inuit concepts of rehabilitation onto a Western, and specifically Danish, system of laws and procedures. The philosophy behind even the enlightened Danish penal system is punishment – a repressive means of social control whose object is forced conformity with society's norms. In contrast to this "conformity model," the object of Inuit customary law is neither punishment nor justice, but the elimination of conflict and the restoration of harmony – a philosophy dubbed the Arctic Peace Model."

One has to ask: Why is it that the example of the Greenland Criminal Code was not followed by others? Why is it that the philosophy that inspired it did not tempt those criminal law reformers who in the past half a century were busy modernizing the criminal codes of their countries? Why is it that the restorative/treatment practices incorporated in the Greenland Criminal Code were never adopted by other countries around the world? Is it the traditional obsession with punishment? Is it Western arrogance that does not allow us to admit that there are certain traditions and certain customs of so-called less "civilized" people that are superior to ours and may be beneficial to our societies? And yet any objective comparative analysis of the various responses to harmful actions and the different means of conflict resolution is bound to show that those people who were labelled by the missionaries as primitive, godless and uncivilized were superior to us in more than one respect. It is certainly to their credit that they used peaceful, non-violent and non-destructive modes of settling disputes and of solving interpersonal and community conflicts. It is to their credit that they were able to realize the futility of punishment, the fact that it does not serve any useful purpose. They were more than cognizant of the detrimental effects of responding to violence with violence, of taking a life for a life or an eye for an eye, and this was long before Gandhi uttered his now famous adage: "An eye for an eye would make the whole world blind"! Those labelled by the missionaries as "savages" realized early on how illogical and unproductive it was to respond to harm by inflicting more harm or to try to alleviate the pain and suffering of the victim by making the offender suffer.

Luckily enough, in Canada we are trying to get rid of our superiority complex and are coming to the realization that when it comes to justice there is a lot that to be learned from Canada's First Nations. As a result, Canada is gradually taking steps that are putting it in the forefront of restorative justice. One initiative has been the development of three Canadian courts for use by the First Nations people only (Lynette Parker, August 2004, online). The purpose of those courts is to bring healing and restoration to the community. Describing one of the three courts, Lynette Parker (2004) wrote:

> "The Tsuu T'ina Peacemaker Court began as a pilot project in 1999. It was developed by the chief and council of the Tsuu T'ina Nation with support from the Alberta provincial court. Its jurisdiction is as a provincial court restricted to reserve offences, and it uses traditional peacemaking methods alongside the normal provincial court process. The judge, prosecutor, court clerks, court worker and the probation officer are all of aboriginal descent. In addition, the court conducted a community consultation process to identify respected individuals for training and selection as peacemakers.
>
> "The court meets twice each month in the reserve's council chambers and begins with a traditional smudge ceremony. The crown council and peacemaker coordinator review all cases before the court to determine those that could be resolved through peacemaking. All adult and youth offences except homicide and sexual assault are eligible. In addition, the offender must take responsibility for his actions and the victim must agree to participate before the case will be referred to peacemaking.
>
> "Cases selected for peacemaking are adjourned and the peacemaker coordinator assigns a peacemaker seen as fair to all sides. Peacemaking is done through a circle process involving the victim and offender, family members of each and helpers or resource personnel (e.g. alcohol, addiction counsellors). Elders are also included in each circle to ensure that peacemaking is conducted properly."

Acceptable?

How Acceptable Is Restorative Justice to the Victim and the Victim's Family?

To my knowledge, there is no empirical evidence to support the claim that victims want revenge or that nothing other than the punishment of the offender will bring them closure or satisfy their thirst for justice. If anything, whatever evidence we currently have does show that victims are not as vindictive or as bloodthirsty as some victim groups would want us to believe (Boers & Sessar, 1991; Pfeiffer, 1993). Healing, recovery, redress and prevention are the foremost objectives of crime victims (Fattah, 1997:270).

Even victims of the most serious and most heinous crimes of violence are not as vengeful as they are usually portrayed in the media or in the manifestos of right-wing political parties. The powerful television documentary *From Fury to Forgiveness*, the experiences of M. Umbreit in the United States and Ivo Aertsen in Belgium, and the recent American television series *The Redemption Project* demonstrate in a vivid and deeply moving fashion that even victims who lose their young children or close relatives to homicidal killers can show genuine forgiveness and can plea with the justice system for the lives of their victimizers (Fattah, 1999:160).

How Acceptable Is Restorative Justice to the General Public?

It goes without saying that a system of restorative justice would have no chance whatsoever to succeed unless it is accepted by, and has the backing of, the general public. Public demands for punishment and the loud cries for vengeance reflect a woeful lack of understanding of the realities of crime and justice. The vast majority of people cannot imagine what would happen to society if every law violator, if every act of violence, if every sexual peccadillo and every property crime were punished by a prison sentence. Just how many citizens would be left out?

Criminologists, who have the responsibility to inform and educate the public about crime and justice, have not been very successful in this respect. As a result, the general public remains largely unaware that only a very small percentage of those who commit crime, even serious crime, end up being punished. Little do they know that the ones who end up in prison are but scapegoats sacrificed at the altar of general deterrence!

What most members of the general public do not realize, or fail to recognize, is that criminal behaviour, as mentioned earlier, is not a unique behaviour, and if it is not, then there is no valid reason to respond to it in a unique manner. Once this point is driven home, once the public is made aware that too many conflicts, too many serious law violations, too many acts of violence, are currently being dealt with outside of the criminal justice system and are not subjected to traditional sanctions, whatever objections or reservations they may have about a general system of restorative justice will gradually but surely disappear. There will still be the odd revolting case that will precipitate a cry for vengeance and will prompt calls for traditional punishments. But in the same way that the abolition of the death penalty has become accepted, and the calls for the execution of murderers have subsided, restorative practices will end up being accepted. And once their positive effects and their superiority over punishment have been amply demonstrated, public resistance to the new paradigm will eventually die down and the new system of justice will become widely accepted and supported. This support will be aided by the fact that restorative justice practices not only involve the community, but they also require the active participation of the members of that community.

What Are the Obstacles Delaying the Full Institutionalization of Restorative Justice?

If restorative justice is a better system, what are the obstacles delaying its implementation and full institutionalization?

Discussions of punishment with politicians, policy-makers, scholars, professionals or with ordinary citizens, more often than not, usually end up with an agreement that punishment is bad, but also with an almost inevitable question: Yes, punishment is bad, but what is the alternative? Underlying this seemingly resigned and helpless attitude that punishment is a necessary evil (or as they say in French, *un mal nécessaire*) is the mistaken belief that it is indispensable to the survival of society. Such a belief makes it difficult to convince members of the general public that there are actually better, less costly and more effective alternatives. The discussions, whether at a high scientific or scholarly level, or at a common-sense, conventional-wisdom level, invariably show that whatever support punishment may have is more out of despair than of any firm belief that it does or may have positive or salutary effects. That punishment has to follow any wrongdoing is a notion that is inculcated in the minds of children in their tender age: "If you commit sin you will go to hell; if you misbehave you will be caned; if you hit your sister you will be spanked; if you break the law you will go to prison." Later on it becomes really hard to break this strong association between crime and punishment. It becomes almost impossible, particularly for the average citizen, to conceive of a non-punitive society, a society without prisons, a community that does NOT respond to harmful actions by the infliction of pain and suffering. Advocating and gaining acceptance for an alternative, non-punitive justice paradigm becomes extremely difficult because the theological notion of a punishment that must follow the fault, the wrongdoing, is too deeply anchored in the minds of most individuals (Fattah, 1999:162).

In fact the idea of doing away with punishment altogether is not even acceptable to most criminologists, many of whom are becoming increasingly punitive, because of a mistaken belief that by so doing they will be taking the side of crime victims. Contrary to this negative view, Kay Harris (1991:94) in her presentation of a feminist vision of justice, questions this seemingly unshakable faith in the need for punishment. She writes:

> "Indeed, we need to question and rethink the entire bases of the punishment system. Virtually all discussion of change begins and ends with the premise that punishment must take place. All of the existing institutions and structures – the criminal law, the criminal processing system, the prisons – are assumed. We allow ourselves only to entertain debates about rearrangements and reallocations within those powerfully constraining givens... The sterility of the debates and the disturbing ways they are played out in practice underscore the need to explore alternative visions. We need to step back to reconsider whether or not we should punish, not just to argue about how to punish."

What is rather surprising is that this uncritical adherence to the archaic institution of punishment remains widespread despite rapid and rather fundamental social evolution. The secularization of society, the liberalization of attitudes towards human misbehaviour, the pursuit of cost-effective social policies and practices, have rendered the metaphysical notion of retribution and the theological concepts of expiation and atonement anachronistic and anathematic to contemporary thinking.

And yet punishment persists and thrives, even in the Scandinavian countries that were, together with Holland, the first to try to do away with it. With the notions of vengeance and retaliation becoming slowly but surely dated and obsolete and having been judged primitive and uncivilized, advocates of punishment are having no choice but to cling to the utilitarian yet unproven argument of deterrence. Yes, study after study has shown that this blind faith in punishment as a deterrent is both unwarranted and unfounded (Fattah, 1976). And even if one ignores the vast volume of scientific research and tries to counter the common-sense argument of deterrence by appealing only to logic and reason, the same conclusion will have to be reached. The practice of punishment suffers from an incorrigible paradox: where punishment may be effective (such as in cases of white-collar crime or other well-calculated rational offences) it is not wanted, and where it is wanted, such as in crimes of violence, acts of terrorism, sexual offences and the like, it is unlikely to have any deterrent effect.

To this it should be added that punishment has tremendous human, social and financial costs. And this is precisely why it is imperative to ask what exactly is being achieved by such a cruel, inhuman and archaic practice. If the ultimate goal of social reaction to harmful actions is the prevention of future harm and the repetition of the violence, then the preventive effects of punishment must be carefully scrutinized and critically analyzed.

Could Restorative Justice and Punitive Justice Co-Exist?

Fearing that replacing the current punitive system entirely with a new restorative one may be a utopian dream, many proponents of restorative justice have resigned themselves to the idea that it is possible to have two parallel systems, operating side by side or at a minimum having a restorative justice component operating within and under the aegis of a dominantly punitive system. In my humble opinion, such vision of a dual system is faulty and misguided. I do believe that since punishment and healing are mutually exclusive, such a double philosophy and dual objective systems can never work in practice. I am utterly convinced that nothing less than a fundamental paradigm change can remedy the deep-seated problems of our current justice system. As a veteran criminologist, I have keenly observed for more than half a century every attempt made to reform the criminal justice system, to correct its shortcomings, to remedy its failings, to lower its costs, to reduce its clientele. To my utter disappointment NOTHING worked! The punitive philosophy that permeates the system defeats any and every attempt at reform. How many alternatives to incarceration were introduced over the decades and hailed as the answer to the overuse of imprisonment and the overcrowding of prisons? Nothing helped! All they did was to widen the net of social control. And many so-called alternatives, such as community service orders, even probation, are being widely used as additives to incarceration instead of being alternatives to prison! Unless there is a radical change in philosophy, unless there is a paradigm shift, all the talk about restorative justice will be in vain. Any attempt to introduce the concepts, the principles and the practices of restorative justice within a primarily punitive system is inevitably bound to fail.

So, does restorative justice have a future?

References

Barnes, H.E. (1972). *The Story of Punishment: A Record of Man's Inhumanity to Man* (second edition revised). Montclair, NJ: Patterson Smith.

Christie, N. (1977). "Conflicts as Property." *British Journal of Criminology*, I. 17(1):1-19.

Christie, N. (1982). *Limits to Pain.* Oxford: Martin Robertson.

Black, D. (1983). "Crime as Social Control." *American Sociological Review,* 48:34-45.

Boers, K. and Sessar, K. (1991). "Do people really want punishment? On the relationship between acceptance of restitution, needs for punishment and fear of crime." In K. Sessar and H.J. Kerner (eds.) *Developments in Crime and Crime Control Research,* 126-49. New York: Springer Verlag.

Fattah, E.A. (1976). *Deterrence: A Review of the Literature.* Published by the Law Reform Commission of Canada under the title *Fear of Punishment,* 119 pages.

Fattah, E.A. (1988). *On Victims, Parole and the Sentencing Commission.* Brief submitted to the House of Commons Standing Committee on Justice and Solicitor General, March, 1988.

Fattah, E.A. (1992). "Beyond Metaphysics: The Need for a New Paradigm – On Actual and Potential Contributions of Criminology and the Social Sciences to the Reform of the Criminal Law." In R. Lahti and K. Nuotio (eds.) *Criminal Law Theory in Transition.* Helsinki: Finnish Lawyers Publishing Company.

Fattah, E.A. (1993). "From a Guilt Orientation to a Consequence Orientation: A Proposed New Paradigm for the Criminal Law in the 21st Century." In J. Welp and W. Küper (eds.) *Beiträge zur Rechtswissenschaft.* Heidelberg: C.F. Muller Juristischer Verlag.

Fattah, E.A. (1994). *The Interchangeable Roles of Victim and Victimizer* (Second Inkeri Anttila's Honour Lecture). Helsinki, Finland: Heuni. 26 pages.

Fattah, E.A. (1995). "Restorative and Retributive Justice Models: A Comparison." In H-H. Kühne (ed.) *Festschrift für Koichi Miyazawa.* Baden-Baden: Nomos Verlagsgesellschaft. Reprinted in E.A. Fattah and T. Peters (eds) *Support for Crime Victims in a Comparative Perspective* (1998). Leuven, Belgium: Leuven University Press.

Fattah, E.A. (1997). *Criminology: Past, Present and Future – A Critical Overview.* London: Macmillan; New York: St. Martin's Press.

Fattah, E.A. (1997). "Some Reflections on the Paradigm of Restorative Justice and Its Viability for Juvenile Justice." In L. Walgrave (ed.) *Restorative Justice for Juveniles: Potentialities, Risks and Problems for Research.* Leuven: Leuven University Press.

Fattah, E.A. (1999). "From a Handful of Dollars to Tea and Sympathy: The Sad History of Victim Assistance." In J.J.M. van Dijk, Ron G.H. van Kaam and Jo-Anne Wemmers (eds.) *Caring for Crime Victims: Selected Proceedings of the 9th International Symposium on Victimology.* Monsey, NY: Criminal Justice Press.

Fattah, E.A. (1999). "Victim Redress and Victim-Offender Reconciliation in Theory and Practice: Some Personal Reflections."" *Hokkaigakuen Law Journal,* 35(1):155-82.

Fattah. E.A. (2000). "How Valid Are the Arguments Frequently Made Against Mediation and Restorative Justice?" In Hedda Giertsen (ed.) *Albanian and Norwegian Experiences with Mediation in Conflict.* Oslo: Institute of Criminology.

Fattah, E.A. (2001). "Preventing Repeat Victimization as the Ultimate Goal of Victim Services." *International Annals of Criminology,* volume 38:113-33.

Fattah E.A. (2002). "From Philosophical Abstraction to Restorative Action. From Senseless Retribution to Meaningful Restitution. Just Desert and Restorative Justice Revisited."

In H.J. Kerner and E. Weitekamp (eds.) *Restorative Justice: Theoretical Foundations.* Devon, UK: Willan Publishing, Culmcott House, pp.308-21.

Fattah, E.A. (forthcoming). *The Monstrous Side of Human Nature: A Chronicle of Man's Inhumanity to Fellow Humans.*

Felson, H.J. and Steadman, H.J. (1983)."Situational Factors in Disputes Leading to Criminal Violence." *Criminology,* 21 (1), pp. 59-74.

Ingersoll, R.G. (1906). *Crimes Against Criminals.* New York: Elbert Hubbard.

Lahti, R. (1990)."Recodifying the Finnish Criminal Code of 1889. A Scandinavian Way to Make the Criminal Law More Efficient, Just and Humane." In R. Lahti and K. Nuotio (eds.) *Towards a Total Reform of Finnish Criminal Law.* Helsinki: University of Helsinki.

Marongiu, P. and Newman, G. (1987). *Vengeance: The Fight Against Injustice.* Totowa, NJ: Rowman and Littlefield.

Parker, L. (2004)."Tsuu T'ina Peacemaking Justice in Canada." *Restorative Justice Online,* August 2004 edition.

Pfeiffer, C. (1993). *Opferperspektiven: Wiedergutmachung und Strafe aus der Sicht der Bevolkerung.* Manuscript, 22 pages.

Post, J. (2004). Interview in *The Globe and Mail,* August 7, 2004 (A6).

Schechter, E. (1983)."The Greenland Criminal Code and the Limits of Legal Pluralism." *Études Inuit Studies,* vol. 7, no. 2, 79-94.

Shaw, G.B. (1946). *The Crime of Imprisonment.* New York: The Philosophical Library.

Woodfox, A. (2019). *Solitary.* New York: HarperCollins Publishers.

Wilkins, L.T. (1964). *Social Deviance.* London: Tavistock Publications.

Wootton, B. (1963). *Crime and the Criminal Law: Reflections of a Magistrate and Social Scientist.* London: Stevens and Sons.

Epilogue
Does Restorative Justice Have *a* Future?

THIS EPILOGUE WILL be used as a vehicle to summarize the main points made throughout this book and to highlight and emphasize some of the most important and salient features of the restorative justice paradigm. Hopefully, it will succeed in providing the reader with a reasonable, believable and acceptable answer to the question: Does restorative justice have a future?

This is undoubtedly a complex and bold question, especially for someone like me who does not have a crystal ball. To try to provide a credible non-speculative answer to this rather challenging question, I will use a combination of history and logic. The lessons of history are among the most useful tools when thinking about and trying to predict the future. Logic, on the other hand, helps us understand where things may be going and why they are moving in this or that direction.

A series of interrogations will hopefully show whether the current punitive criminal law is achieving its primary goals, whether it is in tune with the geist of the times, whether it is compatible with the norms, values, attitudes, realities of post-industrial society, whether the underlying paradigm has become obsolete and thus there is an urgent need for a new paradigm. Hopefully, interrogations will also show whether our present criminal justice system is successful and sustainable or whether it is failing to achieve its fundamental objectives of deterrence and prevention.

Underlying my predictive endeavour is the assumption, which hopefully is true, that human beings are rational beings who will ultimately let their best social and economic interests prevail over their emotional feelings, their traditional beliefs and their instinctive responses.

How and Why Did Criminal Law Emerge as a Distinct Type of Law?

To understand society's response to crime, we need to trace the origins of criminal law and to explore how it emerged as a distinctive type of law. The origins of criminal law can be easily traced to the attempts by the kings and the feudal lords to consolidate their authority, to enhance their powers and to generate revenue for themselves and their estates by imposing fines and by seizing the lands and property of convicted persons. Here is how the process is described by the Law Reform Commission of Canada (1974:8-9 / *Working Papers 5 & 6*):

> "In Anglo-Saxon England there was no criminal law as we know it. Disputes were dealt with by a process greatly resembling our civil law. When an individual felt that he had suffered damage because of another's wrongful conduct, he was permitted either to settle the matter by agreement or proceed before a tribunal. Restitution was the order of the day and other sanctions , including imprisonment, were rarely used.
>
> "As the common law developed, criminal law became a distinct branch of law. Numerous antisocial acts were seen to be 'offences against the state' or 'crimes' rather than personal wrongs or torts. This tendency to characterize some wrongs as 'crimes' was encouraged by the practice under which the lands and property of convicted persons were forfeited to the king or feudal lord; fines, as well, became payable to feudal lords and not to the victim. The natural practice of compensating the victim or his relatives was discouraged by making it an offence to conceal the commission of a felony or to convert the crime into a source of profit. In time, fines and property that would have gone in satisfaction of the victim's claims were diverted to the state. 'Compounding an offence' (that is, accepting an economic benefit in satisfaction of the wrong done without the consent of the court or in a manner that is contrary to the public interest) still remains a crime under the Canadian Criminal Code and discourages private settlement or restitution (sec. 141:1).
>
> "It would now seem that historical developments, however well-intentioned, effectively removed the victim from sentencing policy and obscured the view that crime was social conflict," (pp. 8-9).

This is precisely what Nils Christie meant when explaining in his seminal article *Conflicts as Property* how the conflicts were stolen by the state from their legitimate and rightful owners, the parties involved.

Christie (1977) lamented the fact that victims who used to be entitled to *weregild*/restitution were now left with nothing. Civil remedies were not only too costly and too complicated for most victims, but the majority of offenders were destitute and once they were imprisoned the victim's chances of any compensation were nil. And to add insult to injury when offenders were sentenced to a penal fine it went not to the victim but to the state's coffers.

Answer: an analysis of the emergence and the historical evolution of criminal law clearly indicates that it happened for political and financial reasons rather than a specific need for such type of law.

Is Crime a Unique Type of Behaviour? Is Crime Qualitatively Different from Tort?

The emergence of criminal law as a distinctive branch of law, dispensing sanctions of different kind than civil remedies, suggests that acts and behaviours subjected to those punishments are unique and have their own particular characteristics that justify them being defined as crimes. This begs a series of questions: Is crime a unique type of behaviour? Is crime qualitatively different from tort? Is the distinction between the two based on sound criteria?

Parker (1977:28) affirms that the differentiation between crimes and torts is of relatively recent origin:

> "At this stage of legal development there was no differentiation between what we know as crime or criminal law and tort or civil liability for damage inflicted. All injuries to persons or property were considered as 'wrongs.' The seriousness of the wrong depended upon the disruption caused to the community or the actual or perceived affront to the injured parties. Slowly a distinction emerged between wrongs which were private disputes and required payment to the injured party or his kin and wrongs which had a public quality and required compensation to the whole group."

Any objective analysis and comparison of crimes and torts/civil wrongs is bound to lead to the conclusion that the distinction between the two is both artificial and arbitrary and that the demarcation line separating them is blurred. As Morris and Hawkins (1969:46) point out, very frequently the same act is both a crime and a tort. They add that a large part of criminal behaviour is perfectly "normal," both in the statistical sense and in the sense that it occurs naturally. Howard Becker (1963:9) insists that deviance is not a quality of an act the person commits but rather a consequence of the application of others of rules and sanctions to an offender.

All this is to show that a comparison of acts made illegal by the criminal code or by statutes with similar behaviours that are unregulated by criminal law suggests that there is no qualitative difference between criminal and non-criminal behaviour. This reality indicates that the rationale, the *raison d'etre* of having a criminal law and a criminal justice system with its own arsenal of sanctions is neither logical nor rationally justified.

Answer: It seems an undisputable fact that acts and behaviour defined as crime by the criminal code are not unique, that there is no qualitative difference, for example, between crime and tort, hence there is no logical rationale for having a distinct criminal code or criminal justice system that dispense a different type of sanctions.

Are the Classical Concepts/Notions of Retributive Justice Obsolete?

The Canadian Criminal Code (enacted in 1892), as well as many others dating back to the nineteenth century, is an historical document that mirrors the mentality of the era in which it was promulgated. Most of these documents have undergone some piecemeal changes, but they have neither been overhauled nor replaced by new modern ones that are in tune with the times that we live in, in the twenty-first century. Criminal law is surely the branch of law that seems most resistant to modernization and change!

No century has witnessed more scientific and technological advances, more political changes or more social upheavals than the twentieth century. Unfortunately, the criminal code has not kept pace with social and scientific evolution and remains in most countries as a relic from the past, as a vestige from a bygone era. I certainly find it surprising that in this age of science and technology in which we live we continue to have and to accept a criminal law and a criminal justice system based upon concepts, principles, premises and paradigms dating from the Age of Reason, the Age of Enlightenment.

Isn't it rather surprising that we do not seem to find anything wrong in having an archaic and antiquated criminal justice system that tries hard to dispense justice, not according to earthly criteria, but according to divine criteria? That all the fundamental principles, all the basic notions of the criminal law today have been borrowed from the theology and philosophy of the eighteenth and nineteenth centuries is simply hard to believe – notions such as evil, wickedness, malice, guilt, culpability, retribution, expiation, atonement, redemption, to name but a few. Is it not about time to ask whether metaphysical notions such as "free will," moral responsibility, criminal intent, *mens rea*, premeditation, malice aforethought, as well as many others, do have a place in a modern, secular criminal law? It seems to me that the time has come to ask whether abstract concepts such as those listed above, as well as several others, do have a place in a modern, secular, socially-oriented criminal law that caters to the realities of the twenty-first century. Shouldn't it be time in this age of technology to ask whether legal concepts such as insanity, diminished responsibility, etc. could withstand the test of science? Shouldn't we be asking whether notions such as retribution, punishment, just deserts, redemption are fitting concepts in an evidence-based and secular criminal policy?

Answer: the ever-growing secularization of society has rendered the theological concepts and the religious dictates of the Enlightenment anachronistic and largely obsolete. They are no longer adequate nor compatible with the new realities of the highly technological society of the twenty-first century. There is therefore an urgent need for Western nations to rethink, reassess and modernize the archaic and antiquated criminal codes they have in place to bring them to the standards of the Space Age and to make them capable of meeting the challenges of today's technological urbanized society.

Is There a Need for a Paradigm Shift?

Criminal codes promulgated in the post-French-Revolution eras have become exceedingly inadequate to deal with rapidly changing social realities. Technological discoveries of the Industrial Revolution brought about a rapid urbanization, increased mobilization, mounting communications, etc. Early on it became abundantly clear that strict adherence to philosophical and abstract notions, such as "*mens rea,*" "free will," "moral responsibility," make it impossible to effectively control, sanction and curb a wide variety of socially harmful and dangerous behaviours. These include criminality of negligence, the vast majority of traffic offences, white-collar crime, corporate deviance, crimes against the environment, status offences, offences committed under the influence of alcohol or drugs, and lately we may add cybercrime. Legalists, particularly criminalists, were forced to do some mental acrobatics in order to come up with acceptable deviations, exceptions and exemptions from the metaphysical, yet fundamental, principles of "*mens rea*" and "free will."

As it was necessary in the nineteenth century to come up with legal presumptions and subterfuges that are outright contradictory to the Classical notions of "criminal intent" and "moral responsibility" (such as *dolus eventualis,* irresistible impulse, ignorance of the law is no excuse, etc.), contemporary legal scholars had to invent concepts such as technical guilt, strict liability, absolute liability, vicarious liability, corporate liability, preventive detention, etc. to make it possible to charge, convict and punish those who are responsible for these harmful, injurious and dangerous behaviours.

Most people do not realize the extent of offences to which these new types of criminal responsibilty apply. Already in 1963 Wooton stated that the majority of cases dealt with by the criminal courts in England are cases of strict liability in which proof of a guilty mind is not necessary for conviction. A decade later, the Law Reform Commission of Canada (1974) reported that Canadian federal laws contain about 20,000 regulatory offences, and the laws of the average province another 20,000, and of the combined total ninety per cent (90%) are offences of strict liability. The situation is the same in other Western societies as was shown by Greve (1990).

The problems created by the obsolete notions of *mens rea,* moral guilt and moral responsibility dictated that they be abandoned in a large number of cases in favour of other concepts such as strict liability. But this is not the only problem with a retributive/punitive criminal law that desperately, yet unsuccessfully, tries to find a punishment that fits the crime! Another major failing is the criminal law's inability to curb crime or to deal with the plight of crime victims. This is because our current criminal law is geared towards punishment, not prevention, and reflects a naive and exaggerated faith in the common-sense assumption that punishment deters. Additionally, the punitive/ retributive nature of current criminal law sadly means that crime victims are left without any redress, without adequate financial remedy to the harm, loss or injury they have suffered.

All this has created a host of empirical problems that can only be dealt with effectively through a paradigm shift.

- Research findings supporting the ever-growing scepticism about the deterrent effect of punishment.
- Disillusionment with the medical model and growing scepticism about the efficacy of treatment and rehabilitation programs.
- Enhanced awareness of the pressing need to secularize and sociologize the criminal law and to bring it up to the scientific standards of the Computer Age and Space Age.
- Growing realization and concern about a wide variety of extremely harmful actions that cannot be dealt with effectively through adherence to the philosophical and abstract notions of *mens rea,* moral guilt and moral responsibility.
- Realization that certain behaviours associated with or using modern technologies can cause such extensive and irreparable harm and damage (nuclear disasters, oil spills, to name a few) that no penalty, not even the death penalty, can be made to fit the crime. Meting out the same punishment to someone who is responsible for the death of one individual and another who is responsible for the death of say half a million shakes the foundations of retributive justice and highlights once again the absolute impossibility of making the punishment fit the crime.
- Growing concern about the plight of crime victims and enhanced awareness of the historical injustice done to them when they were unfairly deprived of the compensation to which they were entitled.

Is There a Need for a Modern Criminal Policy?

Present criminal policy, based as it is on punishment as a means of retribution and as an instrument of deterrence, has been a dismal failure. Despite this it has been pushed to its absolute limits. In both traditionally repressive countries such as the U.K. and the U.S.A. as well as in tolerant societies such as Holland, Denmark, etc. the prison population has grown, sometimes to historical levels. Despite this increasingly punitive response, none of the salutary results promised by right-wing politicians who supported and implemented such oppressive and regressive policies has materialized. The manifest bankruptcy of these punitive and highly expensive (financially and socially) policies can no longer be denied or ignored. Right-wing political slogans such as "war on crime" despite being popular with an exasperated public proved to be hollow. Modest initiatives to help crime victims either through compensation or victim-impact statements proved to be nothing more than political placebos or mere palliatives. All this clearly suggests that there is a major policy problem on the hands of those in power, a problem to which a new paradigm can offer a solution.

Enumerating the theoretical, the legal, the practical problems of current criminal policy, its deficiencies and its inconsistencies would require a whole volume! What follows is simply a handful of the most obvious ones:

- Extremely high non-reporting rates shown by victimization surveys indicating that a high percentage, sometimes a majority, of cases are handled outside the official criminal justice system.
- Ridiculously low clearance rates and the usual attrition in the criminal justice process mean that only a tiny minority of those who commit crime face charges before the courts and even a smaller minority end up being punished. Estimates range between five per cent and ten per cent, depending on the offence!
- As a result of the widespread practice of plea bargaining (common in Anglo-Saxon countries) most of those who are punished are punished for offences other than the ones they have committed or are offered a lenient sentence in exchange of a guilty plea.
- A criminal law system that uses the "ability to distinguish right from wrong" as a prerequisite for being held criminally responsible must rely on psychiatric evidence and has to rely on forensic psychiatrists to play an important role in the justice process. It is the psychiatrist who supposedly enlightens the court on issues such as: insanity, partial or diminished responsibility, mental disorder, psychiatric disability, dangerousness and so forth. And yet psychiatry is, in fact, one of the least developed branches of medicine. This explains, in part, the frequency of conflicting psychiatric testimonies. The distinguished Australian psychiatrist Bartholomew (1986) had this to say about psychiatric evidence:

> "Psychiatrists are unreliable in diagnosis, uncertain as to how to treat those conditions diagnosed and often unable to measure any change that the treatment prescribed may have produced. Finally, they more often than not are unable to make worthwhile predictions."

Answer: hopefully the above succinct summary of the woes of present criminal law and the theoretical and practical problems of current criminal policy has provided the needed answers to the two questions posed. Hopefully, it has shown that the current paradigm underlying the criminal law is antiquated and obsolete and in need of urgent modernization and change. Hopefully, it has also shown that the current criminal policy is not only archaic, ineffective, costly but also incompatible with the social realities of the twenty-first century.

What Justice Paradigm Would Be Appropriate for Present Times?

The deficiencies, the shortcomings, the inadequacies of the current paradigm and the inefficiencies and failures of the present criminal justice system should by themselves indicate the major elements of an alternative paradigm to replace the obsolete one that has governed criminal justice for centuries.

Were I to be consulted or asked to propose a replacement paradigm, here are the seven major elements I would suggest as the basic foundations for the new one. As the following brief explanation will show, it is rather misleading to describe the proposed paradigm as a NEW one since most of those elements are by no means new and can be traced to how "justice" has been practised in non-industrial, non-urbanized societies, societies that were not influenced by the abstract, theological, moral, philosophical notions of the dominating religions in Western societies. The proposed paradigm is neither a novel invention nor a radical, revolutionary innovation. It is historically and sociologically inspired. It is meant to adapt justice practices of societies that are as close to nature as possible to the complex realities of modern societies. It is based on the indisputable fact that the roots of human behaviour have not changed. While society itself has undergone radical and fundamental changes over the centuries, the instincts, the needs, the impulses, the urges that motivate human behaviour remain basically the same. The differences between what we observe in those simple societies and what we see in our own are the variations in the means of shaping, controlling, modifying and preventing undesirable behaviours, the list of which enormously varies according to culture and over time. What is subject to historical and cultural evolution are not the behaviours themselves but society's attitudes, definitions of and response to those behaviours.

What follows is a brief description of the seven pillars of the proposed alternative justice paradigm.

From a Guilt Orientation to a Consequence Orientation

As already mentioned, the vast majority of cases dealt with by the criminal courts are offences of strict liability, of negligence, of omission and the like. Why did this come about and why was it necessary to abandon, on such a large scale, the traditional and deeply anchored notions of criminal intent, moral guilt and moral responsibility? The obvious answer is that the social consequences of these behaviours were judged to be more important than the philosophical and religious considerations that required that wickedness, malice, evil intent, be a prerequisite for criminal punishment. The pressing need to regulate those behaviours, because of their actual and potential social harm, overrode the requirement of moral guilt. The growing complexity of society and its ever-growing technologization led to ever declining emphasis on *mens rea* and to a growing emphasis being placed on the consequences of the behaviours. It goes without saying that this tendency was more pronounced in certain sectors of life than in others.

That harm is slowly becoming the primary criterion for criminalization can be seen in the report of the Finnish Criminal Law Committee, quoted by Lahti (1975). The first task the committee performed was to try to locate those forms of behaviour that appear to be most harmful when judged in the light of specific goals of each sphere in life. The notion of harm was the yardstick the committee used in order to judge whether a given behaviour should or should not be criminalized.

A good example of current practice where consequence takes precedence over guilt in determining punishment is that of attempted crime which is punished less severely than completed crime. The same criminal intent (*mens rea*) is present whether the crime is completed or remained at the stage of attempt due to factors external to the offender's will. The lesser punishment is therefore due not to a lesser guilt but to a lesser seriousness of consequences.

As criterion for criminalization, the notion of harm is in perfect harmony with the generally accepted goals of modern criminal law, namely to prevent the occurrence of socially harmful, socially injurious actions. It is only logical, therefore, that the eligibility of any given behaviour for inclusion in the criminal code (as well as the seriousness assigned to various actions) be judged according to their actual and potential harm, not according to the degree of wickedness or malice of the perpetrator. To use as a criterion consequence instead of guilt and harm instead of intent is the best way of correcting the fundamental empirical error of current criminal law, namely the futile attempt to quantify the unquantifiable (degrees of moral responsibility) and to measure the unmeasurable (the degree of freedom of the will, the degree of moral guilt, etc.).

A Switch from Moral Responsibility to Social Responsibility

According to Parker (1977), contemporary criminal law is based on the concept of blameworthiness, which has its foundations in the Judeo-Christian ethic and the notion of free will. I find it surprising that although malicious intent at present applies only to a small minority of the workload of criminal courts, there has been no attempt in recent years to discard it and replace it with a new concept that is compatible with behavioural science research and with another notion that is more in tune with the times. There are, I believe, two compelling reasons that call for abandoning moral responsibility as the fundamental concept of criminal law: one is scientific, the other is practical:

a) moral responsibility is based on the notion of free will which is incompatible with science as it is the negation of causality.

b) moral responsibility has been a major hurdle in the way of dealing effectively with a large number of socially harmful and injurious behaviours. This ultimately led to its rejection in various sectors (such as traffic offences, white-collar crime, etc.) where it was replaced by other types of liability.

The fact that we live in society, that we share the physical environment with others, places several restrictions on our freedom to act and dictates that we respect and obey certain rules of conduct and standards of behaviour. It is our social responsibility to refrain from causing harm or injury to others, to society and to the global environment, either willfully, by recklessness or by negligence, whether by commission or by omission. It is also our social responsibility not to infringe upon the rights of other members of society.

A Move from Legal Fiction to Social Reality

As suggested earlier, the criminal law seems to be the branch of law that is most resistant to change and modernization. No wonder that the metaphysical and philosophical notions underlying current criminal law are far removed from social reality. Many, including the fundamental notion of free will, are philosophical abstractions that are not susceptible to any scientific or empirical validation, let alone measurement. The fact that most of the criminal codes today were enacted in the nineteenth century means that they were neither inspired nor influenced by social and behavioural science. The result is a hiatus between the criminal law and the disciplines of psychology, sociology, criminology and victimology. The anachronism of the principles, concepts and notions according to which the criminal law operates and their incompatibility with the realities of modern society necessitated the invention of many legal assumptions and presumptions. As a result, the criminal law today is governed by what may be rightly described as "legal fiction." Most of this legal fiction is dictated by the need to find some acceptable rational justification for the infliction of or the exemption from punishment.

Many of the theoretical distinctions that were invented over the decades to deal with scientific findings are indicative of the quagmire of present criminal law. And yet in many cases the destiny of the accused depends solely on these hair-splitting decisions, because the distinction often means the difference between conviction and acquittal, and in some cases between life and death! The list is much too long but here are just a few examples of those legal distinctions: distinction between general intent and specific intent; constructive intention and real intention; voluntary acts, involuntary acts and not voluntary acts; purpose, intent and desired result; loss of control, automatism; insane automatism and non-insane automatism; psychiatric disability and diminished responsibility; mental disorder and psychopathic (character) disorder; guilty and sane, guilty but insane, and not guilty by reason of insanity; and fully responsible, partially responsible, not at all responsible.

The new paradigm puts an end to all the practical (and theoretical) problems created by arbitrary, artificial and rather meaningless legal distinctions. Replacing the notion of guilt by the notion of harm, replacing moral responsibility by social responsibility, will remove any need for legal fiction.

A Switch from Penal Repression to Administrative Regulation

The criminal law has traditionally served a repressive function. In addition to its use as an instrument of power, its theological and philosophical origins led to its use as a means of enforcing religious commands and moral standards. As Norval Morris (1973) pointed out, by tradition, America (and the same is true for most Western societies) has relied on the criminal code not only to protect persons and property but also to lead men away from vice and sin, including those vices and sins that injure only the sinner. Morris reports that half of all arrests in the U.S.A. are for crimes without direct victims, crimes which bring no complainant to the station house, no call to the police switchboard. The fact that everything deviant has been criminalized is equally deplored by Anttila (1984).

The lucid arguments made by Jerome Hall (1982) for excluding negligence from penal liability and for narrowing punishable guilt to "voluntary harm-doing" are equally valid for excluding acts that are considered "strict liability offences." And if morality offences, negligent offences and strict liability offences are excluded and removed, what then remains of the criminal law as we know it today?

There is hardly any doubt that the trend towards legalization, decriminalization and depenalization will become more pronounced with every passing decade. And once the paradigm shift has materialized the move will be from repression to regulation. Almost half a century ago, Norval Morris (1973) proposed that we substitute for our present prohibitions strategies diverse strategies of prohibition, regulation and legalization. He predicted that the "criminal" law of the future will be predominantly an administrative law, reserving punishment only for a persistent flouting of regulatory controls.

A Move from Reliance on Deterrence and the Threat of Punishment to Active Social Prevention

Despite overwhelming empirical evidence accumulated over several decades, present criminal legislation continues to be based on a common-sense assumption that punishment deters as well as on an exaggerated faith in the criminal law's ability to influence people's behaviour. Surprisingly, this uncritical reliance on punishment as a powerful deterrent remains the cornerstone of our crime policy despite the lack of empirical support. As a result, our approach to crime prevention is a totally passive one, as if the mere existence of penalties is sufficient by itself to steer people away from committing crime. It is essentially the same conviction as the theological belief that fear of hell will prevent people from committing sin!

But contrary to popular belief and common-sense wisdom, punishment and prevention do not go hand in hand. They are two alternative strategies. Placing the emphasis on punishment detracts from the need for active social prevention. And because too much money is being spent on punishment, there is very little available for effective evidence-based prevention. But since it is much easier to punish than prevent, politicians and the general public have always opted for the former over the latter. For politicians, punishment is an easy alibi because it gives the impression that something is being done about acts that are a source of fear and anxiety to the public. And when years later it becomes evident that the problem has not been solved or has become worse, the typical response is to increase the punishment.

The overconfidence in the intimidating effect of punishment is both misguided and misplaced. It is misguided because there is ample empirical evidence attesting to the severe limitations of deterrence policy. It is misplaced because it puts the stick ahead of, and above, the carrot.

Criminological research has shown that crime rates are closely linked to the available opportunities and are not the least influenced by variations or fluctuations in punishment. All this suggests that abandoning punishment would likely lead to greater emphasis on social prevention. It should also be noted that the efficacy of punishment as a deterrent for negligent, careless or inadvertent actions has been the object of great scepticism.

A Switch from Intimidation to Mediation, from Segregation to Reconciliation

Christie (1977) has observed that the key element in a criminal proceeding is that the proceeding has been converted from something between the concrete parties into a conflict between one of the parties and the state. In this scenario, the victim is a double loser, first *vis-à-vis* the offender, and often in a more crippling manner by being denied the right to full participation in what might have been one of the more important ritual encounters in life. The victim has lost the case to the state.

The criminal law which does not cease to broaden its mandate and extend its boundaries has declared a monopoly on every conflict or dispute falling under its jurisdiction. And yet private dispute settlement and conflict resolution through mediators and third parties have several advantages over criminal court proceedings which simply end in the punishment of the offender.

Since criminal law is centred upon punishment and retribution and because of its avidity to extract revenue from the wrongdoers (in the form of fines), it naturally shuns any initiative for settling disputes, especially when it is done outside the system. As a result the criminal justice system has missed a golden opportunity to reduce its caseload and to stop the repetition of certain offences through the reconciliation of the feuding parties.

A Switch from Retribution to Restitution

One major drawback of retributive sanctions is that they do nothing to heal the injury suffered by the victim or the harm done to the offended party. What they do is to double the pain by inflicting deliberate suffering on the offender. One of the pillars of the new paradigm is a switch from retribution to restitution, a switch aimed at achieving justice through means and methods other than punishment.

The emphasis in the new paradigm is not on the infliction of pain but to help the offended party achieve healing and closure and becoming whole again.

Barnett (1981), one of the many critics of retributive punishment, maintains that the alleged absolute justice of "repaying evil with evil" is really an empty sophism, since Christian moralists have always preached that an evil is to be put right by doing good. Barnett insists that crime is an offence by one individual against another. The armed robber did not rob society, he robbed the victim. His debt therefore is not to society but to the victim and he has an obligation to make things right to the one who has been injured or harmed.

One big advantage of a system of justice centred on restitution is that it would enjoy the unqualified support of most victims. There is in fact overwhelming empirical evidence indicating that victims prefer reparative sanctions (such as restitution) to punitive sanctions such as incarceration or fines.

Does Restorative Justice Have Advantages Over Retributive Justice?

Answer: this is an easy question; the advantages of restorative justice are many and are discussed in some length in Chapter VI. What follows are the titles of just a few of the positive objectives that a restorative justice system could achieve:

1. Restorative justice avoids the inherent arbitrariness of retributive punishment and the enormous disparities in its application.
2. By settling conflicts through a process and outcomes somewhat similar to that of civil courts, restorative justice offers a remedy to the arbitrary and often blurred distinctions between civil and criminal conflicts.
3. Restorative justice avoids the vagaries and inherent injustice of punitive systems.
4. Restorative justice avoids or at least minimizes the inherent bias of punitive justice.
5. Restorative justice would put an end to the unfair and shameful practice of plea bargaining.
6. Restorative justice encourages and enhances victim reporting.
7. Restorative justice minimizes the chances of retaliation and the risks of repeat victimization and by so doing offers more protection to the victims.

8. Restorative justice is the only possible way of dealing effectively with the new blood feuds in modern society, such as gang warfare and sectarian conflicts.

9. Restorative justice personalizes the response, returns the conflict to its legitimate owners and provides injured or harmed parties a central role in the justice process.

10. Restorative justice offers some remedy to victims whose offenders have not been identified, arrested, convicted and punished.

11. Restorative justice is the most appropriate model for cases of undisputed harm.

Can the History of Social Reaction to Harmful, Injurious Acts Give Any Hints About the Future?

Do Prisons Have a Future?

Regardless of how imaginative they may be, most people simply cannot conceive of a society that does not hold persons captive behind bars in cage-like cells! Hence the question I am constantly being asked: So what is the alternative?

The reason is that free people who have never experienced the horrific pains of captivity have very little understanding of how cruel, inhuman and torturous deprivation of liberty is. It is surely not a coincidence that most of those who struggle for prison reform or for prison abolition are people who personally experienced the harrowing life in prison.

Having studied thoroughly and extensively the tragic and painful history of penal sanctions, I came to the conclusion that no punishment is transcendental, permanent or immutable. Social change is inevitable and unstoppable. All punishments appear only to disappear when they become incompatible with the new mentalities, the modern views and attitudes of the time and once suitable and acceptable alternatives, in harmony with the geist of the era, have been developed. This is why I deeply believe that the future of incarceration is no different. Imprisonment, like other antiquated, medieval and abandoned punishments of the past, will eventually decline and ultimately disappear. I know this will not happen in my lifetime or any time soon, but I am utterly convinced that it is inevitable and unavoidable. Yes, I am convinced that deprivation of liberty will eventually join other cruel and unusual punishments and will eventually be abandoned. Prisons will become only a historic relic like the gallows. Like the fate of medieval castle dungeons, many prisons will undoubtedly be converted into horror museums.

Answer: the fact is, modern-day technology provides sophisticated tools and instruments making it possible to control the behaviour and movements of dangerous individuals without having to lock them up or to deprive them of the most valuable asset to humans and animals alike, namely their liberty. Two major hindrances are delaying the inevitable abolition of prisons and penitentiaries: (a) the first stems from the general public's religious beliefs and punitive attitudes, their mistaken conviction that prisons are indispensable and irreplaceable and their firm insistence that punishment is the proper response to crime; (b) the second stems from the ideology of powerful conservative and right-wing politicians combined with the lucrative economic interests of a thriving prison industry.

Does Restorative Justice Offer a Viable Alternative to and a Feasible Replacement for the Current Justice Model?

Question: What is restorative justice? A simple answer: It is a rational, peaceful and constructive way of restoring harmony and order that were disrupted by the harmful or injurious act.

Restorative justice offers a great promise. It offers to move us, or rather to remove us, from the medieval system of punishment that has been in place for centuries to a new era of social reaction to harmful, injurious behaviours, to more peaceful and less onerous means of settling personal conflicts and disputes. It promises a constructive, less costly, less wasteful, less painful way of dealing with those who offend. It offers justice without caging those responsible. It promotes forgiveness, not revenge. It restores harmony while ensuring redress to the victim. It promises to put an end to the big penal mess we are in right now.

Unfortunately, there is a widespread yet mistaken belief that punishment is indispensable and irreplaceable. Another erroneous belief is that an institutionalized restorative justice system is neither feasible nor viable. Both those beliefs suggest that there is a huge need for education through mass information and effective communication.

Not only is there widespread ignorance about what restorative justice is, there is also a great deal of confusion about its modalities and what does qualify as restorative justice and what does not. This means there is a pressing need for an accurate definition of restorative justice and detailed explanations of its practices. In an attempt to gain support for restorative justice and to counter or minimize the perception that it is lenient or soft on criminals, there has been a tendency to sell it as a harsh mode of dealing with offenders. Even the Supreme Court of Canada in the Gladue decision maintained that when combined with appropriate probationary conditions restorative justice may impose a greater burden on the offender than a custodial sanction.

There is no denying that restorative justice is a more humane mode of doing justice than retributive sanctions. But my favouring of restorative justice over punishment is not merely a humanitarian stance. It is based on a deep conviction that it is a better, viable, constructive and more effective response to harm than punishment.

In my personal opinion, restorative justice, in its true form, has nothing in common with punishment. There is a basic difference between the goals being pursued by both. I see punishment's primary aim as the deliberate infliction of pain on a wrongdoer, a sinner, a criminal offender. Punishment was invented to create on earth a fireless equivalent to hell, and it survived because prisons admirably succeed in doing that.

This, however, is not one of the goals of restorative justice. Restorative justice rejects the notions of retribution and expiation, which are often offered as the moral justification for making the criminal/sinner suffer. It preaches tolerance and forgiveness, not harshness and vindictiveness. Unlike punishment, restorative justice does not deal with or respond to some moral fault or some theological concept of guilt. It responds to the actual injury or harm done and attempts at healing the injury and repairing the loss. Punishment has abstract and unattainable goals. Restorative justice has realist and achievable objectives.

A stark difference between deprivation of liberty as a penal sanction and restorative justice is the inevitable arbitrariness of the former compared with the latter. In fact arbitrariness is a structural, innate and irremediable defect in retributive systems that try to follow *The Mikado's* lighthearted verse in Gilbert and Sullivan's operetta: "My goal is all sublime; I shall achieve in time; to make the punishment fit the crime." To maintain that a given number of days, months or years in prison is a fair and equitable punishment for offences such as assault, rape, kidnapping, robbery or anything else strikes me as the height of arbitrariness, and it is rather difficult for me to understand how intelligent people – lawyers, scholars, academics and others – could believe and maintain that pain can be measured and dispensed according to some kind of mathematical formula. How could they believe it is possible to create some kind of equation that would make a prison sentence fit a crime that has caused physical or psychological injury, material harm or loss? That a seriously flawed concept and a fundamentally defective sentencing model like "just deserts" could be accepted and implemented for so long is a mystery. Except in a purely theological perspective, retribution is not, and can never be, an instrument of justice. To speak, therefore, of retributive "justice" is a contradiction in terms, since it is impossible to establish a fair equation between the punishment and the crime, between the pain to be inflicted upon the offender and the pain caused by the offence to the victim and his/her family, associates and friends.

Despite these obvious and glaring defects and shortcomings, it is very difficult to convince the majority of people, who were born and raised under a punitive justice system, to accept a desirable switch to a non-arbitrary mode of doing justice. Punishment is inculcated in people's minds since a very young age. They are repeatedly told, "If you lie, you will be punished; if you hit your sister, you will be spanked; if you steal, you will go to prison; etc." This creates in their minds a strong association between punishment and wrongdoing that is much too difficult to abandon when they grow up. This, in turn, creates an almost insurmountable obstacle in the way of replacing the existing punitive system with a fundamentally different one, a system that has its own philosophy, its own goals and its own modalities. Hence the piecemeal attempts we are witnessing to introduce restorative justice practices here and there.

When promoting restorative justice, I have always maintained that creating a restorative justice system parallel to the punitive one will not work, that it will doom restorative justice to become eternally a peripheral or secondary system. I argued that we have to convince the public that the present system, despite its enormous human, social and material costs, is not working, is not achieving its avowed goals, and thus has to be replaced by a different and superior system.

Unfortunately, realist that I am, I know that the chances of this happening in the near future are quite remote. It will take a revolution like the one that made the French people storm the Bastille to achieve this radical yet necessary change.

Conclusion

The deep dissatisfaction with the punitive/retributive justice system is universal. Offenders complain that it is cruel and inhuman. They deplore the flagrant disparities in sentencing. They point out to the countless errors the system makes even when a human life is at stake. They decry the fact that the punishments inflicted, whether prison or fines, are never personal but inevitably extend to and affect innocent family members, work associates and friends. Victims' dissatisfaction stems largely from the fact that they were excluded from the justice process, have very little say in the outcome and, whether the punishment at the end of the trial is prison or fine, they get no restitution and hardly any compensation from the state. The general public, the taxpayers, are distressed by the system's inefficiency, ineffectiveness and its failure to prevent crime despite its huge costs both socially and financially. For those with punitive inclinations, the system is never harsh enough. To those with a humanitarian bend and those who do not believe punishment is the right answer, the system is on the wrong track and its sentences are much too harsh.

Objective assessments and empirical evaluations tend to confirm the validity of all those complaints. Scholarly criticism of the current system tend to focus on a couple of questions:

If punishment is not an effective deterrent (and there is ample empirical research showing it is not) and if it is not an effective means of prevention (and the record number of offenders incarcerated proves it is not), what useful purpose does it serve? What is society getting in return for the billions of dollars being wasted on punishing wrongdoers? The conclusion is inevitably the same: there has to be another and better way of dealing with those who break the law.

Yes, I do believe there is, and to the countless students and others who always asked me: What is the alternative? – my answer is ***restorative justice.*** Hopefully, this brief essay will give them a good idea of the compelling reasons for my deeply held faith in it.

References

Anttila, I. (1984). *Crime Control and Freedom.* Paper presented at the George Orwell Year International Colloquium (April 2-4), Strasbourg.

Barnett, R.E. (1977). "Restitution: A New Paradigm of Criminal Justice." *Ethics: An International Journal of Social, Political and Legal Philosophy,* vol. 87, no.1, pp. 279-301.

Christie, N. (1977). "Conflicts as Property." *British Journal of Criminology.* Vol. 17, no. 1, pp. 1-19.

Canada, Law Reform Commission (1974). *Working Paper No. 2: The Meaning of Guilt-Strict Liability.* Ottawa.

Canada, Law Reform Commission (1974). *Working Paper No. 3: The Principles of Sentencing and Dispositions.* Ottawa.

Canada, Law Reform Commission (1974). *Working Papers Nos. 5 & 6: Restitution and Compensation-Fines.* Ottawa.

Fattah, E.A.

1982a "Making the Punishment Fit the Crime: The Case of Imprisonment – Problems Inherent in the Use of Imprisonment as a Retributive Sanction." *Canadian Journal of Criminology,* 24:1, pp. 1-12.

1992 "Beyond Metaphysics: The Need for a New Paradigm – On Actual and Potential Contributions of Criminology and the Social Sciences to the Reform of the Criminal Law." In R. Lahti and K. Nuotio (eds.) *Criminal Law Theory in Transition.* Helsinki: Finnish Lawyers Publishing Company.

1993 "From a Guilt Orientation to a Consequence Orientation." In F. Denker et. al. (eds.) *Beiträge zur Rechtswissenschaft.* Heidelberg: C.F. Muller.

1995 "Restorative and Retributive Justice Models: A Comparison." In H-H. Kühne (ed.) *Festschrift für Koichi Miyazawa.* Baden-Baden: Nomos Verlagsgesellschaft, pp. 305-15.

1997a "From Crime Policy to Victim Policy: The Need for a Fundamental Policy Change." In M. McShane and F. Williams III (eds.) *Victims of Crime and the Victimization Process.* New York: Garland Publishing, pp. 75-92.

1997b "Towards a Victim Policy Aimed at Healing, Not Suffering." In R.C. Davis, A.J. Lurigio and W.G. Skogan (eds.) *Victims of Crime* (second edition). Thousand Oaks, CA: Sage Publications, pp. 257-72.

1998a "Restorative and Retributive Justice Models: A Comparison." In Fattah, E.A. and Peters, T. (eds.) *Support for Crime Victims in a Comparative Perspective.* Leuven, Belgium: Leuven University Press, pp. 99-110.

1998b "Some Reflections on the Paradigm of Restorative Justice and Its Viability for Juvenile Justice." In Lode Walgrave (ed.) *Restorative Justice for Juveniles: Potentialities, Risks and Problems.* Leuven: Leuven University Press, pp. 389-401.

1999a "Victim Redress and Victim-Offender Reconciliation in Theory and Practice: Some Personal Reflections." *The Hokkaigakuen Law Journal,* vol. XXXV, no. 1, pp. 155-82.

1999b "From a Handful of Dollars to Tea and Sympathy: The Sad History of Victim Assistance." In J.J.M. van Dijk, Ron G.H. van Kaam and Jo-Anne Wemmers (eds.) *Caring for Crime Victims: Selected Proceedings of the 9th International Symposium on Victimology.* Monsey, NY: Criminal Justice Press, pp. 187-206.

1999c *Mediation in Penal Matters.* Report for Correctional Services Canada. Ottawa. 44 pages.

2000a "Victim Redress and Victim-Offender Reconciliation in Theory and Practice: Some Personal Reflections." *Resource Material Series No. 56.* Fuchu/Tokyo: UNAFEI (Asia and Far East Institute for the Prevention of Crime and the Treatment of Offenders), pp. 87-101.

2000b "How Valid Are the Arguments Frequently Made Against Mediation and Restorative Justice?" In Hedda Giertsen (ed.) *Albanian and Norwegian Experiences with Mediation in Conflict.* Oslo: Department of Criminology, University of Oslo, pp. 25-36.

2002 "From Philosophical Abstraction to Restorative Action, From Senseless Retribution to Meaningful Restitution: Just Desert and Restorative Justice Revisited." In H.J. Kerner and E. Weitekamp (eds.) *Restorative Justice, Theoretical Foundations.* Devon, UK: Willan Publishing, Culmcott House, pp. 308-21.

2004 "Gearing Justice Action to Victim Satisfaction, Contrasting Two Justice Philosophies: Retribution and Redress." In Hendrik Kaptein and Marijke Malsch (eds.) *Crime, Victims and Justice: Essays on Principles and Practice.* Burlington,VT: Ashgate Publishing Company.

2007 "Is punishment the appropriate response to gross human rights violations? Is a non-punitive justice system feasible?" In E. van der Spuy, S. Parmentier, A. Dissel (eds.) *Restorative Justice: Politics, Policies and Prospects.* Published under the auspices of the Faculty of Law, University of Cape Town: Juta and Company. Originally published in *Acta Juridica* (Cape Town), 2007, pp. 209-227.

2011 "Is Restorative Justice a Viable Option in Crimes of Violence?" Published in a special issue of *Keio University Law Journal* dedicated to the memory of Prof. Koichi Miyazawa, pp. 713-730.

End of Fattah's references

Greve, V. (1990). *Negligence in Danish Law.* Helsinki (mimeographed).

Hall, J. (1982). *Social Science and Criminal Theory.* Littleton, CO.

Lahti, R. (1975). *The Utilization of Criminological Research in Finnish Criminal Law Reform.* Paper presented at the 9th International Congress of Criminology, Vienna (mimeographed).

Morris, N. (1973). "The Law Is a Busybody." *The New York Times* (reprinted by the World Correctional Service Center).

Parker, G. (1977). *An Introduction to Criminal Law.* Toronto.

Wooton, B. (1963). *Crime and the Criminal Law: Reflections of a Magistrate and Social Scientist.* London.

About the Author

Ezzat A. Fattah was born in Egypt. He graduated from the Faculty of Law, Cairo University, in 1948. For the next twelve years he worked in the justice system in various Egyptian cities as a prosecutor and investigating judge. Fed up with the oppression of the Nasser's regime and disillusioned with punitive criminal justice, he left Egypt and headed to Austria where he studied the social sciences at the University of Vienna, focusing on criminology and victimology. In 1964, seeking a graduate degree in criminology he enrolled at the University of Montreal where he obtained an M.A. in 1965 and a Ph.D. in 1968. He taught at the School of Criminology until 1974, when he was invited by Simon Fraser University in Vancouver to set up the first School of Criminology in Western Canada, where he currently is professor emeritus.

Ezzat Fattah has been a guest professor at several universities in Canada and abroad, including University of Muenster, Westphalia; Catholic University of Leuven; University of Gran Canaria; University of Abidjan, Ivory Coast, etc. He was also honoured by invitations from Keio University and Tokiwa University in Japan. And in Tokyo in 1999 he was on the faculty of the 112 International Training Course organized by The United Nations Asia & Far East Institute for the Prevention of Crime and the Treatment of Offenders.

Among the many awards Ezzat Fattah received over the years is a doctorate *honoris causa* from the University of Liège in Belgium; the Sterling Prize in support of controversy; the Commemorative 125th Anniversary of Canada Medal; the Hermann Mannheim Prize awarded by the International Society of Criminology and the International Centre for Comparative Criminology; and the Hans von Hentig Award by the World Society of Victimology. Ezzat Fattah has been a fellow of the Royal Society of Canada since 1990.

In 1993 the Konrad Adenauer Research Award in the social sciences and humanities was bestowed on Ezzat Fattah by Chancellor Helmut Kohl to study first-hand the rise of crime in the former police state of East Germany following the reunification of the country.

Decriminalization of drugs, modernization of the criminal law, abolition of the death penalty and of prisons and the struggle for human rights have been central issues of Fattah's research and social activism. Staunch defender of human rights and keenly aware of the need to protect citizens against the abuses of power, Ezzat Fattah was one of many scholars leading the successful fight in Canada against the death penalty. His well-known association with Amnesty International resulted in several missions on behalf of the organization to several countries, including the U.S.A., Libya, Brazil, Jamaica, etc. It also generated a number of invitations to international conferences to campaign for the abolition of the death penalty and the commutation of the sentences of those on death row.

Ezzat Fattah is the author, co-author, editor and co-editor of more than a dozen books and has published over a hundred scholarly papers and book chapters in learned journals and edited collections. He is a harsh critic of punishment and retribution and a strong advocate of restorative justice. A pioneer in victimology, he strongly argues for a new criminal law paradigm for the twenty-first century, a paradigm that discards nineteenth-century metaphysics and reflects the social realities of post-industrial society.

For More Information About the Author

Fattah, E. A. (2017). "From the Land of the Pharaohs to Lotus Land: The Life and Criminological Achievements of Ezzat A. Fattah." In J. Winterdyk (editor) *Pioneers in Canadian Criminology*, pp. 44-75. Oakville, ON: Rock's Mills Press.

www.ingramcontent.com/pod-product-compliance
Lightning Source LLC
Chambersburg PA
CBHW071443230926
51846CB00001B/323
9781999215606